Restoring Safe School Communities

Restoring Safe School Communities

Brenda Morrison

THE FEDERATION PRESS
2007

Published in Sydney by

The Federation Press
PO Box 45, Annandale, NSW, 2038.
71 John St, Leichhardt, NSW, 2040.
Ph (02) 9552 2200. Fax (02) 9552 1681.
E-mail: info@federationpress.com.au
Website: http://www.federationpress.com.au

National Library of Australia cataloguing-in-publication

Morrison, Brenda.
Restoring safe school communities: a whole school response to bullying, violence and alienation.

Includes index.
ISBN 978 186287 477 0.

1. Restorative justice. 2. Bullying in schools.
3. bullying – prevention. I. Title.

371.78

Text printed on
100% recycled paper

Typeset by The Federation Press, Leichhardt, NSW.
Printed by Southwood Press Pty Ltd, Sydney, NSW.

Foreword

Bullying, violence and alienation are major problems in schools. Brenda Morrison shows they are connected to many other problems such as youth suicide and crime. The research evidence in this book also suggests bullying and violence is preventable. In making a fresh contribution to this literature, Brenda Morrison advances our thinking in the fields of education and psychology. But she also progresses thinking in restorative justice – a sub-field of criminology that is now influencing many domains of regulation beyond criminal law. In a wonderful clarifying reformulation of what restorative justice is, Morrison argues that restorative justice is about building positive affect (interest and excitement) and providing mechanisms to discharge negative affect (shame).

Bullying, while a serious problem, can create a special kind of opportunity to enrich democracy and our struggle for a world with less domination and more care in it. This book represents educational innovation in the philosophy of restorative justice, an approach that enables us to be more responsive and more restorative to the needs of those affected by bullying and violence. The contribution of this book occurs both at the level of how to better meet the individual needs of students and how to transform institutions to accomplish this. It is path-breaking in illuminating the hopes and hazards of the journey to building safe schools and communities.

Brenda Morrison is a compassionate and inspiring leader of educational practice communities. In this book she combines that experience with genuine depth of theoretical and empirical insight.

John Braithwaite
Founder, Regulatory Institutions Network (RegNet)
Australian National University

This book is dedicated to:
Valerie Braithwaite, who opened the door
John Braithwaite, who held the door open
Damien, Hamish and Anna Bryan, who shared the journey

The royalties from this book are being donated to the Dalai Lama
Center for Peace and Education, whose vision I share:
"to develop the heart, be compassionate, work for peace in your
heart and in the world".

Love and compassion are necessities, not luxuries.
Without them humanity cannot survive.
His Holiness, The Dalai Lama

Contents

Preface

This book has been an amazing journey, covering a range of territory and a range of ideas. Some of these ideas have survived the journey, others have not. In the time that it has taken for these ideas to take shape, I have lived and worked in three different countries, wearing a range of disciplinary and institutional hats, all the while sharing the highs and lows of working towards safe school communities with many. With me every step of the way, has been my family – Damien, Hamish and Anna – riding out the highs, the lows, and the endless days of revisions and editing. Their love and support are the foundation of my life, as well as this book.

The initial vision for this book on school bullying and restorative justice was nurtured by my work with Valerie Braithwaite and John Braithwaite, at the Regulatory Institutions Network at the Australian National University. I will be forever thankful for their faith in me and this book.

In my early days of learning about restorative justice, I was introduced to Terry O'Connell, Peta Blood and Julei Kirner, who were introducing restorative justice into inner city schools in Sydney, Australia. Inspired by their work, I began the research and development of what was to become the Responsible Citizenship Program (in hindsight, maybe it should be called Project, as the practice of restorative justice in schools can not be sustained by a single program and I would encourage a range of projects, wherein schools develop a program that fits their community). With funding support from the Criminology Research Council, Hawker Primary School in the Australian Capital Territory became the partner school for this project, through the support of Jeff Sheridan, the principal, and Jan Spencer, the Year 5 teacher. Together, with two thoughtful and enthusiastic facilitators, Charlotte and Jean, we developed a program, based on AVP (Alternatives to Violence Program) and HIPP (Help Increase the Peace Program). Sadly, this program was wrapped up a couple of weeks into the school year; due to a number of factors, the dynamic was not working for everyone involved, most notably the students. Yet, with this initial step of working restoratively with schools came a huge amount of learning for us all.

I spent the next week giving the Program a new face and headed out to the school with a fresh team – Jacko, Ali, and wee Hamish (my eight-week-old son). We had great fun with the students and I learnt a lot from being directly involved with the students and the program. The students were our guide to getting the program on a fun and productive course. It was pleasure to share the journey with such a great crew. Following each session, we enjoyed some great debriefs and development sessions at Cornucopia bakery. Food is an important ingredient to many restorative justice programs, including this one. Many thanks must also go to the Australian Institute of Criminology for promoting the Responsible Citizenship Program in their Trends and Issues in Crime and Criminal Series (No 219).

Overtime, between numerous other projects, I developed, revised, and revised again this book. It was my move to Philadelphia, to work with Larry Sherman at the Jerry Lee Center of Criminology at the University of Pennsylvania, that particularly impacted me and the development of this book. My heart was deeply touched by this troubled yet hopeful city, in particular its young people and schools. This time it was my daughter Anna who travelled with me from school to school. Philadelphia offered me the highs and lows of the most enriching of experiences – the worst and the best of everything. It almost tore my heart out to leave Philadelphia when I was offered a position at the Center for Restorative Justice at Simon Fraser University and a chance to move home to Vancouver, where I had left 20 years previously in search of adventure. What an adventure it has been. My life has been enriched by many and I am truly thankful.

Federation Press has stuck with me from the beginning, riding the highs and the lows. I am forever grateful to them for their patience and faith, in particular Margaret Farmer, Chris Holt and Clare Moss. Peta Blood shared this journey in many ways too, not only inspiring and sharing those early days in Australia but also providing extensive feedback on an earlier draft of this book.

There are so many others who I can thank: good friends in many places; strangers in coffee shops and libraries; family in Vancouver and Australia. Throughout this journey, I have been blessed with an abundance of love – something I wish for each and every child. The weft and warp that constitutes the fabric of my life offers me much to draw on as my journey continues with new opportunities and new ideas to explore. With every step, the vision has remained a constant: restoring safe school communities.

Brenda Morrison
Vancouver
February 2007

Introduction

Safe school communities

There is no trust more sacred than the one the world holds with children. There is no duty more important than ensuring that their rights are respected, that there welfare is protected and that their lives are free from fear and want and that they grow up in peace.

Kofi Annan (2000, p 4)

Education can never merely be for the sake of individual self-enhancement. It pulls us into the common world or it fails us altogether.

Robert Bellah (1991, p 176)

How do we secure and nurture safe school communities, where students, teachers, parents – all members of the school community – feel safe to learn and grow, free from the destructive forces of bullying, violence and alienation? In recent years, securing school safety has become a priority for schools, communities and governments. The tragedy of *Columbine*– the high school in Colorado where in April 1999 two teenage students, Eric Harris and Dylan Klebold, shot and killed 12 students and a teacher, wounding another 24 – resonates with at least 10 school rampage shootings in the late 1990s, with the 2005 Red Lake rampage shooting in Minnesota shattering any illusion that these events are behind us. Around the world, *Columbine* harnessed the attention of students, parents, teachers, school administrators, governments, academics and the clergy. It's ongoing emotional impact compels us to find how we can best secure and nurture safe school communities.

In 2002, Michael Moore's award-winning documentary *Bowling for Columbine* re-iterated the many questions that remained unanswered: Why? How could this happen? How can we prevent it from happening again? And now, the tragic incident in Red Lake suggests that these questions, and more, remain unresolved. The stark emotive reality of *Columbine* still holds. *Bowling for Columbine*, while controversial, tapped an emotional pulse. The film vividly re-tells the story and impact of 20 April 1999, a day that began much like any other day but ended with the social and emotional landscape of Columbine High School in Littleton, Colorado – indeed, in schools and communities around the world – changed forever. For the story of *Columbine* does not stand alone but amplifies a hidden chord of alienation that continues to be experienced by school communities. The reverberating stories and incidents echo the inner turmoil that plagued the lives of Eric Harris and Dylan Klebold. While subsequent investigation revealed the early warning signs of their distress and intentions, on the morning of 20 April 1999 their emotional turmoil was tightly masked as they began their day bowling with their classmates. These same emotions were then boldly exposed when they ended their day, taking the lives of 12 students, a teacher, and eventually their own. The events of that day changed the way schools are secured and regulated throughout the world and revealed a disturbing culture of alienation in the social and emotional lives of children.

Columbine repositioned the high bar of school violence, but it was fuelled, at least in part, by a more insidious form of violence that affects students every day – bullying. Whether it be physical, social or emotional bullying, it occurs more often than we are aware of, securing its power in the corners and everyday nuances of school life. While more covert, the emotional scars of bullying can last a lifetime. In the past decade or so, the mounting evidence about the ill effects of school bullying has brought that concern to the forefront of schools, communities and governments globally. School bullying is no longer tolerated as a normal part of growing up. Recent court cases have awarded victims of bullying large cash settlements where schools have failed to respond to incidents of bullying. When we look closely at what bullying is, and the effects that it has, it helps us to understand that it is part of a wider cycle of violence and alienation.

Robert Fuller recounts the story of Tommie T in his influential book, *Somebodies and Nobodies*, quoting a federal official:

> I often think of Tommie T. I may have had a tough time, but he suffered bullying several orders of magnitude worse. Fat and ashamed, he could not stave off the attacks. I remember kids putting pats of butter down his shirt collar in the lunchroom. He just sat there crying, not defending himself.
>
> While I survived, Tommie's high school experience probably killed him. He ended up working at a lumberyard, never moved from the house in which he grew up, and became a recluse. The last time I saw him he was almost 50. I stopped by his house and we talked for a few minutes. He had eczema, was obese, just a miserable creature. He died soon after that. Bullying can be fatal, even without shootings. (2004, pp 48-49)

Short- and long-term effects of bullying can manifest themselves in a wide range of harmful behaviour, towards one's self and others. Here are the words of one young girl in Canada who was bullied at school:

2

It is killing me Mom. I'm sorry. I love you so much but I can't live any more.

XXX has too many people after me and the one who will kill me is YYY.

Please give this message to them and ask them if they are happy now. I never knew it would get this far, but I'm so depressed. If I tried to get help it would have gotten worse. They are always looking for a new person to beat up.

If I ratted on them I would get kicked out of school and then there's nothing stopping them. (Middleton, 2000):

This 14-year-old girl hung herself after one last phone call from the girls she had often called her friends. Her parents had no idea just how bad things were for her. Neither did the school community. They characterised her as bright and cheerful. When she left school on that Friday, she talked to the school staff about a course change, not about being bullied, nor her feelings of depression. The principal believed: "Dawn [Marie] would be the kind of person who would tell us". But she didn't, she masked her emotional turmoil well. Initially, the girls responsible for the bullying were suspended and were required to go through one-on-one counselling, but the principal added: "Sometimes I wonder if it does any good" (Middleton, 2000). Beyond the school's response, this case set a legal precedent: the first criminal charges associated with bullying in Canada were laid. The three girls involved were only 16 at the time.

In a case in Australia, a 16-year-old youth bought a crossbow over the Internet with his mother's credit card, went to school and maliciously wounded his former girlfriend and another student. At his sentencing, the trial judge said he had been "bullied into isolation" at school and by his older brother, and was "at his wit's end" when he attacked the girl. He is now serving his sentence and will be eligible for parole in 2008 (Wallace, 2004).

In British Columbia, Canada, the Children's Commissioner, Paul Pallan, looked closely at 22 child fatalities in that province. Of the 15 children who committed suicide, one-third had been identified as being systematically bullied. It could be more; it is hard to know now that these children are gone and we can no longer listen, learn and respond to the great hurt they felt. In the United States, studies of the school rampage shootings revealed that two-thirds of the shooters had been bullied at school, all but one suffered from social marginalisation, and in that one case there was evidence of the loss of a significant social relationship (Newman, 2004).

Each of these tragic stories raise a number of questions:

1. Why are so many young people taking their own lives, and others? Why are they not speaking out? Why can't they express their feelings? Why do they feel there are no effective means to help them?

2. Why is bullying in schools such a problem? What is activating and legitimising this behaviour? What is the pathology of this behaviour? What are the antecedents?

3. How can we better respond to the seriousness of bullying, violence and alienation in schools? How can we respond effectively before it is too late? How can we proactively respond to better meet the concerns of the next generation?

4. Does school counselling, or any other intervention for that matter, really make the difference we want it to make? When is one intervention more appropriate than another intervention? How do we decide?

Schools and communities continue to grapple with these questions, suggesting that we are still in need of better answers.

Once a student's feeling of alienation strikes deep enough the consequences can be devastating: some students mask their shame in various unhealthy behaviours; others strike back by attacking themselves and others, or attacking the institution that failed to protect and honour their dignity. While many people survive the emotional impact of bullying, the evidence suggests the emotional scars remain. The problem of bullying has hidden costs, across a lifetime, for individuals and society.

Many psychologists and psychiatrists have tried to make sense of what happened at Columbine and other schools, and what needs to be done to prevent such tragedies from happening again. Well known social psychologist, Elliott Aronson, wrote *Nobody left to hate: Teaching compassion after Columbine*; the distinguished American psychiatrist James Gilligan writes extensively about the case in his book *Preventing Violence;* and James Garbarino and Claire Bedard wrote *Parents Under Siege*, after being contacted by Tom and Sue Klebold, Dylan Klebold's parents. More recently, Julie Webber has written *Failure to Hold: The Politics of School Violence*; and Katherine Newman has written *Rampage: The social roots of school shootings*, both of which closely examine the school massacres of the 1990s. These books focus on the issue of school safety and challenge us to think and act differently in securing and nurturing safe school communities.

Largely, *Columbine* has fuelled the advancement of zero tolerance policies in schools, as well as a host of other knee-jerk reactions, which often amount to no more than band-aids on deeper wounds. These responses are typically highly visible, "tough on crime", help calm concerned parents and communities, and fulfil accountability standards. But are they effective? And for whom? There is yet to be a rigorous test of zero tolerance policies, the best studies we have are retrospective (Skiba & Noam, 2001). More rigorous tests have been carried out in the context of school bullying, however, recent meta-evaluations of bullying intervention programs show marginal effects at best (Rigby, 2002; Smith, Schneider, Smith and Ananiadou, 2004).

This book offers some further insights and understanding of the culture of bullying, violence and alienation, and presents a comprehensive whole school response to addressing these harmful behaviours. Research interest in bullying in schools began in Norway in the 1970s and for almost three decades the subject has been studied widely internationally. A lot of work has been done to build an understanding of the causes and effects of bullying and we are increasing our knowledge about the effectiveness of interventions (see Smith, Pepler and Rigby, 2004). There is little doubt that the issue of school violence and school safety are hot topics in education (see Gerler, 2004; Jimerson and Furlong, 2006), as is the topic of classroom management (see Evertson & Weinstein, 2006). We still have more work to do, however, and the hope is that this book will add further substance to this issue.

The approach developed is distinct from many currently in practice in that it focuses on dealing with the social and emotional harm caused by bullying, as well as other behaviour, in schools. The approach is based on principles of restorative justice and responsive regulation and provides a framework that is both *responsive* to the concerns of the school community, and *restorative* to those affected by harm and wrongdoing. The practice of restorative justice grew out of dissatisfaction with traditional juvenile and criminal justice systems for victims, offenders and communities. These practices have more recently been applied to schools.

At the heart of restorative justice is healing – the fundamental premise being that in order to restore the social fabric of our communities, the social and emotional void associated with bullying, violence and alienation must be addressed. The process aims to repair the harm done to individuals and to restore healthy relationships within the community. To achieve this end, the web of relationships that bond an individual to their community is put at the centre of the process.

Addressing the social and emotional harm caused by bullying and other harmful behaviour is not usually the focus of many traditional responses, which typically downplay or sidestep the emotional issues. Indeed, students are often separated from each other or removed from the school community in order to avoid emotional encounters. Sometimes the "offender" is removed from the community; at other times the "victim" is removed. Either way, there is no emotional closure and no opportunity for the individuals and the community to take responsibility, and to heal and learn.

As author Daniel Goleman (2003) tells us, learning and using better ways to navigate our feelings – becoming emotionally intelligent – is part of the answer. Feelings are important messages about the state of our social relationships but they can also be a destructive force. The Dalai Lama challenges us to take responsibility of our emotions which, when out of control, can be devastating to the whole community (see Goleman, 2003). We need to listen and respond to the highs and lows of school life, as both individuals and a community; and we need to create safe spaces and opportunities to do this. Students, parents, teachers, administrators, counsellors, cleaners, canteen staff, etc must all have an opportunity to become socially and emotionally intelligent and to learn to navigate emotions in productive ways. Honest and productive expression becomes possible when we create safe spaces where communities of care, that foster mutual respect through listening and learning, can gather.

This is the essence of restorative justice: creating safe spaces for dialogue through building communities of care, where story telling and listening are valued and emotional understanding is developed, so individuals are enriched with the capacity, and given the opportunity, to take responsibility for the harm done, and to repair it.

This book seeks to build understanding and practice around three main issues that relate to addressing bullying, violence and alienation in schools:

1. Understanding individuals' behaviour in the context of group life.

2. Affirming and building socially and emotionally healthy relation-ships when establishing and regulating behavioural expectations.

3. Re-affirming, re-pairing and re-building the social and emotional well-being of individuals, and their communities, when responding to harmful behaviour.

In summary, for interventions to be effective, they need to move beyond mere information campaigns that address the deed over the doer; they need to respond to individuals, as well as the relational dynamics between individuals; moreover, they need to seek out reason while navi-gating emotions. In other words, effective interventions need to address the social and emotional culture of the school community.

This book is a journey, in three parts. Part I looks at harmful beha-viour and harmful responses through building our understanding of bullying, violence and alienation (Chapter 1). It then moves onto the social and emotional dynamics of alienation, shame and humiliation

(Chapter 2). The book then examines traditional responses to harmful behaviour, typified by neglect, quick fixes and zero tolerance initiatives, which can further exclude and alienate (Chapter 3). Part II offers a way forward through the practice of restorative justice (Chapter 4) and responsive regulation (Chapter 5). In Part III a whole-school approach to restorative justice and responsive regulation is offered, proposing a continuum of restorative responses across three levels intervention (Chapter 6), as well as a regulatory framework for responsive implementation, development and sustainability (Chapter 7). The end of the journey is marked by a short epilogue on reflections and revelations (Chapter 8). No doubt the journey will continue beyond this book; there is much for us to learn, and much for us to do, to address these complex problems. The hope is that the chapters ahead will offer some signposts to the next steps, as individuals, schools and communities continue to navigate the territory of restoring safe school communities.

This book is for students, parents, teachers and all concerned members of our schools and communities.

Our children are powerful teachers. They are the mirrors to our social world. When our children are hurting themselves and others, they are sending us important messages. We need to listen, individually and institutionally. We also need to ask what messages, as individuals and institutions, are we sending to our children in our words, our actions and our inactions. How are we building the hope that will sustain our children's strength to move confidently into their future? Schools and communities are laying the foundation for the future of the next generation. It is important that that foundation be strong and safe.

Chapter 1

Bullying, violence and alienation

It is a fundamental human right for a child to feel safe in school and to be spared the oppression and repeated, intentional humiliation implied in bullying.

Olweus (1999, p 21)

Man is wedged between being a social creature and being an individual. I think the *nemo*, the sense that you are nothing or nobody, can drive us all to violence or unreason. Through all human history it had been the hidden motive – that unbearable desire to prove oneself *somebody* – behind countless insanities and acts of violence.

John Fowles (1998, p 374)

School bullying

This chapter focuses on the relationship between bullying, violence and alienation, beginning with a focus on bullying in school. This focus is intentional for a number of reasons:

1. Bullying is one of the most insidious and common forms of violence in schools.

2. Bullying feeds the wider cycle of violence in schools.

3. Bullying can leave emotional scars that can last a lifetime.

4. The study of school bullying helps us to understand the practice of restorative justice, given that bullying has been defined as the systematic abuse of power and restorative justice seeks to responsibly empower those affected by harmful behaviour.

5. In practice, restorative practices have been found to be effective in addressing school bullying, as well as other harmful behaviours in schools.

There is an interesting synchronicity to the emergence of bullying and restorative practices as new fields of study. Both fields have a recent history, emerging strongly in the 1990s, which parallels with Braithwaite's analysis of the decline of democracy, where: "The lived experience of modern democracy is alienation. The feeling is that elites run things, that we do not have a say in any meaningful sense" (2002, p 1).

These observations concur with Putnam's (2000) analysis on the decline of social capital in contemporary society, and provide a context for building our understanding of bullying, violence and alienation. Thus, this chapter begins with a close look at bullying and examines the lives of students who bully and are bullied at school, focusing on the influence of family, peers, the school and wider institutions on the development of bullying behaviour.[1]

What is bullying?

While there have been a variety of definitions of bullying, the following is often cited: bullying is the "repeated oppression, psychological or physical of a less powerful person by a more powerful person or group of persons" (Rigby 1996, p 15; see also Olweus, 1999). Rigby (2002) has subsequently developed his definition, but the three main critical points remain:

- *Power*: Those who bully acquire their power through various means: physical size and strength; social status within a peer group; and the imposition of social and emotional oppression and exclusion on others. Power imbalances are not necessarily fixed across time and place; the imbalance is relative to the actors involved and must always be understood in context.

- *Frequency*: Bullying is not a random act; it is characterised by its repetitive nature. Because it is repetitive, those who are bullied not only have to survive the humiliation of the attack itself but live in constant fear of its re-occurrence. Having said this, bullying can be used to describe a one-off experience, as Randall (1996) has argued.

- *Intent to harm*: While not always fully conscious to those who bully, causing physical, psychological and emotional harm is a deliberate act at some level. In other words, it is a "means to an end" to achieving a sense of personal agency and security in one's social world.

At its core, bullying can be thought of as "the systematic abuse of power" (Rigby, 2002). In other words, bullying is the assertion of power through

---

1   For a fuller development of the literature on school bullying there are many excellent books and papers written by scholars around the world, including Ken Rigby in Australia; Wendy Craig, Shelley Hymel and Debra Pepler in Canada; Helen Cowie, David Galloway, Sonia Sharp and Peter Smith in England; Christina Salmivalli in Finland; Mona O'Moore in Ireland; Dan Olweus and Erling Roland in Norway; and Dorothy Espelage, Richard Hazler, Susan Limber, Tonja Nansel and Susan Swearer in the United States.

oppressive behaviour that harms another person or persons. It happens in government, corporate boardrooms, workplaces, and in our schools. While the intent to dominate remains consistent across these institutions, the social dynamics of bullying change over the course of life: from playground bullying and gang violence, to sexual and workplace harassment, to child abuse and domestic violence, as well as abuse of our elders and disabled people (Pepler & Craig, 1997). The exertion of power can take many forms: through the overt use of physical size, strength and numbers; the use of status within a group or community; or through social and emotional abuse. The form can be face to face or insidiously indirect, through rumours, exclusion, stalking and setting people up through others (Olweus, 1991). The repetitive nature of bullying sets up an ongoing relationship of dominance and oppression, which can have a negative impact on the perpetrator(s), the victim(s), bystanders and the wider community.

How pervasive is school bullying?

Bullying in schools is a worldwide phenomenon as data from a number of countries shows; see for examples, Australia (Rigby, 2002); Canada (Bentley and Li, 1995; Pepler et al, 1997); England (Withney and Smith, 1993; Blaya, 2001); Ireland (O'Moore, 1986), Scotland (Mellor, 1990); Scandinavia (Olweus, 1991); and the United States (Nansel, Overpeck, Pilla, Ruan, Simons-Morton and Scheidt, 2001). Smith et al (1999) wrote one of the first international reviews.

The percentage of school children bullied varies from 4 per cent to 20 per cent, but however you slice the pie, the numbers amount to thousands of students being victimised by bullying every year. Be it overt physical bullying, or insidious social and emotional bullying, all are hurtful. Rigby (2002) conducted a study of just how hurtful different forms of bullying were for boys and girls. While the expectation in this study was for boys to rate physical aggression as the most hurtful to them, and relational abuse as "girls' stuff", this was not the case. As Rigby (2002, p 64) stated: "What is most striking about these results is that the most hurtful aggressive acts were those that we had categorised as relational, such as 'somebody trying to break up my friendships', or 'people ganging up on me' and 'being excluded'. 'Being deliberately hit or kicked' was way down on the list. From this study we were left to conclude that we could have greatly underestimated the effects of relational aggression, especially on boys". The irony here is that the old defence against name-callers that many of us grew up with – "Sticks and stones may break my bones but names will never hurt me" – is far from true (see Garbarino & deLara, 2002).

To understand the problem of bullying and of being bullied, we must consider the life patterns of children who seek to dominate others and the patterns of the children who become their victims. We must also examine the social systems in which bullying occurs, such as in the family, peer groups, schools and other social institutions.

Life paths of students who bully and are bullied

There is now a large body of evidence that both children who bully, and those who become victims of bullying, experience poorer psychological adjustment than children who are not involved in bullying (Kumpulainen, Raesaenen & Henttonen, 1999; Nansel, Overpeck, et al, 2001). While there are similarities between these two groups of children, there are also differences.

Students who bully

The life trajectories of children who bully are not straightforward; likewise, there isn't a single path that leads a child to bullying others. Children bully for many different reasons. Each develops this behavioural pattern through many different life experiences. Some bullies stand alone, while others come to the fore in groups, some are more likely to initiate, while others are more likely to join in (Salmivalli, Huttunen & Lagerspetz, 1997). Bullies are not necessarily those who lack academic ability or a secure family environment. While some bullies tend to be impulsive (Lowenstein, 1978; Olweus, 1987), others can be extremely clever about how they craft their place in the world (Sutton, Smith & Swettenham, 1999a). Generally, bullies behave aggressively towards others: this can include their peers, teachers, parents or siblings, but they can be very selective about who they target (Olweus, 1991). Likewise, students who bully can be clever about the manner and the place in which they choose to bully. For example, a Finnish study found that children who were nominated as socially intelligent were also more likely to bully others in indirect and relational ways (Kaukainen et al, 1999). Further to this point, an English study found a correlation between students' ability to guess what others were thinking and the type of bullying they engaged in. Students who verbally bully have a greater ability to guess what other people are thinking, while those who physically bully have a lower ability (Sutton, Smith & Swettenham 1999b). The inference is that the social skills of some students who bully can be highly developed, while others are less skilled in this area.

Fulfilling the stereotype of the school bully, academic underachievement and poor social skills can also characterise some students who bully. In terms of academic achievement, a number of studies have found that students who bully have: below-average school attainment, intelligence and reading ability; negative attitudes toward school work; and find it hard to concentrate at school (Lowenstein, 1978; Olweus, 1984; O'Moore & Hillery, 1991; Stephenson & Smith, 1989). In terms of social competency, research on students who bully has found these students: lack social skills and interpret social skills incorrectly; and are rated lower than average in popularity among their peers, being regarded as controversial, disruptive and uncooperative and thus can be socially rejected and ostracised, and participate in subsequent antisocial behaviour (Boulton & Smith, 1994; Rigby, Cox & Black, 1997; Larson, 1994; O'Moore & Hillery, 1991; Rican 1995; Rigby & Slee, 1993).

Reflecting these mixed findings, some bullies have very high levels of self-esteem, while others don't. For some students who bully, the social skills and aptitudes they possess are often more than adequate for attaining their social standing. For these students, their self-esteem is no different than students who don't bully (Olweus, 1978). They've defined their place within their social world. For others, their social life is more of a challenge as they struggle, even battle, to find their place in the world. These students suffer from lower self-esteem (O'Moore & Hillery, 1991; Rigby & Cox, 1996). Likewise, severe depression has also been associated with bullying behaviour (Slee, 1995; Roland, 2002). In line with the old adage, "like attracts like", children who bully are not only aggressive themselves, they are attracted to situations with aggressive content and view aggression as being quite a productive means to an end (Stephenson & Smith, 1989).

Without doubt, children who bully have life trajectories that are multifaceted and complex. At the same time, there are a range of factors that are indicative of the path they are treading. Early studies found that children who bully had little empathy for their victims and showed little or no remorse and understanding about their actions (Olweus, 1987). Subsequent studies have found that children who bully also tended to be involved in alcohol consumption and smoking, had poorer academic records than non-involved students, displayed a strong need for dominance, and showed little empathy for their victims (Roberts & Morotti, 2000). Children who bully at school are more likely to drop out of school, use illicit drugs and engage in delinquent behaviour (Farrington 1993; Gottfredson, Gottfredson & Hybl, 1993). Longitudinal studies have also shown that up to one-half of first graders who are disruptive, unable to get along with other children, and are disobedient to their parents and resistant to teachers, will become delinquent in their teen years (Offord et al, 1992 cited in Goleman, 1995). These same behaviours can be attributed to young bullies. The path they tread generally reflects a pattern of poor social adjustment, as later reflected in the areas of marital and occupational relations (Wolfgang, Figlio & Sellin, 1972; Jessor & Jessor, 1977). A relationship between bullying and crime has also been found – in Norway approximately 60 per cent of boys who were characterised as bullies in Grades 6 to 9 had at least one criminal conviction by the age of 24 (Olweus, 1993).

Students who are bullied

Boys and girls are equally likely to be victims of bullying (Charach et al, 1995; Pepler et al, 1997). Unlike students who bully, whose numbers peak in the middle years of schooling, more children report being victimised in the early years of schooling (see Rigby, 2002). One way of understanding this discrepancy is to look at the profile of the children who bully. In general, younger students are more likely to be victims of older bullies. As children get older the number of children who are in a position to dominate them decreases. Furthermore, as students grow older, indirect bullying such as exclusion and rumour-mongering replaces direct bullying (Olweus, 1993). As boys grow older there is an increased tendency to claim that they are "not bothered" by bullying and are more likely to ignore it (Smith & Shu, 2000).

While a good number of students experience being bullied at some time in their school life, it is those who are chronically victimised who are most severely affected (Juvonen, Nishina & Graham, 2000; Kochenderfer-Ladd & Wardrop, 2001). These victims of bullies often stand alone in some way and experience low self-regard (Egan & Perry, 1998). Often physically weak, relatively introverted, socially unskilled and unassertive, they do not engage with any particular peer group on a regular basis (Olweus, 1993; Rigby, 1996). Victims are prone to be withdrawn and anxious, characterised by tenseness, worry and loneliness (Burks, Dodge & Price, 1995; Neary & Joseph, 1994; Slee, 1995). As a result, victims report lower self-esteem and depression that is characterised by sadness and loss of interest (Besag, 1989; Craig, 1998; Egan & Perry, 1998; Slee, 1995). The anxiety and depression associated with victimisation has also been linked to lower immunity to illness and higher levels of headaches, stomach aches, sore throats and other somatic symptoms (Cox, 1995; Rigby, 1998, 1999; Williams et al, 1996). Victimisation has also been associated with suicidal ideation (Rigby, 1998). While students who are emotionally weak can become attractive targets for bullies, it has also been shown that a history of victimisation and poor social relationships predicts the onset of emotional problems in adolescents. In other words, bullying can be the cause of emotional problems (Bond, Carlin, Thomas, Rubin & Patton, 2001). This is supported by Cynthia Pfeffer's work on suicide:

> Probably one of the most critical factors in precipitating suicidal ideation arising from interpersonal problems is humiliation – feelings of disgrace and public disparagement may shatter a youngster's healthy sense of narcissism and sense of identity, and loss of a basic sense of one's worth-whileness is a powerful force to increase thoughts of self-annihilation. (1990, p 81)

Tragically, we know from the stories of Columbine, Dawn Marie and others (highlighted in the Introduction) that students who have been bullied sometimes take their own lives and the lives of others. Those that take the lives of others can do so in very public displays of rage; while for those that suicide, the act can be a very private one, in a very private setting, or more public, in a community setting. Regardless of the means, the pain of social rejection is immense, as can be heard in the words of this 15-year-old who was teased for being overweight and killed himself at school with his father's handgun: "They see me as an insignificant 'thing', something to be traded, mangled, and mocked … In the shadow, I can sleep without dreams of despair and deception" (Garbarino & deLara, 2002, p 83).

The suicides of three boys, within a short period of time, led to the first systematic anti-bullying interventions in Norway in 1983. The rates of adolescent suicide are significant (see De Leo & Evans, 2004) and in many Western developed countries, suicide is reported in the top three leading causes of death among 15 to 24 year-olds. The rate of suicide has increased significantly since 1960 (by as much as five times), with the rate for males being much greater than the rate for females. However, young women are more likely to attempt suicide, while young men are as much as four times more likely to succeed. It is estimated that rates of attempted suicide are as much as 20 times greater than completed acts of suicide.

These suicide trends point to a hidden problem. Thoughts of suicide are closely guarded secrets. Garbarino and Bedard (2001) found that one quarter of the 275 first-year undergraduate students they surveyed had considered suicide. Of that quarter, 87 per cent said that their parents were unaware of their thoughts. A recent study in the United States found that suicidal ideation and homicidal ideation are highly correlated (Harter, Low & Whitesell, 2003).

A number of general points can be made about the trajectory of children who are victimised. Over time, they are less inclined to relate positively to the school environment and may exclude themselves. Rigby (1998) found that 9 per cent of girls and 6 per cent of boys reported staying away from school at least once because of school bullying. The National Association of School Psychologists estimates that 160,000 students in America miss school each day because of fear of attack, intimidation, or bullying (Newman, 2004, p 64). The high anxiety levels that these children report interfere with their ability to concentrate and their capacity to learn. Finally, their health, mentally and physically, is affected, both short- and long-term. Interestingly, students who are bullied and rejected by other students are not unlike the students who bully them; both are more likely to drop out of school, experience mental and physical health-related problems and engage in delinquent and criminal behaviour (Parker & Asher, 1987; Kupersmidt, Coie & Dodge, 1990). Both tread the path of alienation.

Students who bully and are bullied

A number of studies have identified students who report being both bullies and victims (see Craig, 1998; Espelage et al, 2001; Nansel et al, 2001). There is also a category of victim called "provocative victims" (Pikas, 1989; Roland & Idsoe, 2001). Relative to other categories (that is, bullies, victims, non-bullies/non-victims) this category covers the smallest percentage of students. A recent Australian study found it to be just over 8 per cent of students (Ahmed et al, 2001). By comparison, a Canadian study (Pepler et al, 1997) found that 2 per cent of students fitted into this category and a British study (Stephenson & Smith, 1989) reported 6 per cent. In Ireland and Archer's (2004) review of bullying categories, they found that while pure bullies were more likely to be aggressive in conflict situations, bully/victims were more likely to displace their aggressive behaviour onto others, such as peers and others not directly involved in the conflict. More research needs to be done to understand and define this group of children. Do victims become bullies out of anger and frustration? What facilitates the tide turning? Do bullies become victims of their own targets? We are only beginning to scratch the surface in understanding this complex group of students.

Given that students in either one of these categories are already at high risk of maladjustment, students that are both victims and bullies are at an even higher risk of developing a range of adjustment problems and subsequent antisocial behaviours. While the research is mixed, the evidence suggests that these students are the most insecure, the least likeable and the most unsuccessful in school (Stephenson & Smith, 1989); they have also been characterised as strong and easily provoked (Besag, 1989).

Social influences on bullying behaviour

Family

Two features of family life are particularly influential on the social development of bullying behaviour: parenting style and family disharmony. When the parenting style is authoritarian, characterised by punitiveness, domination and control, children are more likely to use this dominating style when relating to others (Manning, Heron & Marshall, 1978; Olweus, 1980, 1984; Strassberg et al, 1994). In contrast, when the parenting style is authoritative, characterised by support for the autonomy of the child while providing clear behavioural boundaries, children are less likely to engage in bullying behaviour (Rican et al, 1993). The parent-child relationship itself, has also been shown to be important. Children with positive relationships with their parents are less likely to participate in bullying (Rican et al, 1993; Rigby, 1993). Likewise, children who are insecurely attached to their parents are more likely to bully their peers (Troy & Sroufe, 1987). It has also been shown that children who perceive their families to be less cohesive and less caring for each other are more likely to participate in school bullying (Bowers, Smith & Binney, 1992, 1994; Berdondini & Smith, 1996).

Children's interaction with their siblings also fuels this developmental path (Patterson, 1986). Aggression between siblings has been found to be the most common form of family violence (Straus et al, 1981). By not intervening when siblings fight, parents can inadvertently support bullying. Parents often attribute this behaviour to sibling rivalry and see it as a normal part of growing up, believing that their children will learn best from sorting out their own problems.

Broadly, the family life of children who bully can be characterised by neglect, dominance, hostility and harsh punishment (Olweus, 1993; Rigby, 1993, 1994). This family dynamic can be overt or insidious, and the children of these families enact the conflict-resolution style to which they have been exposed.

Interestingly, a number of studies have found that the family life of victims of bullies can be similar to the family life of those who bully, characterised by control, dominance, hostility and rejection (Rican, Klicperova & Koucka, 1993; Finnegan, Hodges & Perry, 1998; Shields & Cicchetti, 2001). At the same time, the research findings have been contradictory (Bowers, Smith & Binney, 1992). Families often don't know about their child being a victim of bullying. Victims often keep the problem to themselves, either feeling they should be able to handle the problem or worrying over possible revenge and disapproval. Overall, these children believe that there is little others can do to help them (Garfalo et al, 1987; Olweus, 1991).

Peers

Peers play an important role in understanding bullying and victimisation. An interesting finding shows that 85 per cent of bullying episodes occur in the context of a peer group (see O'Connell, Pepler & Craig, 1999). While most students (83 per cent) report feeling uncomfortable when confronted with an incident of bullying, they have been observed to adopt many roles: joining in, cheering, passively watching and, on occasion, intervening (see Salmivalli, 1999). Observational research has spotted the following pattern of interaction between peers. More often than not, positive attention is given to the bully over the victim. This reinforces the bully's dominance over the victim and their position within the peer group. Peers attracted to aggression become excited and join in, more often in the case of boys than girls (Salmivalli et al, 1996). But even by doing nothing, and not intervening in some way, bystanders unwittingly condone the bullying behaviour. Rigby (1997) found that a good number (15 per cent) of students thought their friends would support and approve of their bullying behaviour. For victims of bullying, having friends lowered the levels of distress felt.

Schools

Family and peers do not wield all the power in influencing students who bully at school. School culture also contributes significantly to the reduction of bullying. Schools differ significantly in the amounts of reported bullying, even when socio-economic and other variables are controlled (Rigby, 1996; see also Galloway & Roland, 2004). It is important for everyone in the school to be committed to reducing bullying. Without the support of those in positions of authority and power in the school, addressing bullying in a systematic way can be an uphill battle. In particular, teachers need the support of the principal if school bullying is going to be reduced (Charach et al, 1995). Positive and supportive school relationships between all members of the school community (principals, teachers, students, and parents) can have a positive impact on reducing school bullying. Having all members of the school community share in the decision-making that affects their lives has also been found to be particularly effective (Olweus, 1987). This process has been applied to the development of school bullying policies, as it assists in making the message clear that bullying behaviour is not condoned and ensures that follow through is consistently applied (Olweus, 1991).

It is also important that schools and their classrooms are well-structured physically and well-integrated culturally. More behaviour problems occur in classrooms where this is absent (Doyle, 1986). Teachers' organisational skills are essential to the goal of maintaining order. Effective teachers have a very clear communication style; monitor and respond to student behaviour; and endorse student responsibility and accountability for their work (Evertson & Emmer, 1982; Duke, 1989). In contrast, disorderly schools are characterised by: teachers with punitive attitudes; rules that are loosely enforced and perceived to be unfair or unclear; ambiguous responses to student misbehaviour; a non-consensual attitude between school staff about appropriate responses to misconduct; and general staff disagreement. Lack of appropriate resources within schools is also associated with higher levels of school bullying (Gottfredson & Gottfredson, 1985). The parallels with the risk factors associated with family life are clearly evident. Schools need to be consistently authoritative, rather than authoritarian, supporting students while not condoning harmful behaviour.

Schools also play a role through recognising where bullying occurs. Generally, students are much more aware of bullying than teachers. When there are consequences for bullying at school, children who bully are careful about where and how they exert their dominance. One study showed that teachers intervene in only one in every 25 bullying episodes (Craig & Pepler, 1997). There are times and places at school where bullying is most likely to occur; generally where there is little or no supervision, such as in the school playground (Olweus, 1991; Pepler et al, 1997). Bullying is also more likely to occur during more competitive or aggressive activities (Murphy et al, 1983). This highlights the importance of the supervision of students during non-classroom time and the maintenance of behaviour codes during all school activities. While some members of the school community support the "principles of free play", with minimal intervention from teachers, this actually encourages bullying behaviour in young children. Just like reading, writing and arithmetic, children need to be taught social skills that encourage safe and productive play.

Social institutions

Our social institutions regulate and legitimate our tolerance for bullying and violence in society. They set limits on what is acceptable and define the regulatory structure that aims to build compliance through encouraging certain behaviours and discouraging others. In essence, they shape the norms that we live by. The assertion of power, be it through physical force or status, is an avenue for resolving social problems that is often proposed, carried through, and rewarded. Bullying and violence can be an avenue to compliance legitimised by governments, corporate bodies, workplaces and families. The media, too, is a source of influence, be it the evening news, the latest blockbuster production, or morning cartoons – a common theme is that bullying works. In other words, domination of others is an effective means to an end. The message has particular appeal to those who see violence as consonant with their view of the world. Aggressive children are more likely than non-aggressive children to be drawn to and imitate media violence (Huesmann et al, 1984). Those developmentally predisposed to aggressive behaviour are also predisposed to seek out aggressive acts in the media and others who perpetrate it, be it through the Internet, television or street gangs.

It is impossible to isolate bullying in school from other social influences that perpetuate the problem. Bullying is a global problem that demands global attention. At the same time schools have an important role to play, as Goleman (1995, p 278) stated:

> Family life no longer offers growing numbers of children a sure footing in life, schools are left as the one place communities can turn to for correctives to children's deficiencies in emotional and social competence. That is not to say that schools alone can stand in for all the social institutions that too often are in or nearing collapse. But since virtually every child goes to school (at least at the onset), it offers a place to reach children with basic lessons for living that they may never get otherwise.

In summary, we can see that both children who bully and who are bullied are treading a path that we should be concerned about. Being a bully and being a victim are risk factors for subsequent antisocial and violent behaviour that have serious personal and social consequences. We can also see that there are a number of risk factors associated with becoming a bully and a victim. This pattern of behaviour is often set early in life and can secure itself as the child moves from the family environment to school and into the workplace. Given this analysis, early intervention seems the most productive path to take. Children, and their families and communities, must be given opportunities to learn that there are alternatives to bullying, and our schools, as our primary developmental institution, are well placed to support them in this learning process. This said, schools need broader institutional support in addressing the problems of bullying, violence and alienation within their confines.

A schoolyard lesson in the ways of life?

It could be that the lesson for schools, despite the growing evidence of the harmful effects of bullying, is that bullying really is "a lesson in the ways of life", "character building", "kids being kids", "playground rough and tumble" and "learning how to stick up for yourself". Maybe instead of addressing the problem, schools just need to embrace the problem. These are attitudes and sentiments that are widely held. As a case in point, a senior politician in the United Kingdom was quoted as saying that bullying had done him no harm and was preparation for life (*The Guardian*, 25 January 1996, p 5). Indeed, bullying is a commonly used tactic and there is evidence that it always has been. There are numerous historical and fictional accounts of bullying, such as in the works of Charles Dickens (*Oliver Twist*, 1837; *Nicholas Nickleby*, 1838) and Thomas Hughes (*Tom*

Brown's School Days, 1857), as well as other historical tales (see Ross 1996). Even today, the exploits of the orphaned boys in *Oliver Twist* are alive and well in the hearts and minds of contemporary society, for the same issues continue to present themselves. More recently, James Moloney's (1998) award winning *Buzzard Breath and Brains* tells the contemporary tale of dominance and submission, in other words, bullying. Further, besides these stories there is mounting empirical evidence that most bullying intervention programs are largely ineffective (Rigby, 2004, p 287):

> In a meta-evaluation of 12 well-planned interventions conducted bet-
> ween 1986 and 2001 in different countries, the programs were generally
> found to have had significant but relatively small effects in reducing the
> proportion of children being victimized and little or no effect in the
> reduction of children bullying others.

Likewise, Smith, Schneider, Smith and Ananiadou (2004, p 559) carried out a meta-review of 14 different bullying intervention programs from around the world and concluded: "we can only make a cautious recommendation that whole-school antibullying interventions be continued until they are evaluated further".

Does this evidence convince us that it is time to concede defeat, that bullying really is a normal part of life? Many researchers think not: "the overarching message is that intervention can succeed, but not enough is known to indicate exactly how and when. Psychologists should be proactive in promoting carefully evaluated interventions in which the whole-school approach is implemented with precision and compared with other potentially useful interventions" (Smith et al, 2004, p 560). In other words, each school must think and act very clearly and strategically when implementing a whole school approach that will work for them.

Bullying may have been common through the ages, but this is as much a reflection on having institutions that tolerate (or even condone) bullying, as on the nature of children. Bullying is not just "kids being kids". Bullying is the systematic abuse of power meant to oppress another. The acceptance of bullying as a normal part of life signals that intimidation, dominance and violence are acceptable ways to resolve differences and conflict, as well as to inflate our own standing in the world. The evidence shows that tolerance and acceptance of bullying leads to lifelong problems, for the victim and the bully, and the community around them. Further, we know that some schools have been able to significantly address bullying behaviour (see Smith, Pepler & Rigby, 2004). The question is where to from here? Given the large and comprehensive research that was done following the school rampage shootings in the United States, where bullying behaviour had been clearly implicated early in the analysis, this research may provide some clues to a larger picture of school life.

School rampage shootings: The findings of the Secret Service in the United States

In the United States, the Secret Service's National Threat Assessment Center (NTAC) examines and builds knowledge around incidents of targeted violence to provide leadership and guidance in its prevention. In the wake of the school shootings in the United States (and elsewhere), the Center examined 37 incidents of school shootings, involving 41 perpetrators (Vossekuil et al, 2002). They looked at a number of the variables that we have reviewed and found mixed results:

- Family background: some perpetrators came from intact cohesive families; some from broken homes or lived with foster parents.

- Academic achievement: some were excellent students; others were failing.

- Peer support: some were loners; some had a close circle of friends.

None of these standard predictors were helpful in unravelling the puzzle of "why". Was there a common theme at all? Yes, depression. Three out of four perpetrators had tried or talked about suicide. More than two-thirds felt victimised through ongoing bullying. The Secret Service asked Luke Woodham, who killed his mother and two students in 1997: what would it have taken for a grown-up to know what you felt? Woodham replied: "Pay attention. Just sit down and talk with me". The Secret Service then asked: "What advice do you have for adults?" Woodham's advice was, "they should try to bond more with their students ... Talk to them ... It doesn't have to be about anything. Just have some kind of relationship with them".

The school rampage of Kip Kinkel – who shot and killed both his parents and two students, and wounded 22 other students – was the case that most puzzled the experts because his profile reflected a number of protective factors, and not risk factors, for violent behaviour. Responding to early warning signs in Kip's behaviour, his parents "were considered, concerned, attentive parents who knew their son was troubled and did everything in their power to help him" (Newman, 2004, p 259). They monitored both his media influences and access to firearms, and provided Kip with academic support. Kip's parents had a good relationship with the school and were also teachers. Kip also had a close circle of friends, including girls who liked him. In other words, he had all the right institutional supports in place.

But if you scratched the surface of this profile the pattern becomes more complex: parental discipline was uneven, his father had been the "controlling" factor and his mother had struggled to get him more support, such as psychiatric assistance and anti-depressant medication. As in others cases examined by the Secret Service, public social ridicule and bullying at school finally got to Kip. His response was a coldly rational plan of attack, disgracing those who had disgraced him. Like many of the other perpetrators, he was both homicidal and suicidal. He wanted his own life to end the day of the rampage, but that wish was not fulfilled.

In contrast to the cases of Kip Kinkel and Luke Woodham, Harris and Klebold were concerned about their parents (see Aronson, 2000, p 40). The videotape they made a few weeks prior to the Columbine shootings makes this clear: "They're going to be put through hell once we do this", Harris said. He even addressed his parents directly, stating: "There is nothing you guys could do about this". Both Harris and Klebold wanted to make sure their parents would not be blamed for what happened, quoting from the Tempest: "Good wombs hath borne bad sons". They clearly thought their situation had more to do with their school life than their home life.

In each of these cases, the common denominator was public humiliation. The perpetrators struck back at the institution, and the community therein, that failed to honour them with a sense of respect and dignity (see Leary, Kowalski, Smith & Phillips, 2003; Webber, 2003). These perpetrators were not being impulsive. There was a coherent, understandable, and often coldly rational pattern to their thinking and behaviour. Typically, they told others about their plan and even asked for help and advice. This information wasn't taken seriously, or never got to a person who had the means, skills and resources to take appropriate action. If schools had in place appropriate mechanisms to channel this type of information, and once received, take it seriously, they would be more able to respond in ways that make a difference.

There is no one specific profile that targets the next likely perpetrator, however, there are key indicators that typify the social life of perpetrators of mass school violence. Instead of profiling, the Federal Bureau of Investigation's Critical Incident Response Team recommends a threat assessment approach using a four-pronged model that takes into account personality, family dynamics, school dynamics and social dynamics, and then specifies the level of threat at one of three levels – low, medium and high (O'Toole, 2000). Dewey Cornell and his team have field-tested guidelines for a student threat assessment process, which has been found effective in assessing the level of threat and determining the appropriate response (see Cornell et al, 2004). Thus, it seems productive to examine these incidents within a larger social dynamic.

Mark Leary and his colleagues empirically tested the claim that the school shootings of the late 1990s were precipitated by teasing, ostracism and social rejection. In their analysis of 15 school shootings in the United States, Leary et al (2003, p 212) concluded: "Without discounting other explanations, we believe that the primary motive in most of the school shootings seems to have been retribution, either for an ongoing pattern of ostracism and teasing or for an acute rejection such as a romantic breakup". This is consistent with the findings of Katherine Newman and her team: "School shooters are not all loners and they are not all bullied, but nearly all experience ostracism and social marginality" (Newman, 2004, p 242). Based on their conclusions, Leary and his colleagues make two broad points that warrant attention:

1. The school shooters were typically male students, who were ostracised and had been chronically taunted, teased, harassed and publicly humiliated. They were also characterised by one or more of the following:

   - an interest in firearms or bombs;

   - a fascination with death or Satanism;

   - psychological problems involving depression, impulse control or sadistic tendencies.

2. Bullying and malicious teasing is a serious problem in schools that:

   - affects the majority of students in primary and middle schools;

   - causes a good number of students to stay home to escape social torment, and, in extreme cases, take their own life;

   - induces feelings of shame, humiliation, depression, anxiety, and low self-esteem.

These researchers, like others, also make the point that many young people who share the characteristics of the school shooters are not likely to endanger their peers, thus affirming that profiling along these lines is not likely to be effective (see also Mulvey & Cauffman, 2001; Reddy et al, 2001). They also make the point that bullying in schools is a behaviour that is likely to be ignored.

The general conclusions that can be drawn are that: (a) bullying behaviour is important to understand and address and (b) to intervene effectively we must understand the wider social and emotional dynamics of students' lives at school, particularly the social and emotional dynamics of ostracism, shame and humiliation. These forces are largely social constructs that cannot be understood in terms of individual factors alone. The evidence suggests that violent behaviour is relational in nature and must be understood in terms of the social and emotional dynamics in play, and across a range of social contexts that shape the lives of children. Strong and healthy relationships are a protective factor against violence; weak and fractured relationships are a risk factor for violence.

As a case in point, it was a strong and healthy relationship that saved the life of a teacher and ended a school rampage in Germany. This teacher knew he had a relationship with the masked gunman: "Go ahead and shoot me, Robert, but first look me in the face". That instant, instead of becoming the 14th teacher shot that day, along with two students and a police officer, Robert responded with respect for the teacher, "That's it for today Herr Heise", (*International Herald Tribune*, 29 April 2002, p 7). Sadly, shortly thereafter, when contained and isolated in a schoolroom, Robert ended his own life, crossing the grey line from perpetrator to victim.

Beyond pathologising and blaming

Bullying and victimisation in schools is a systemic and multifaceted problem. It is important that we get beyond the impulse to find simple solutions to complex problems. Pointing fingers at one factor is not an option: be it the child, the parent or the school. Dismissing a child as "just like that", is pathologising the child and thereby abating responsibility for the problem. Likewise, parents are also at risk of being pathologised by themselves, and others, for their children's behaviour. Further, it is not uncommon to claim that it is the school's problem alone. Blame in any form is not productive; it merely shifts responsibility, when typically some form of collective responsibility is the only way forward. There are many influences that shape a child's life. Not discounting individual factors, it is the wider social and emotional dynamic found in the web of relationships we weave around the lives of our children, that has been found to be important to understanding the cycle of violence.

This perspective highlights the fact that "intervention" is an ongoing process as relationships develop and that it is possible to intervene at different points in the developmental cycle. While the optimal path would be for students, families and schools to work together in a coordinated and participatory framework, it is also the case that parents can intervene where schools fail to take responsibility, and schools can intervene where parents fail to take responsibility. Further, the cycles of bullying, violence and alienation, which are related to the social and emotional dynamic of shame and humiliation, arise at any stage of life. Understanding these social and emotional processes is crucial for navigating the way ahead. Thus, the social psychology of, and the relationships between, alienation, shame and humiliation are explored in the next chapter.

Chapter 2

Alienation, shame and humiliation

To be overwhelmed by shame and humiliation causes the destruction of self-esteem; and without a certain amount of self-esteem, the self collapses and the soul dies.

James Gilligan, 1996, p 48.

Much human suffering stems from destructive emotions, as hatred breeds violence or craving fuels addiction. One of our most basic responsibilities as caring people is to alleviate the human costs of such out-of-control emotions.

The Dalai Lama (in Goleman, 2003, p xii)

Bullying and violence: The social dynamic

The previous chapter highlighted how the social and emotional dynamic of school life can lead to the escalation of violence. Through examining bullying and violence in schools in terms of individual risk factors and pathways, the aim was to highlight that school violence also needs to be understood in terms of the social and emotional dynamic that underpins the processes of social inclusion and exclusion. The main premise was that it is important to understand an individual's social behaviour in the context of group life. This chapter seeks to further examine the social dynamic of school life, in terms of the impact of social exclusion and the associated emotions of shame and humiliation.

There is an inherent tension to the social life of individuals, each of us is capable of being both compassionate to others and narrowly self-interested. This tension suggests that individuals need both a sense of belonging and a sense of significance. When the balance between belonging and significance breaks down, we become motivated, psychologically and socially, to address this imbalance. We can either manage this process in socially adaptive ways, or socially maladaptive ways. When individuals develop socially maladaptive responses, this pattern of behaviour could allow for a process of alienation to establish itself. Alienation, in turn, can lead to feelings of shame and humiliation. These feelings are often masked, as revealing them exposes our vulnerabilities to others. Yet, at the same time, these hidden emotions can become a destructive force for the individual and their community, particularly when they begin to fester. The process is complex, both psychologically and socially, yet important to understanding the dynamics of bullying, violence and alienation. The aim of this chapter is to build a better understanding of these dynamics, so to better address these problems.

A good starting point in building this understanding is acknowledging that we all have a basic need to be "somebody" – this requires both a sense of *individual* significance and a sense of *collective* affirmation. Being "somebody" is carefully navigated throughout life. For some, this can be a difficult and tenuous journey, as Fuller (2004, p 49) recounts:

> As the hunger for recognition mounts, the undernourished may become desperate. An outcast starved for recognition who attacks others or himself is giving expression to the unendurable indignity of feeling inconsequential. A confidant of one of the boys who killed a dozen of their Colorado schoolmates at Columbine High said of his friend, "He was afraid he would never be known".

Both students who bully and students who are victimised are caught up in cycles of alienation, although their patterns of behaviour are different. For some, the social cycle of alienation and the associated psychological void continues to widen, affecting themselves and others through different life stages and social domains, becoming evident in behaviours that reflect poor psychological and social adjustment. For others, this cycle is broken through tragic means – suicide and revenge. Still, there are many others who are able to move beyond bullying and victimisation and break the cycle of alienation. These stories give us hope and we have as much to learn from these stories of hope as we do from stories of harm.

Emma's story: A story of hope

Emma started to push other girls around when she was in Grade 3. The pattern of behaviour began, she says, because she felt excluded from the "popular" group. She wanted in. Whatever it took. ... She says it was the death of [a student in another school], as well as her school's antibullying programme, that convinced her that kids can play at schoolyard politics with a little more compassion: "I didn't have a group. This is a huge impact on people and I don't think people understand how much impact it has". "There's a way out. You don't have to get to the point where you're killing yourself". (Clough, 2001)

Emma's story makes an important point. She bullied because she wanted to belong, to be part of a group. We often forget this basic need in our increasingly globalised and individualistic society, where we rely less on local communities and more on our economic status.

Eric Debarbieux (2003), Director of the International Observatory on School Violence, makes a strong case for the link between school violence, social exclusion and globalisation. Building on the work of Giddens (1990), he argues that a narrow global focus on building economic capital poses a danger for democracy, in particular local democracies, where social inequities are realised. These effects are now being played out in our schools and are characterised by increasing alienation and violence. Debarbieux's analysis offers an implicit solution: If social exclusion, characterised by alienation, is associated with increases in school violence, can social inclusion mitigate against school violence? In other words, can a sense of connectedness with family and schools protect us against violent and harmful behaviour?

School connectedness

In the United States, a national longitudinal study of adolescent health looked at the effects of school connectedness, the belief by students that adults in the school care about their learning and about them as individuals. It found that students who felt connected to school (McNeely, Nonnemake & Blum, 2002; see also Blum and Libby, 2004) were less likely to:

- use alcohol and illegal drugs;

- become pregnant;

- engage in violent or deviant behaviour;

- experience emotional distress.

The inference is that through building the capacity for schools to foster supportive relationships within the school community, schools can address the feelings of estrangement and hopelessness that some students feel. Kelm and Connell (2004) have made the point that "by high school as many as 40% to 60% of students become chronically disengaged from school – urban, suburban, and rural – not counting those who drop out" (p 262). Their research finding support the importance of school engagement for students, created through a "caring, well structured learning environment in which expectations are high, clear and fair" (p 270). This research contributes to "the mounting body of evidence supporting school connectedness as an important protective factor in the lives of young people" (Blum and Libby, 2004, p 231). The Wingspread

Declaration on School Connections presents a statement by an interdisciplinary group if education leaders, based on the best empirical evidence to date. Core elements of the statement include:

1. Student success can be improved through strengthened bonds with school.

2. In order to feel connected, students must experience high expectations for academic success, feel supported by staff, and feel safe in their school.

3. Critical accountability measures can be impacted by school connectedness such as: academic performance, fighting, truancy, and drop out rates.

4. Increased school connectedness is related to educational motivation, classroom engagement, and better attendance. These are then linked to higher academic achievement.

5. School connectedness is also related to lower rates of disruptive behaviour, substance and tobacco use, emotional distress, and early age of first sex.

6. School connectedness can be built through fair and consistent discipline, trust among members of the school community, high expectations from the parents and school staff, effective curriculum and teaching strategies, and students feeling connected to at least one member of the school community. (Blum and Libby, 2004, p 232)

Social exclusion and belonging

Roy Baumeister and his colleagues have done some compelling work building on their thesis that the need to belong is one of the most basic and fundamental human motivations (Baumeister & Leary, 1995); consequently, exclusion from a community could be a powerful blow to self-esteem. Indeed, Twenge, Catanese and Baumeister (2002, p 614) found that social exclusion resulted in self-defeating behaviour, and the relationship was causal, not correlational.

> Apparently the desire for social connection operates at a motivational level that precedes the rational pursuit of enlightened self-interest. At very least, our results suggest that a strong feeling of social inclusion is important for enabling the individual to use the human capacity for self-regulation in ways that will preserve and protect the self and promote the self's best long-term interests of health and well-being.

Baumeister and colleagues have made the link between social rejection and strong emotional distress, providing evidence of its effects on a variety of behaviours. For example, their studies have found that social exclusion and rejection:

- reduced intelligent thought (Baumeister, Twenge & Nuss, 2002);

- increased aggressive behaviour (Twenge, Baumeister, Tice & Stucke, 2001);

- reduced pro-social behaviour (Twenge, Ciaracco, Cuervo & Baumeister, 2005);

Each of these studies makes the argument that social exclusion has caused breakdowns in self-regulation. In other words, social exclusion is the basis for *deflating* human potential and social responsibility, while social inclusion is the basis for *building* human potential and social responsibility (see also Williams, Forgas & Hippel, 2005). The inference is that who we are as individuals is intimately caught up with who we are as a member of society, and the many different social groups that make up society. Social identities, understood as the psychological link between individuals and social groups, mould who we are and how we behave.

Social identity and the self: Bridging the individual and society

A coherent framework through which to understand the self and behaviour is important when building understanding of behaviour change to effectively to break the developmental cycles of bullying, violence and alienation. Two conceptual frameworks that help to make sense of how the psychology of individuals is linked to the psychology of group membership are social identity theory (Tajfel & Turner, 1979) and self-categorisation theory (Turner et al, 1987). As Turner (1996, p 8) states:

> [The theories suppose] that the self-process works to socialize cognitive functioning and individual behaviour and ensure that cognitive activity is closely tied to the current realities of individual's social environment.

In other words, students' behaviour is intractably linked to the social realities of home, school and community life. The theories provide a framework for thinking about the self at both the individual and collective level. Simply put: an individual's sense of significance and belongingness. This theoretical framework for thinking about the individual and society enables us to move beyond the dualistic stance between individualism – which underlies the legalistic traditions of social regulation, and collectivism – which underlies the moralistic traditions in social regulation. This alternative framework acknowledges that who we are is intractably caught up with our sense of self at both the individual and collective levels; in other words, our sense of significance and belongingness.

Social identity and delinquency

If significance and belonging are important, what can students do when they don't feel valued within the school or they don't identify with what the school values? One option for such students is to develop a counter-culture, a gang that values delinquent behaviour. Delinquency is defined as the behaviour of adolescents who have violated the norms and rules of society (Calhoun et al, 1989 or literally defined, is the deficiency of social links and social bonds (Tomoric, 1979). Koh (1998) has investigated the development of the delinquent social identity. Her research addresses a number of issues: the role of social comparison processes in the creation of counter identity; the role of the peer group in delinquency; and the context-specific nature of the delinquent social identity. Thus, delinquency arises within a specific social context through social comparison; but, a delinquent is not necessarily a delinquent in all social contexts, as peers influence the identity in play at any given time.

Emler and Reicher (1995) have made similar claims. They understand delinquency in terms of the collective management of reputation. Their argument incorporates three main elements. First, an individual only defines how they relate to an institutional order, such as a school, once they come to participate in that order. Secondly, delinquent acts signal opposition to the institutional order, while conformist acts signal identification with the institutional order. Thirdly, self-definition is a collective process and depends on the reputation that an individual is able to negotiate with significant others. Therefore, in the case of students who bully, their identity is negotiated in the context of the social relationships that sustain them within an institutional order – at school and home. If institutions have the capacity to legitimate and support harmful behaviour, they also have the capacity to counter harmful behaviour.

Social identity, social institutions and cooperation

As previously stated, social identity can be thought of as the psychological link between an individual and a social group or collective. Within an institutional framework, Tyler & Bladder (2000) have applied a social identity analysis to the understanding of cooperative behaviour, linking cooperation within organisations to levels of pride and respect held by individuals within the organisation. It is argued that an individual's self-worth is both collective (taking pride in group membership) and individualistic (having discrete respect within that group). They argue that an individual's self worth is a function of both collective (pride in group membership) and individual (respect within the group) dimensions within that organization or institution. Compliance and cooperation within an institution can be predicted by an individual's self-worth within that institution. Thus, the more an individual feels a sense of pride and respect within an institution, the more they are likely to comply and cooperate with that institutional order. In the context of school safety, a bully may find it difficult to take pride in certain aspects of school life (such as academic achievement) but counter this through gaining respect by dominating others and involving him or herself in subcultures that condone (passively or actively) their behaviour. Further, if domination of others is valued (and legitimated by principals, teachers and parents), then the bully has a legitimate source of pride. When students cease to take pride in their accomplishments at school and instead gain respect through the domination of others, delinquency often follows (Farrington, 1993). Yet some bullies are not necessarily viewed as delinquents, and may not take on this persona, in part, because institutional orders – be they home, school or broader social forces – may normalise and legitimise bullying as a form of accepted behaviour.

This research suggests that healthy cooperative behaviour in schools is a product of a positive social identity within the school community. To this end, it is important to develop students' sense of pride and respect within the school community. At the same time, there is growing evidence that suggests that we need to do more than focus on the positive aspects of school life. When school communities focus on the positives, while neglecting to address underlying social and emotional issues, a shallow social veneer is created and engagement with the community becomes superficial. True engagement with the school community requires addressing the deeper issues. To this end, the thick emotional stew underlying areas of contention must be addressed. School communities need effective strategies to manage negative emotions, while building positive emotions. The importance of emotions in negotiation has been recognised by two of the world leaders in developing effective negotiation strategies – Roger Fisher and Daniel Shapiro of the Harvard Negotiation Project (Fisher & Shapiro, 2005).

> Although emotions are often thought of as obstacles to a negotiation – and certainly can be – they can also be a great asset. They can help us achieve our negotiation purpose, whether to find creative ways to satisfy interests or to improve a rocky relationship (p 6).

Fisher and Shapiro emphasise that the emotional tone of a negotiation can either make, or break, a mutually productive outcome. They outline five universal human concerns that need to be addressed to establish a productive emotional tone: express appreciation (of thoughts and feelings); build affiliation; respect autonomy; acknowledge status; choose a fulfilling role. Establishing a productive emotional tone is, of course, most difficult when addressing the emotive issues of bullying, violence and alienation.

As Douglas Stone (1999) argued, we need to learn how to have those "difficult conversations" such that we can harness the negatives as opportunities for growth, understanding and reconnection. To get to the heart of these "difficult conversations", school communities need to become emotionally literate, increasing their capacity to navigate a range of emotions including shame and humiliation.

Bullying and violence: The emotional dynamic of shame and humiliation

Humiliation was one of the key factors discussed in Julie Webber's (2003) analysis of the school shootings and Leary et al's (2003) analysis, as described in Chapter 1. Yet, as Harter and colleagues (2003, p 13) noted in their recent review of the literature on humiliation:

> Surprisingly, in the literature on emotion, in general, and in the literature on adolescence, in particular, there is scant attention to humiliation ... This is especially surprising given the fact that adolescence is a psychologically fragile period of development, where youth have heightened levels of self-consciousness and a vulnerable sense of self ... making them prone to reactions of humiliation.

While these researchers acknowledge the contributions of William Pollack and James Garbarino, there are others who are also building our understanding of shame and humiliation as it relates to social behaviour. This literature does not sit squarely within the field of adolescent development, but it is certainly relevant. For example, from the fields of criminology and sociology, John Braithwaite's theory of reintegrative shaming theory is notable (see Ahmed, Harris, Braithwaite & Braithwaite, 2001; Braithwaite, 1989), as is Tom Scheff's work on shame, rage and violence (1990, 1994, 2000; see also Scheff and Retzinger, 1991). From the clinical literature a number of others come to mind[1] and from the field of social psychology, the work of June Tangney stands out (see Tangney, 2002, 2003; Tangney & Dearing, 2003). While these authors do not necessarily agree on a common understanding of shame and humiliation (indeed there is a healthy level of debate within the literature), each is engaged in a field of analysis that is gaining interest and influence. The framework to be developed in this chapter does not seek

---

1   From the clinical literature see Paul Gilbert (1998, 2000, 2002); James Gilligan (1996, 2001); Gershen Kaufman (1992, 1996; Kaufman & Raphael, 1990); Helen Block Lewis (1987, 1995); Donald Nathanson (1987, 1992, 1997); and Silvan Tomkins (1963, 1987).

to work through the current debates within the literature; nor does it seek to be comprehensive, there are other sources that do this well (see Ahmed et al, 2001; Harris, Walgrave & Braithwaite, 2004; Martens, 2005; Tangney & Dearing, 2002; van Stokkom, 2002). The aim is to build a basic foundation so as to understand the relationships between alienation, shame and humiliation.

Social identity, the self and emotion

Through one's life course, individuals develop a range of social identities. Kaufman (1996), building on Tompkins script theory (1987), argues that the process of identity development involves the conscious differentiation of the self. Social identities can be congruent with one another and they may also express a divergent aspect of one's self. For Example, as Eli Anderson (1999) explains in "Code of the Street", the safety of poor inner city black youth in America is dependent of their ability to "code switch" – where a person behaves by different sets of rules, depending on the situation. For these young people the "code of the street" operates by a different set of rules than the code of home life or even school life. The "code of the street" developed in a social context of alienation as Anderson explains:

> The hard reality of the world of the street can be traced to the profound sense of alienation from mainstream society and its institutions felt by many poor inner city black people, particularly the young (1999, p 34).

As Anderson further explains:

> At the heart of the code is the issue of respect – loosely defined as being treated "right" or being granted one's "props" (or proper due) or the deference one deserves … The rules of the code in fact provide a framework for negotiating respect (1999, p 34).

In this context, an identity that keeps one safe on the street may get one in trouble with many of society's mainstream institutions. Negotiating the interplay between this range of identities requires careful attention to one's social world. When these identities come into conflict, feelings of shame will also need to be managed by one's internal sanctioning system.

Kaufman (1996) argues that shame is healed when we offer a genuine and honest human relationship that provides for an individual's deepest needs, in particular care and respect. Through building and affirming positive relationships shame is healed, hope is instilled and individuals are freed from the hold of counterproductive identity patterns. He concludes: "Central to the resolution of shame is the development of a *self-affirming* capacity … This capacity to affirm oneself translates into having esteem for self, valuing self, respect for self, pride in self" (1996, p 216). Simply put, for Kaufman identity re-growth and the healing of shame leads to reintegration of the self.

This analysis helps make the link between the social dynamic of pride and respect, and the emotion of shame, each of which is bound up with the other. While Tom Tyler's work, reviewed above, highlights the importance of building pride and respect in fostering healthy social identities, Kaufman's work helps us to understand the role of shame in these same processes. The work of John Braithwaite and his colleagues brings further insight into the centrality of shame; specifically, in the context of a process that enables individuals and communities to have those difficult conversations that are often heavy with emotion. In particular, Braithwaite's theoretical work has helped ground our under-standing of successful reintegration ceremonies (Braithwaite & Mugford, 1994) that aim to restore individuals to communities following harm and wrongdoing. These conversations are also known as "community con-ferences", and are a form of restorative justice.

Restorative justice and reintegrative shaming

The success of a community conference, according to Braithwaite and colleagues, is predicated on acknowledging and discharging shame such that, parties affected by harmful behaviour can move towards social and emotional healing. A restorative justice conference is a practice that brings "victims" and "offenders" together to listen and respond to the impact of individuals' behaviour upon others. Creating safe social and emotional spaces enables victims and offenders to take responsibility for their behaviour and to lay the foundation to repair the harm done; thereby reducing the risk of harm re-occurring. The aim is to restore victims and offenders to their communities and, through this process, increase responsibility and resilience within the community. Indeed, these are high hopes, but there is building evidence that these hopes are being realised (see Chapters 4 and 6). The strength of these practices lay in the structure, process, and values of the community conferencing process.

During a conference, both "victims" and "offenders" come together with their respected supporters. These supporters are often an indivi-dual's family members but could also include other members of their community, such as the football coach, music teacher, neighbour, and so on. The important ingredient to the success of the conference is that these people are highly respected by the person being supported (see Harris, 2001). Thus, in community conferences individuals are supported through the involvement of a positive reference group. Both victim and offender are supported by the esteem that these individuals provide to get them through the difficult process of confronting the shame and humi-liation caused by the wrongdoing.

By bringing the affected community together, the aim is to develop a common understanding of what happened, who was affected and how, and what needs to happen to collectively address the harm caused. The dynamics of the conference are complex and there is usually an ebb and flow in the connections between participants as the process develops. For example, the parents may identify with each other, as could siblings, as each individual's story of how they were affected by the incident unfolds. However, the collective frame of reference that is hoped for typically does not emerge until the expression of shame is brought to the fore, through individuals taking responsibility for their behaviour and acknowledging how it has affected others. It is here that the stage is set for affected parties to begin a healing process.

Reintegrative shaming theory (Braithwaite, 1989) has informed social and emotional understanding of restorative justice. This analysis of restorative justice argues that there are two main features inherent in the process of successful reintegration ceremonies. First, a community of sup-port must be offered to the "offender" and the "victim". This community would be made up of the people who are most significant in the lives of the individuals involved. Second, the wrongdoing must be addressed in a manner that exposes how each party present, including supporters, has been affected by the action. It is through this process that the shame over the wrongdoing emerges (see Braithwaite, 1989, 1999). This process puts the behaviour, and not the person, in the centre of the proceedings. This inclusive process, where all parties that have been involved and affected participate: (a) makes it clear to the offender that their behaviour is not condoned within the community; and (b) is respectful of the individual while not condoning the behaviour. The first point constitutes the shaming aspect of the intervention while the second point provides the basis by which the shaming process is reintegrative, rather than stigmatising.

Reintegrative shaming theory suggests that both shaming and the emotion of shame are of considerable importance in regulating social behaviour (see Harris, 2006). When a member of a community has done something that the community does not condone, the act can be dealt with in two ways: those affected can belittle both the person and the behaviour, or those affected can respect the person while not condoning the behaviour. The former is known as stigmatised shaming, a process that gives negative labels to both the person and the act, the latter is known as reintegrative shaming, a process that supports the person while not condoning the act. Separating the person from the behaviour allows communities to confront the shame and humiliation without stigmatising those involved. The process aims to create a space wherein participants are given the opportunity to touch each other's humanity, acknowledging that they share some level of commonality with the other participants. This sense of commonality has been described as a sense of "collective vulnerability" (see McDonald & Moore, 2001). The process prioritises the dignity and worth of the individuals involved. Indeed, it is the value of human relationships that is the true influence mechanism in the process, and which mitigates against further harmful behaviour. There can be the sense of a collective epiphany, or a turning point, for a community brought together through a community conference.

McDonald and Moore (2001) were among the first to move to an understanding of community conferencing as a mechanism by which the negative emotions associated with conflict could be transformed into the positive emotions associated with cooperation (see also Abramson & Moore, 2002). They argue that the expression of shame occurs at a turning point in a restorative justice (or community) conference, and emphasise that a significant part of the experience of shame seems to be collective. It is at this collective level that emotional transformation allows the shame to be acknowledged and forgiveness to be expressed. This point has been described as the time when a process of emotional transformation occurs.

Offenders generally seem to express a sense of shame most strongly when everyone affected has an opportunity to openly parti- cipate in the process and share their story of what happened and how they were affected. This is the moment when the extent of the harm done has been most thoroughly communicated. Offenders, as the primary cause of the harm, are now at their most vulnerable. It is at this moment that a relationship common to all participants comes to the fore, through a sense of collective vulnerability, wherein participants feel that they are a community of people each harmed by the same incident. This sense of empathy for each other suggests a sense of identification with each other, and that shame has been acknowledged and resolved. (See Harris et al (2004) for a more detailed explanation of the emotional dynamics of community conferences.)

Bullying and shame management

Building on reintegrative shaming theory, Ahmed (2001) has found that a student's ability to manage shame over wrongdoing to be an important mediating variable in the understanding of bullying and victimisation. Ahmed (2001) defines two broad categories of shame management styles: shame acknowledgement and shame displacement.

These styles differentially characterise the four bullying status categories – bullies, victims, bully/victims and non-bullies/non-victims.

- Non-bullies/non-victims acknowledge shame and discharge it.

- Victims acknowledge shame but are caught up in self-critical thinking, through ongoing feelings of rejection from others. Shame becomes persistent, despite acknowledgement of wrongdoing.

- Bullies are less likely to acknowledge shame. Shame is more likely to be displaced, often being expressed as anger towards objects or individuals.

- Bully/victims capture the worst of these two troubled groups. They feel shame but, like bullies, fail to acknowledge it. As such, they are also more likely to displace shame into anger. Further, like victims, they are caught up in ongoing self-critical thoughts, through feelings of rejection from others.

Shame management has also been found to be related to some of the earlier risk factors for bullying behaviour (Ahmed & Braithwaite, 2004). For example, one family factor which has been found to be significantly influential is how wrongdoing is dealt with in the family. Is the process punitive or reintegrative? Does the process stigmatise the child into a certain pattern of behaviour or does the process allow the child to make amends while maintaining their dignity as a respected member of the family? The evidence is consistent with the theory outlined. Parents of children who bullied others reported using stigmatised shaming more often as a child-rearing practice (Ahmed et al, 2001).

Shame management can be adaptive or maladaptive. Shame management is adaptive when it activates an internal sanctioning mechanism that allows individuals to discharge shame in a manner that maintains the health of social relationships. The process can be understood as follows. Shame comes to the fore when we behave inappropriately in respect to an important community of support, for example our family or school. Through taking responsibility for the wrongdoing and making amends, shame is acknowledged and discharged. Through this process, feelings of connectedness with others in our community remain intact and our social relationships are not damaged. Shame can be maladaptive when our internal sanctioning mechanism is functioning in such a way that does not allow shame over wrongdoing to be discharged. Why the sanctioning system is not operating at an optimal level can be a product of a number of processes. While much more work needs to be done in this area, a good overview is detailed in *Shame Management Through Reintegration* (Ahmed, Harris, Braithwaite & Braithwaite, 2001).

Shame that has not been discharged remains internalised. This has consequences for feelings of connectedness with others in the community, and can reduce both feelings of community pride and respect. Further, unacknowledged shame has the potential to be expressed as anger towards the community and significant others, thus further propagating the cycle of shame and alienation. The community that has evoked the shame can contribute to its negative manifestation if the individuals involved are subjected to further feelings of rejection, through the way members of the community, particularly authority figures, manage shame themselves.

Pride, shame and conflict

In the first chapter, bullying was defined as a form of conflict where there is a power imbalance. Scheff (1994) argues that pride and shame play central roles in the escalation and resolution of conflict. Scheff conceptualises pride as the obverse emotion to shame, as each is conceptualised as an emotion grounded in the collective knowledge of self. Pride is associated with achievement and success while shame is associated with failure and wrongdoing. Scheff (1994, p 34) rests his argument on three main principles that build upon one another.

1.   Protracted conflict often oscillates between silent impasses and interminable confrontation.

2.   The alienation between the two parties takes the form of unity (engulfment) during impasses and separation (isolation) during confrontation. The denial of shame is a key aspect in the alienation of the self from others. The result is a feeling trap within and between each party.

3.   Protracted conflict is resolved when alienation is transformed into solidarity through the acknowledgment of shame. Parties are able to self-regulate the social distance between themselves and others when shame is acknowledged.

Building on Durkheim (1897), Scheff (1994) argues that there must be a balance between the emphasis given to individuals in society and the emphasis given to groups. Scheff uses the terms "solidarity" and "alienation" to explain social integration. Solidarity is a product of a balance between the "I" and the "We" (see also Elias, 1987). Alienation has two forms: isolation and engulfment. When there is too much emphasis on the "I" in conflict, isolation results because there is little basis to establish common ground; when there is too much emphasis on the

"We" in conflict, engulfment results because the individual fails to communicate their own distinctive point of view. As Scheff states:

> Effective cooperation between human beings involves the ability to deal rapidly with complex and novel problems as they arise. Because of the complexity and novelty of the problems we face, solidarity requires that we draw upon our whole selves, and connect with the whole selves of other participants. Alienation occurs if important parts of self are withheld (engulfment) or if participants are completely divided (isolation). (1994, p 29)

Retzinger and Scheff also argue:

> [S]hame plays a crucial role in normal cooperative relationships, as well as conflict ... shame signals a threat to the social bond, and therefore is vital in establishing where one stands in a relationship. Similarly, pride signals a secure bond. Shame is the emotional cognate of a threatened or damaged bond, just as threatened bonds are the source of shame. (1996, p 5)

It may be that students who are victims of bullying and students who are bullies are both alienated in different ways. Those who are victims are engulfed; there is too much emphasis on the "We" and not enough on the "I". Those who bully, on the other hand, may be alienated from the school community as a whole through isolation; there is too much emphasis on the "I". For both, internalised shame alienates these students from their communities. In summary, shame that is acknowledged reconnects individuals with their social world, while shame that is internalised and transformed underlies shame-rage cycles that characterise the worst types of conflict (Scheff, 1994).

Bullying, shame and identity

Braithwaite and colleagues (cited in Ahmed et al) argue that effective regulation of social conduct should be governed by the following principles:

- shaming of bad acts that averts shaming of the actor's character;
- praise of good character that uncouples praise from specific acts.

In this way, we achieve:

- shaming acts but not persons that repairs identity;.
- praising virtues of the person rather than just their acts that nourishes a positive identity.

Moral balance requires both processes. Hubris is the risk of unremitting praise of the person that is never balanced by shaming of specific moral failures. Shaming without praise risks a failure to develop a positive identity for the moral self. (2001, p 16)

Restorative justice aims to capture the balance between shame and praise. In theory, the process rests on the premise that shame must be acknowledged for reconciliation between the conflicting parties to ensue.

In a broader sense, the collective shame for victims and offenders, once acknowledged, is used to harness the collective pride that is built through moving forward together. Restorative justice is about discharging negative affect, such as shame, and building positive affect, through the interest and enjoyment that flourishes through connecting with others. The process takes individuals from positions of alienation through to positions of affiliation and engagement. It seems that the negative affect of shame is best mobilised in the context of the collective most affected by the wrongdoing; these people, collectively, are the "keepers" of the shame. It is they who hold the capacity to release the shame and move forward. Through the process of discharging shame within the community affected by the harmful act, the shame no longer acts as a barrier to the process of social identification and reconciliation. It is these strong emotional bonds which reflect interest and excitement that we want to nurture and foster in the everyday life of school communities.

Building on the theoretical propositions developed thus far Morrison (2006) tested the proposition that processes underlying shame management (that is, shame acknowledgement and shame displacement) are closely tied to processes underlying identity management (that is, pride and respect). Using the four bullying status categories (non-bullies/non-victims, bullies, victims, bully/victims), it was shown that shame management and identity management follow a predictable pattern of disengagement for the four groups. The shame management styles of these four groups replicated Ahmed's (2001) findings, with the measures of identification (pride and respect) complementing this analysis, making further sense of the process of alienation and how it is distinct for students who bully others and students who are victimised by bullying. While the table below over-simplifies the process, it provides an understanding of how the process of identification with the school community can break down.

The students who are non-bullies/non-victims, who rate high on both pride and respect, see the school as a positive reference group. These students feel good about their relationship with the school community and identify strongest with the school. The other bullying status groups are less positive about their relationship with the school. For students who bully others, they rate high on respect but lower on pride. Often for these students it is pride in achievement within the school, or at home that comes hard. For some, they may not perform well on the traditional indicators of achievement within the school, whether that be academically

Table 2.1. Bullying status categories in reference to levels of respect, pride and shame management

	Respect	Pride	Shame management
Non-bullies/ non-victims	High	High	Acknowledged (discharged)
Bullies	High	Med	Displaced (by-passed)
Victims	Low	Med	Acknowledged (persistent)
Bullies/victims	Low	Low	Acknowledged/displaced (denied, by-passed)

or on the sports field. They gain their sense of respect within the school through their bullying activities, or sense of power over others. The school, in the worst of cases, may become a negative reference group for these students, as the process of alienation takes hold and a delinquent identity is moulded. For victims, the school is often an insecure reference group; they can be cooperative members of the school community but fit in awkwardly. They can be self-critical and insecure about their place in the school. They can rate moderately high on pride but low on respect. Finally, for the bully/victims, the school is an unstable reference group, managing their connection with the school community in awkward, unhealthy ways. Overall, they rate lowest on both pride and respect. Interestingly, on another comparative dimension, students who bully, like students who are neither bullies nor victims rate schools communities high on emotional value. On the other hand, students who are victims or bully/victims rate the school community low on emotional value. Thus, bullying at school does seem to have some emotional pay off for students.

This evidence suggests that individuals have a basic need to belong and this is best secured when individuals hold a respected place within a community where there is a pride in group membership. This said, shame may be a barrier to nurturing and restoring a safe school community if building pride and respect are the sole focus. As Braithwaite and colleagues conclude:

[O]nce we have reached the point where a major act of bullying has occurred or a serious crime is being processed by the justice system, it may be that shame management is more important than pride management to building a safer community, as our data indeed suggest. (see Ahmed et al, 2001, p 17)

'In other words, the evidence suggests that discharging internalised shame is a critical aspect to restoring safe school communities. Without enabling the discharging of shame over wrongdoing, the fostering of healthy and responsible engagement within the school community could prove difficult, as shame has fragmented the integrity of an inclusive social identity within the school community. The shame must be discharged to create a healthy foundation through which to promote a positive social identity that reflects a good sense of pride and respect within the school community as a whole.

Social norms and bonds: Shame and behaviour in context

There have been a number of perspectives reviewed here, with the unifying theme being the importance of emotionally healthy social relationships. Others have also made this point. For example, Lewis (1981, 1983) has argued that connections with others is a primary motive in human behaviour. The maintenance of bonds is reciprocally related to and involves emotions: emotions are a means of cohesion. Nathanson (1997), building on the work of Silvan Tomkins (1963, 1987), has argued that shame arises from feelings of failure, rejection, exposure and social embarrassment. He identifies four reactions that individuals adopt in order to deal with internalised shame: withdrawal, attack self, attack other, and avoidance. Nathanson defines these four shame responses in terms of a compass of shame. "Withdrawal" is characterised by removing one's self from the social sphere and the relationships that embody the shame; thus, becoming a recluse is an example of this type of shame reaction. "Attack self" is characterised by negative "self-talk", where the individual denigrates themselves publicly and privately. As this negative self-talk escalates, it can trigger harmful behaviour directed towards the self. "Avoidance" is characterised by other harmful behaviours such as alcoholism and drug abuse that mask shame. Finally, "attack other" is characterised by showing others that one's self is more powerful than someone else, as in the school rampage shootings. These reactions help resolve, albeit in unhealthy ways, the internal tension that has arisen through shame. Shame, as such, is associated with feelings of social isolation, withdrawal, difficulties in interpersonal communication, and feelings of hopelessness and depression.

Shame, as such, is intimately connected with solidarity (in-group cooperation) and alienation (out-group competition). Humans are inherently social animals and lapses in important social bonds affect us as individuals. Threatened or damaged bonds create an environment for

42

shame. Chronically unacknowledged shame arises from and generates a failure to socially connect (Retzinger, 1991). As such, shame can be conceptualised as a thermostat that measures the health of our social relationships. Large measures of internalised shame signal that the regulation of healthy social relationships is becoming tenuous. In other words, shame management involves the search for coherence of identity. Acknowledgment of shame can lead to greater integrity of the self and our social world; shame displacement, and its persistence, can lead to social alienation and internalised conflict for the self, as individuals navigate their social world.

Shame is a strong emotion, and one that is associated with guilt over a wrongdoing (see Harris, 2001). While shame reflects the state of our social relationships, guilt reflects our actions and behaviours. The two are related through the social norms of behaviour that we share through social identification with others. When an individual feels guilty about a particular action this can be emotionally powerful; when the act carries the additional burden of severing social relationships, individuals can become highly motivated to address the internal pressure of shame. The options are limited. One can acknowledge and discharge the shame in healthy ways or lapse into unhealthy relationship patterns. As such, shame can act as a powerful social regulator at a personal and community level.

Elster (1999) has argued that shame is the key emotion underlying the power of social norms. At the same time the relationship between the two is not straightforward; norms are regulated by emotions, which in turn regulate them. The following vignette by Tomkins shows the importance of social norms in generating shame:

> Our hero is a child who is destined to have every affect totally bound by shame. We see him first with his age equals. He is a friendly, somewhat timid child, who is being bullied. He is not angry with the bully, indeed he is a little afraid of him. His reluctance to fight evokes taunts of "sissy", "chicken", "yellow" from those who themselves may be shamed by his timidity. Rather than tolerate his shame he will permit himself to be coerced into flying in the face of fear and fight the dreaded bully. The same timid one, coerced into tolerating fear by his age equals and into fighting the bully, may be shamed into mortification for having fought. "Nice little boys don't fight like ruffians. Mother is ashamed of you. Whatever got into you? You know better than that". The timid one now starts to cry in distress. The feeling of shame has passed into critical density, and tears well up in the eyes and add to the intensity of his sobbing. At this point his father, attracted by the childlike, even effeminate display of tears, expresses manly contempt for such weakness. "What are you crying for, like a two-year old? Stop it – you make me sick". (1962, pp 228–29)

This descriptive account highlights the context-specific nature of shame. In each of the three interpersonal situations described above, the norms of appropriate behaviour shift depending on the social context and, so too, do the associated feelings of shame. Thus, it is important to resolve shame within the context of the relevant social sphere. Those closest to the person involved and those directly involved in the event, are best able to resolve and discharge the shame over the wrongdoing. As Howard Zehr (2000, p 10), one of the founding fathers of contemporary restorative justice, tells us:

> Be it a person who has been a victim, or one that has victimized others, either way both need the social support through a journey that allows each to "re-narrate our stories so that they are no longer just about shame and humiliation but ultimately about dignity and triumph".

Zehr describes restorative justice as a journey to belonging. An important part of this journey involves the discharging of internalised shame; a further part of this journey involves the building of pride and respect as communities and individuals work together to right wrongs while securing and nurturing the safety of the community as a whole.

Social behaviour: The self, social identity, and emotion

From this analysis, ten basic assumptions about the behaviour of individuals can be used to build a conceptual framework to think about securing and restoring healthy relationships and behaviour within schools:

1. An individual's self-worth is developed in the context of their social relations with others.

2. Individuals choose, implicitly and explicitly, how they behave in a particular situation.

3. The options available to individuals are shaped by social institutions, role models, social norms, social identities and values.

4. A central criterion in the choice of behaviour is protection and enhancement of self.

5. The self is complex and dynamic.

6. The self is socially responsive.

7. The self is constantly evolving in reference to its social relations with others, as regulated through the process of social identification with a range of social groups.

8. Emotions (that is, positive and negative affect) regulate relationship patterns of the self.

9. Shame management, along with the management of pride and respect, are important social regulators.

10. Self-regulation is optimised in the context of emotionally healthy social relationships.

Reflections on the victims of school violence: What were they telling us about shame?

The Columbine tapes (Gibbs & Roche, 1999) revealed to us that Harris and Klebold were socially marginalised at school. Based on what they wrote, said, and did, psychiatrist, James Gilligan, provides us with an analysis of how this affected them:

> The effect ... was shame, leading to rage, leading to violence, in a desperate attempt to replace shame with respect so as to stop the social and psychological annihilation they were undergoing. The tragedy was that neither of them found a way to rescue his self-esteem, and hence his self, except at the expense of his body (his physical survival), and the bodies and physical survival of others. (2001, p 72)

As Eric Harris states in one of the videos that they made prior to the school rampage, while holding the sawn-off shotgun he would then use: "Isn't it fun to get the respect that we are going to deserve?" He also wrote, "God I can't wait till I can kill you people. I'll just go to some downtown area and blow up and shoot everything I can. Feel no remorse, no sense of shame. I don't care if I live or die in the shootout, all I want to do is kill and injure as many of you as possible" (*New York Times*, 1 May 1999). Gilligan makes four important points, which emerge as themes from these remarks:

1 The need to gain respect.

2 The absence of feelings of remorse, or guilt. Violence always represents self-defense to those who engage in it – defense of that vulnerable and threatened psychological construct, the self. Furthermore, any experience that specifically intensifies feelings of shame simultaneously diminishes feelings of guilt and remorse.

3 Absence of feelings of shame over the plan to kill everyone. Violence from the point of view of those who engage in it, does not intensify shame, it diminishes it and even reverses it into its opposite, namely self-respect, and respect from others, which is why the most violent people boast of their violence rather than apologising for it.

4 The willingness to sacrifice one's own body when that is seen as the only means by which one can rescue one's soul (or psyche, or self). Or, when one's self has already died, to kill one's body as well (along with other people's), since that may be seen as the only means of escape from an intolerable degree of shame. (2001, pp 72–73)

Other scholars have heeded the relationship between shame, humiliation and violence. For instance, Feshbach (1971) concluded: "violations to self-esteem through insult, humiliation or coercion are probably the most important source of anger and aggressive drive in humans". Indeed, the grandfather of psychology, William James, heeded more than a century ago:

> If no one turned round when we entered, answered when we spoke, or minded what we did, but if every person we met "cut us dead", and acted as if we were non-existent things, a kind of rage and impotent despair would ere long well up in us, from which the cruellest bodily torture would be a relief. (1890, p 281)

Building healthy relationships in schools

What can we conclude? It seems clear that securing and nurturing safe school communities is both sublimely simple and dauntingly complex. At the individual student level it seems simple. We need to use the ups and downs of school life as opportunities to build positive social relationships within the school community. The building of positive regard aims to foster pride and respect. Working through conflict restoratively can provide students with learning opportunities to effectively discharge negative affect, such as shame, as well as build positive affect associated with affiliation. Students' confidence in themselves, and compassion for others, will be developed and sustained by these relationships.

At the institutional level it becomes more complex. How does one institution meet these needs for hundreds of students? This is where the hard work needs to be done, for the evidence at hand suggests that we are not achieving this, on the whole, for our students. The needs and concerns of both individual students and the community as a whole must be the focus of our school health and safety policies; because the research shows it is a matter of "fit" between the individual and the community that is the issue in maintaining health and safety within schools. We need to ask ourselves a number of questions: what is the institutional message when safety concerns regarding individual students come to the attention of the school, (be it a case of everyday niggling behaviour or a very serious infraction of school safety). What is the institutional response? Does this response meet the concerns of those affected, restoring the dignity, health and safety to the school community? Short- and long-term, does the response secure the school safety or does it eat away at the foundation of our schools and communities?

In answering these questions, this chapter asks school communities to consider the role of shame, humiliation and alienation in

46

restoring safe school communities. One lesson from the theory and practice of restorative justice within schools is that it is helpful to conceptually separate the student from the behaviour. It is the behaviour, and not the person, that should not be condoned within the community and it is the behaviour, and not the person that needs to be confronted by the community. It is the behaviour, *and not the person*, that should not be condoned within the community; hence, it is the behaviour, *and not the person*, that needs to be confronted by the community. To this end, the behaviour needs to be confronted in terms of how it has affected the individuals within the community involved, such that social and emotional healing can take place. The broad aim is to build understanding and collective resolve. Throughout this process, both victim and offender need to be involved and supported. This process is important if we hope to instil a sense of sound judgment and self-regulation for students and other members of the school community. This analysis has placed alienation, shame and humiliation front and centre in understanding the cycle of harmful behaviour in schools. With this in mind, we can now examine the ways we typically respond to harm and wrongdoing in the school community, questioning whether these responses address the issues of alienation, shame and humiliation.

Chapter 3

Beyond ignorance,
band-aids and zero tolerance

If you punish a child for being naughty, and reward him for being good, he will do right merely for the sake of the reward; and when he goes out into the world and finds that goodness is not always rewarded, nor wickedness always punished, he will grow into a man who only thinks about how he may get on in the world, and does right or wrong according as he finds of advantage to himself.

Immanuel Kant (1803)

If you have the end in view of ... children learning certain set lessons, to be recited to a teacher, your discipline must be devoted to securing that result. But if the end in view is development of spirit of social co-operation and community life, discipline must grow out of and be relative to such an aim.

Dewey (1943, pp 16–17)

Schools are among the safest place for youth, at the same time, we cannot ignore the reality of school violence, be it school bullying or rampage shootings (Jimerson & Furlong, 2006). Over the past two decades, a range of anti-bullying programs has emerged, emphasising awareness-building and the consistent use of sanctions to no-blame and problem-solving approaches (see McGrath and Noble, 2005; Smith et al, 2004). The success of these programs varies widely, from intervention to intervention, as well as from place to place. For example, while the seminal Norwegian program, which emphasises the consistent use of sanctions, reduced bullying by 50 per cent, the replication of this program elsewhere has failed to achieve this result. Modest success rates of reductions of 15 per cent are more typical (see Rigby, 2005). All in all, anti-bullying policy and practice are highly variable, with little consistent evidence of what works for whom, and under what conditions. The school rampage shootings, at the extreme end of school violence, produces stronger policy direction. While these events are rare, they send emotional shock waves, garner national and international attention, and change policy directions overnight. This was particularly true for Columbine, and particularly true in the United States. While other countries have not gone to the same policy and practice extremes, internationally the mind-set seems to have shifted to a zero tolerance approach to managing school safety.

As the range and severity of incidents in schools increase internationally – be it a crossbow incident in Australia; growing insubordination and swearing in classrooms in England; retaliation with a switchblade in Canada; or guns at school in America – each of these incidents, and more, has led to exclusion from school, fast-tracking the move from schoolhouse to jailhouse (Advancement Project, 2005). Regardless of the country, and whether the focus is on bullying or a school rampage, many students today do not feel safe at school. In Australia, Ken Rigby "estimates that the number of children who do not feel safe at school is at least 125,000" (Higson, 2005, p 12). In America, students report that 22 per cent had been physically bullied, and 25 per cent teased or emotionally bullied in the past year. This amounts to 13.7 to 15.7 million students reporting being bullied (Finkelhor et al, 2005). Internationally these numbers are significant, with the issue of school safety at the forefront of schools, communities and governments.

This chapter examines how schools respond to harmful incidents in their efforts to maintain safe school communities. While school rampage shootings are rare, they evoke fear. In the wake of Columbine, Aronson reported:

> [F]ifty-two percent of teenagers from relatively benign communities ... live with the fear that a Columbine-style attack could strike their school. And it is not only the students living with that fear; their parents also show a great deal of stress and anxiety around the issue of school safety. (2000, p 5)

With this heightened concern came a range of political reactions that capitalised on parents' and schools' fears for the safety of their children. Responses, across administrations, ranged tremendously from country to country, State to State (or province to province), city to city, and school to school. Overall, the response was unprecedented: everything from quick fixes and band aids; to metal detectors, police and security guards; to fences and other surveillance tactics; to zero tolerance and blatant ignorance. For some countries, the main focus is on lethal violence, while for others the focus is on bullying; regardless of form, these behaviours are harmful and must be addressed. This chapter reviews these responses and the theories underlying the general approaches.

Beyond quick fixes and band-aids

The media provoked and revealed numerous ad hoc and shallow responses by school and government administrations following Columbine. Some responses offered nothing more than band aids on deep wounds, others potentially exacerbated an already bad situation for many young people. The typical band aid approaches came quickly. For example, the United States Congress voted to tack on an amendment to the Crime Bill, giving States the right to allow the display of the Ten Commandments in schools. This response parallels the emergence, in the 1980s, of the war on drugs and the rise of the DARE Program (Drug Abuse Resistance Education). This program is highly visible, sounds good and receives significant funding, but has yet to be found effective in addressing the drug problem (Greene, 2003). These are basically moralistic information campaigns that dare us to say "no" and offer a set of rules to live by. Band aid approaches fail to address the underlying problem, and in doing so, offer a false sense of security and potentially compound the problem by doing nothing.

Other knee-jerk reactions in response to Columbine made the problem worse, by directly soliciting and condoning further harmful behaviour. For example, one school principal sent around notices asking students to report any students who are "dressing strangely, behaving weirdly, appear to be loners, or out of it" (see Aronson, 2000, p 14). If a school is already exclusionary and cliquish in nature, which would make it at higher risk for retaliatory behaviour to begin with, asking students to point out "strange" students, could well make the situation worse. Asking students to identify the "odd" student(s) encourages students to act on their worst prejudices and sanctions stigmatising behaviour. So, if a student, or group of students, were already targets in the school this would make their life even more unbearable, increasing the risk of suicide, revenge, withdrawal and avoidance. As highlighted in Chapter 1, profiling is unreliable, even when carried out by professionals, let alone students.

When individuals and administrations are in distress but need to look responsive, they will find all sorts of creative, often ineffective, ways to deflect the emotional impact, potentially causing further harm. In reality, band aid responses do nothing, and by failing to address the problem at its root cause, they perpetuate the problem and waste time, money and other resources. These are downstream responses to problems that have their genesis upstream. If time and resources were spent upstream to address the problem closer to its root cause, it might free up time and resources downstream. These types of responses are characterised by short-sighted ignorance, bystander apathy and fear. Reflecting on Columbine, 16-year-old Caleb Cornell knew that the issues at hand where not going to be solved lightly: "It was not the music that caused this or the lack of metal detectors at the school. And even though the Nazism that these kids were reportedly involved in more than likely played a part, the real problem lies deeper" (Cornell, 1999, p 3). Cornell could relate to the suffering of Harris and Klebold, and with a strange synchronicity left school that very same day himself, out of a fear that he would hurt someone, if nothing was done to stop the bullying and taunting that he had been subjected to. As Cornell points out, our responses must go deeper than quick fixes, but typically they do not; instead, schools have adopted law and order, or legalistic, approaches. Indeed, the response that quickly gained momentum in the United States, and went onto influence school policy internationally, was zero tolerance, and along with this mind-set, the installation of metal detectors, higher fences, video cameras and other increased security measures. In summary, most school safety policies took on a traditional policing model of social control (National Center for Education Statistics, 1998).

Beyond metal detectors, security officers and fences

In what way do metal detectors, security officers, surveillance cameras and fences keep schools safe? They generally aim to isolate individuals who are a threat to themselves and others. For example, schoolyard scraps between rival gangs from different high schools have prompted the immediate installation of a six-foot high perimeter fence to keep some students in and other students out. But are they also useful for self-inflicted harm? A 17-year-old Australian student stood on the sports ground of her high school and shot herself in the head with a starter pistol. The response on the evening news from distressed parents and concerned authorities was to call for the immediate installation of metal detectors in schools. These security devices, while often seen as preventative measures, treat the problem at a behavioural level, not the relational level; that is, they stop guns from being brought to schools. Rather than work on relational issues, it is much easier to erect barriers and other devices that separate "us" from "them", even when the enemy is one's self.

Metal detectors and security guards aim to keep schools safe through detection and deterrence; their presence in schools is to detect harmful weapons before they hurt someone and, when they are detected, to legitimate the imposition of harsh penalties to deter possible future offenders. Typically, school security policies and practices that include metal detectors also include school security officers and surveillance cameras. These automated and impersonal security systems, typical of airports, have become commonplace in large urban schools in America. Each of these measures is predicated on one assumption: expect the worst from some members of a school community (and the community at large) and impose external monitors to establish measures of law and order. But is an impersonal airport security system the type of security we want for our schools? Is this the type of security that nurtures and fosters safe school communities, where students feel safe and secure to learn at their best?

Clearly, some do think this is a good way to move forward. In 1999, in the wake of Columbine, the Office of Justice Programs in the United States Department of Justice issued a report, *The Appropriate use of Security Technologies in US Schools*. The Department recommended that security cameras and metal detectors should be an important component of school security plans, while acknowledging that these security measures would not address all aspects of school violence. However, there is little or no systematic evidence that these measures are, in there own right, effective. Prior to Columbine, in the United States, the 1995 National Crime Victimization Survey, which looked at the responses of 9000 youths, found that when schools emphasised physical security, such as metal detectors, and over-developed a normative environment that clearly spelt out rules and consequences, the result was more victimisation and disorder (for example, fights and theft), as well as an overall feeling of less safety in the school.

At the same time, despite the tragic school shooting, it has been shown that schools are physically safer today than they were at the beginning of the 1990s. This positive trend is often attributed to the *Gun-Free School Act* in 1994, which legitimated the use of metal detectors and zero-tolerance policies (see Furlong & Sharkey (2001) for a good overview). However, while schools may be physically safer at the end of the 1990s, this does not mean that students today feel socially and emotionally safer in schools.

A recent study (Gastric, 2006), using data from the National Longitudinal Study of Adolescent Health in the United States (Udry, 2003) has found that some security measures make some students feel less safe, particularly "at-risk" students. For example, African American students report feeling significantly less safe at schools with security guards than their white peers. Further, metal detectors only had a positive effect on the feeling of school safety when the school was in crisis.

Beyond zero tolerance

Even more sweeping than the installation of metal detectors, fences and security guards, in the reform of safe school policies, is the mind-set of zero tolerance. While zero-tolerance policies can be broad or narrow in scope and definition (Day et al, 1995; Gabor, 1995), a typical policy would be "intended primarily as a method of sending a message that certain behaviours will not be tolerated, by punishing all offences severely, no matter how minor" (Skiba & Peterson, 1999, p 373). The form of punishment is typically an out-of-school suspension or expulsion, both of which have increased with the establishment of zero-tolerance policies and mindsets (see Skiba & Rausch, 2006).

This form of regulation in schools was driven by similar policies in policing and law that grew from the broken-window theory of crime control (see Kelling & Coles, 1996), which was made popular by the policies of former New York Mayor Rudolph Giuliani. This theory is based on evidence that high crime neighbourhoods also have high rates of relatively minor crime, and that many crimes are committed by a minority of people. The imagery of broken windows is used to make the argument that if "broken windows" aren't repaired, this sends a message of loss of order, and this becomes the turning point of urban decline. Extending the metaphor, all acts of anti-social behaviour, including minor incidents, are firmly and consistently enforced, as failing to uphold these standards leads to a breakdown in social order and increases in serious crime. In New York City, through targeting minor incidents such as graffiti, roadside car window washers, fare evaders, and offensive behaviour on public transport systems, dramatic reductions in serious crime have followed, resulting in a 67 per cent reduction in homicides over eight years. Subsequently, zero-tolerance policies of policing quickly spread throughout the world and, more recently, started to emerge in our school communities. And while the use of metal detectors, along with zero-tolerance policies, may be most prominent in American schools, zero-tolerance policies and mind-sets can also be found in international educational policy and practice.

The genesis of zero tolerance began with the "war on drugs" in the 1980s, was then applied to policing to counter the rising juvenile crime wave in the late 1980s, then jumped the institutional line from law and order to education. It is now regularly applied to school discipline in the United States. The *Gun-Free School Act* 1994 federally mandates States to have disciplinary policy that requires the expulsion of students (for one calendar year) when found in the possession of a firearm on school property. Failure to hold such a policy can result in the failure to receive federal funding. This Act was amended in 1997 to include any instrument that could be used as a weapon, as well as drug infractions. At the State level the categories have been broadened to include alcohol, fighting, threats, swearing, and dress codes, whether or not they happen in the schoolyard. Since the passage of the *Gun-Free Schools Act* in the United States, some form of zero-tolerance policy has been found in most schools: 94 per cent of all schools have zero-tolerance policies for weapons or firearms, 87 per cent for alcohol, and 79 per cent for violence and tobacco (Heaviside, Rowand, Williams & Farris, 1998; for the National Center for Education Statistics).

While these formalised regulatory policies aim to maximise consistency they seldom do. The greyness over interpretation of certain aspects of the Act, such as "instruments that could be used as a weapon", has lead to some extreme examples of interpretation. For example, in Florida, an 18-year-old senior high school student spent a day in jail, was suspended for five days, and missed her graduation, when a kitchen knife was found in the backseat of her car. In Pennsylvania, a five year-old was suspended from school, when a five-inch plastic axe was used as part of a firefighter's costume at a school Halloween party. And, in Illinois, a high school junior was expelled, jailed for seven hours and was encouraged to drop out of school, when a paper clip, shot from a rubber band, hit a cafeteria worker instead of the intended friend. Many more examples abound (see Skiba & Noam, 2001).

In England, zero tolerance was federally introduced in 1999, giving greater powers to the 1944 *Education Act* in England that enshrined the practice of exclusion in schools, and which grew rapidly in the 1990s: from 2910 in 1990–1991 to 12,7000 in 1996–1997 (see Hayden, 2003). Following the election of the Labour Government in 1997, the Social Exclusion Unit (SEU) was established with the aim of reducing truancy and exclusion by one-third. This target was met in 1999–2000 but subsequent targets have been dropped and the rate of exclusion is again rising, and inherent to the tensions within the wide range of ever-changing educational policies. For example, in 2002, carrying an offensive weapon and serious bullying were added to the list. Previously, students could only be expelled immediately for sexual misconduct, drug dealing, or serious violence. In 2005, zero tolerance in schools became a major campaign issue, with the Labour Government announcing:

> Behaviour is good in most schools most of the time ... But any poor behaviour is too much and should not be tolerated. We need to re-draw the line on what is acceptable ... Where parents do not take responsibility for their child's unruly behaviour, then it is right that action is taken to ensure that they do, through Parenting orders administered by the courts. Every pupil and every teacher has the right to expect a safe,

secure and orderly classroom, so that teaching and learning can flourish. (Department for Education and Skills, 2005)

Hence, the zero-tolerance strategy is not only getting tougher on students, it is getting tougher on parents as well.

While there is no federal mandate in Canada, a range of policies have been enacted at the provincial level. Zero-tolerance policies, including mandated suspension for serious offences, are required in the provinces of Ontario and Nova Scotia, and are recommended in the provinces of New Brunswick and Newfoundland. Within each of these provinces sanctions are required. However, there has been continual confusion over the zero-tolerance policy since it has been implemented (see Shannon & McCall, 2001). For example, Ontario's *Safe Schools Act* 2000, which explicitly adopted a zero-tolerance policy in 2001, has been very controversial and was reviewed in 2004. After much controversy the provincial minister announced the Act would be "fixed" and not dropped (*Globe and Mail*, 11 May 2004).

Indeed, there remains considerable confusion over what "zero tolerance" means, as was evident from focus group discussions held by the Canadian Association of Principals in 2000–2001:

> There were questions about whether it meant zero tolerance for the behaviour or zero tolerance for the student ... There were also concerns around the interpretation of the severity of incidents. The principals realized that the same incident in different contexts can mean quite different things, and also that not all individuals would necessarily have the same interpretation of a given incident. (Shannon & McCall, 2001)

While there seems to be more policy variation across and within provinces in Canada, and more questioning of policy, notable examples of policy extremes are evident. For instance, in Ontario, one student was suspended for bringing a bread knife (to spread cream cheese on his bagel) to school, and another suspended for possession of a purple squirt gun he used as a prop in a French class skit; in Nova Scotia, an A-student and former peer mediator, was suspended for pushing her friend into a snow bank (see Hoffman, 2001).

As with American policy reform, zero tolerance in Australia was originally introduced within the context of the Australian Drug Strategy; however, when the issue was raised in Parliament the Australian Drug Foundation (ADF; 2001) made its position on zero tolerance very clear:

> Of real concern is how the use of the term, zero tolerance, and its hard line connotations, lends itself to a shift by some sectors of the community towards a more conservative, fundamentalist, moralistic approach towards drug use and drug users. This does not support consideration of drug use as a health issue rather than a legal issue. A "war on drugs"

is really a war on people. Using phrases like zero tolerance only serves to confuse and polarize the debate about responses to drug problems. It may be in the public interest if this term were avoided in relation to drug strategy. (See also Munro, 1999)

This stance set some precedence in Australia, and for the most part the term "zero tolerance" is avoided in the context of schools, with some variation from State to State. Despite the lack of explicit zero-tolerance policies, there is growing reference to the term, particularly in regard to bullying in schools.

The examples raised in these four countries highlight the impact of, and range of responses to, zero-tolerance policies and practices. One commentator suggested that zero tolerance is like baseball: "Americans invented it and, while we play too, it's their national pastime" (Hoffman, 2001). Given the prevalence of zero tolerance in America, it is not surprising that the most systematic writing on zero tolerance also comes from America. This research makes a clear case that despite the wide-spread mind-set and practice, the more surprising fact is that there is zero evidence of the effectiveness of zero tolerance. Skiba and Knesting (2001, pp 7–8; see also Skiba & Rausch, 2006) make the following conclusions:

1. Although punishing both major and minor incidents is central to zero-tolerance philosophy, community and national reaction has grown as increasingly trivial incidents receive progressively harsher penalties.

2. Although expulsion may be reserved for more serious incidents, school suspension is used for a wide range of misbehaviour, including disruption, attendance-related issues, and non-compliance.

3. Suspensions and expulsions are used inconsistently across schools, often primarily as a function of classroom over-referral or poor school climate.

4. Minority over-representation in suspensions and expulsions has been documented for over 25 years. There is no evidence that this is explainable by either student poverty status or increased disruption on the part of the minority student.

5. A high rate of repeat offending indicates that school exclusion is not a particularly effective punishment. In the long-term, suspension and expulsion are associated with an increased risk of school drop-out and juvenile delinquency.

Indeed, from a range of professional bodies, there is little support for zero tolerance. For example, Tebo (2000) in the *American Bar Association Journal* made a strong argument that zero tolerance makes "zero sense", and this was followed by the American Bar Association (2001) passing a resolution condemning the use of zero tolerance. Similar sentiments have arisen in Canada: "Zero tolerance operates on the wrong side of the behaviour. If you look at suspension as a response, it's too late. You already have a victim" (see Hoffman, 2001).

In the end, the problem with zero tolerance is its "one size fits all" mentality, and like the other downstream solutions described above, it allows school administrations to act on their worst prejudices. Which kids get picked out and targeted for zero-tolerance violations? Who gets picked out for swearing? Bringing a plastic gun to school? The data clearly indicate that the policy works to discriminate against the most vulnerable students at school – minority students already at risk (Hayden, 1997; Parsons, 1999). Thus, the policy encourages schools to discriminate against those who are already potential targets of discrimination. Fine and Smith argue:

> Zero tolerance is, intuitively, a reasonable policy – until you look under the veil. Ideologically it is part of a larger political project of "accountability", in which youth of color, typically, but not only, the poor and working class, are held "accountable" for a nation that has placed them "at risk". Systematically denied equal developmental opportunities, they are pathologized, placed under surveillance, and increasingly criminalized.
>
> Indeed, this blanket approach to complex social problems offers little, if any, insight into the problem. It is, indeed, one of the best examples of "throwing the baby out with the bathwater". When we cast the child out of school and into the wider community through zero-tolerance polices that condone exclusion, the problem is also cast into the wider community, which, on the whole, has a lower capacity to deal with the problem. (2001, p 257)

Anderson in the *University of Pennsylvania Law Review* puts it this way:

> As authorities increasingly relinquish responsibility by simply removing students from school, these youth find themselves distanced from the exact social institutions charged with teaching them the conformist norms necessary to become successful citizens. this social disconnect not only isolates them from mainstream conformist voices but also leaves them vulnerable to the call of deviant, sub-cultures, thus encouraging further delinquency and disadvantage. (2004, p 1182)

When we cast children out of school we also increase their chances of befalling the effects of violence, be it as victim or perpetrator. Schools remain one of the safest places for most children. The out-of-school death rate for children in the United States is four times higher than it is at school, with the greatest risk being at home (see Dohrn, 2001). Further to this point, research has shown that effective community-building programs that keep communities safe, put the school at the centre of the community-building process (Schorr, 1997).

As our primary developmental institution, schools are a micro-cosm of society; when children are cast out from school, the impact is felt by the individual, in the short-term, and society, in the long-term. The process of exclusion from school can be stigmatising, thereby giving children a loud and powerful message: you are not like us; you do not belong with us. So these young people find other ways to belong, through gangs on the street, or virtual gangs, taking on personas very different from those you typically find in schools. Further, given that zero-tolerance policies have been found to be discriminatory, schools are sending students, both in and out of schools, the wrong message: one that promotes prejudice and discrimination. Justice Einfeld, in his keynote address to an Australian national conference on safe schools, recognised the important role that schools play in imparting a sense of justice to the community:

> If it is the obligation of society as a whole to address the social injustices that confront the disadvantaged and the victims of discrimination, it is the responsibility of schools to impart to children the equal worth of all peoples ... Knowledge is the key to overcoming prejudices and igno-rance, and school is the environment to which society has entrusted the responsibility of providing the foundations of a lifetime of learning. (Australian Council of State School Organisations, 1998, p 5)

The evidence suggests that not only does zero tolerance make zero sense, but zero tolerance promotes intolerance, through discriminatory practices that license discrimination. In this way, schools can fail society as the central developmental institution in the promotion of civil society (see Morrison, 2001). In summary, while zero tolerance sounds clear and precise – clear on the unsanctioned behaviour and precise on the appro-priate punishment – the reality is that it promotes intolerance and discrimination, due to the grey haze that lies between the black and white print of the policy. The bottom line is that the exclusionary fail to address the deeper issues, build understanding and foster responsibility.

Beyond school exclusion:
Expulsion and suspension

While one of the central features of zero-tolerance policies is the use of suspension and expulsion, zero-tolerance policies are not necessary for the use of suspensions and expulsions, as Hayden argues:

> Exclusion from school might be seen as the more extreme end of the con-tinuum of disciplinary responses to behavior that is seen as unacceptable

within school. Exclusion thus represents the limits of adult tolerance, but it is also the "tip of the iceberg" in terms of the problematic behaviour (from both adults and children) that might be found in a school setting. (2002, p 627)

While suspensions refer to temporary exclusion from school, expulsion refers to permanent exclusion. As with data on zero tolerance, the data on suspension and exclusion are sparse and impoverished, with only a few studies beginning to appear in the 1970s and 1980s. From what researchers can piece together the national trends are worrying for example:

- England – for expulsions, there was a fourfold increase from 1990– 1991 to 1996–1997; very little national data on suspension (Hayden, 2003, p 629).

- Ontario released suspension and expulsion data for the first time in 2005, using provincial data from the 2003-2004 school year – 152,626 students (7.2%) were suspended (at least once) and 1,909 students (0.08%) were expelled. The year before the introduction of the *Safe School Act*, 113,778 students were suspended and 106 students expelled. There is no systematic national data.

- Australia – New South Wales reported a 27 per cent increase from 1993 to 1994; South Australia reported an increase of 100 per cent for the same period; and Queensland reported a 16 per cent increase from 1996 to 1997 (Taylor, 1995; Slee, 1998). There is no systematic national data.

- United States: 4.2 per cent of all students in the United States have been suspended at least once (Royer, 1995); in Chicago, expulsions increased from 14 to 737 between 1992 and 1999 (Civil Rights Project, 2000); in Massachusetts, expulsions increased by 35 per cent between 1993 and 1997 (Brooks, Schiraldi & Ziedenberg, 1999). Nationally it has been reported that 3 million students are suspended each year from Kindergarten to Grade 12 and nearly 100,000 more excluded (Fuentes, 2003). Further, the National PreKindergarten Study (Gilliam, 205) found that pre-school students are expelled at a rate more than three times that of their older peers in Kindergarten to Grade 12.

There may be an even darker side to these numbers. Stirling (1993) estimated that only 10 per cent of all exclusions were officially recorded, due to: (a) unofficial cooling-off periods that were arranged with parents (Vulliamy & Webb, 2001); and (b) massaging of figures to make schools look good (Le Grand & Bartlett, 1993). Of those students excluded from the school community, boys, those of lower socio-economic status and minority groups, were typically over-represented. What happens to those who are excluded? Research shows that these students: (a) experience further disruption to their schooling (Hayden & Ward, 1996); (b) are not deterred in the future (Sugai & Homer, 1999); (c) are involved in greater levels of disruption (Wu et al, 1982); (d) experience hardening of social sensitivity (Morrison et al, 2001); and (e) experience anger and feelings of unfairness (Costenbader & Markson, 1994). Indeed, suspension puts students at greater risk of entering the formal criminal justice system. Suspensions disconnect students who may already have fragile connections with their school community and peers, and they place them at risk of self-harm and of harming others. Suspension begets further suspension, through harmful behaviour being promoted through harmful responses, which further entrenches the cycle of alienation.

Beyond punishment

Underlying zero tolerance, suspension and exclusion is the belief that punishment is a just consequence for misbehaviour. Interestingly, there has been a growing shift back to punishment over the past two decades, following the welfare or rehabilitation approach of the 1960s and 1970s. This trend is particularly evident in the United States (see Whitman, 2003; Fowler, 1995). Wronged parties, individuals and communities, can expect to have their wrongs redressed by having the offender punished. While this is a largely held sentiment, in the United States in particular (Tyler, 2006), punishment has been found to increase re-offending. For example, an analysis of 500 delinquency treatment programs in the United States found that punitive programs such as "Scared Straight" tended to increase recidivism, whereas family and mentoring programs showed more promising results (Gibbs, 1995).

While it has been found that as the intensity of punishment increased, the level of unwanted behaviour decreased, the total suppression of the undesired behaviour required a level of punishment that was deemed to be inhumane (see Azrin & Holz, 1966; Parke & Walters, 1967; Turner & Solomon, 1962). These studies suggest compliance is being gained for all the wrong reasons. Further, as punishment increases, so too does the emotional impact of the punishment, such that the emotional harm affects other areas of learning and wellbeing (Clarke, Montgomery & Viney, 1971). Sherman's (1993) theory of defiance showed that punishment that was deemed by the recipient to be excessive or unjust, provoked defiance and increased the rate and severity of offending. Further, if the offender, or the group to which the offender belongs, is treated with disrespect, regardless of how objectively fair the punishment is, there is a strong risk of defiance rather than deterrence. Indeed, it has been shown that locking kids up does not deter crime, and may increase it (Tolan & Guerra, 1994).

In parallel with these findings, in the context of families, a substantial body of research has found that harsh and punitive parenting styles have been associated with higher levels of child aggression (Leach, 1993; Strassberg, Dodge, Pettit & Bates, 1994). In the context of schools, a review of 500 studies concluded that the least effective responses to violence in schools were counselling, psychotherapy, and punishment (Lipsey, 1991). Likewise, if no school-wide system of support is in place, the consequences of punishing problem behaviour are an increase in aggression, vandalism, truancy, tardiness, and drop-outs (Mayer & Sulzer-Azaroff, 1990). Thus, while punitive measures have long been used as a behavioural deterrent, there is now an expansive body of literature that establishes its ineffectiveness in shifting behavioural patterns. As such, schools now argue that suspensions are used to keep the school community safe, rather than shift behaviour. The evidence is now clear that they do not shift behaviour in a positive direction; however, these punitive measures may shift behaviour in the opposite direction, thereby increasing the risk to school communities. Schools, through capitalising on approaches that developed out of law and order concerns, have compounded the biggest mistake of the justice and penal system – that punishment keeps communities safe. James Gilligan makes a compelling argument that:

> [P]unishment increases feelings of shame and humiliation, and decreases feelings of guilt; and those are exactly the psychological conditions that give rise to violent behavior, in which the rage that has been provoked by being humiliated is not inhibited by feelings of guilt. (2001, p 116)

In conclusion, this section has reviewed both moralistic and legalistic responses to harmful behaviour in schools. A moralistic approach is typified by the post-Columbine display of the 10 commandments in classrooms, offices and corridors. The idea is to establish clear standards about school expectations and then to model and reinforce positive behaviour that reflects these standards. The moralistic approach is often augmented by the legalistic approach, which imposes negative sanctions when the moral standards are violated. In this vain, many schools have adopted a zero-tolerance policy for a range of behaviours. James Gilligan (2001) argues against these approaches in preventing violence; that is, making moral judgments about behaviour and legal judgments about appropriate penalties. These approaches are clearly not effective in deterring harmful behaviour, further, it could also be argued that while they may keep the school community safe in the short-term, they may put the school community at risk in the long-term.

Empowering victims

What is evident in our typical responses is that when harmful behaviour occurs in schools, the spotlight is clearly on the offender – not the victims, nor the teachers, nor other members of the school community, who are often deeply affected by the harmful behaviour. The main focus has been to reform, or at least address, the behaviour of the person, or persons that have caused the harm. The general belief is that the safety of victims and communities is best addressed through applying negative sanctions or consequences to the offender, or excluding that individual from the school community. When we simply exclude offenders from the school community, or transfer them to another school, we fail to address the emotional scars of the harmful behaviour. In the end, with all the focus on the individual offender, and not the social and emotional dynamics between those harmed and involved, the result is usually less than optimal. For instance, focusing on the offender can lead to further bullying behaviour and less understanding and empathy about what happened, how to repair the harm done, and how best to take responsibility for future behaviour.

As in other jurisdictions, moralistic and legalistic approaches typically fail to involve the victim in the resolution process. In the end, this is undesirable as the victim often needs to reconcile their relationship with the community; further, as was demonstrated in Chapter 1, the emotional scars can deeply affect an individual over a lifetime and need to be addressed. In recognition of the emotional scars of victimisation, legal processes typically adopt a third-party system, wherein victims never speak for themselves and barriers are erected around the victim. This is a carry over from our criminal justice system (see Strang, 2002).

Humanistic approaches

Besides moralistic and legalistic approaches to school safety, schools use a variety of strategies to maintain a climate of discipline that fosters an orderly learning environment. These approaches, driven by a range of philosophical and theoretical assumptions, regulate behaviour and power relations in schools. Some theoretical approaches argue that the balance of power should favour students, some argue that it should favour teachers, and some argue that it should be equal. In general, autocratic and authoritarian approaches favour the teacher, liberal and laissez-faire approaches favour the student, while authoritative, humanistic and democratic approaches favour both (see Porter, 2000).

For the most part, schools have long favoured an authoritarian approach, wherein the teacher holds the power. Some examples of this type of approach include limit-setting approaches (for example, Canter & Canter, 1992); applied behaviour analysis (for example, Alberto & Troutman, 1999); and cognitive-behaviourism (for example, Kaplan & Carter, 1995). At the other end of the continuum, few schools endorse the laissez-faire approach, although some come close. While there was a shift towards some form of an authoritative, humanistic or democratic approach in the 1980s and early 1990s, events such as Columbine quickly forced a swing back to an authoritarian approach, particularly in the United States, and along with this an increase in punitive attitudes and behaviours, as detailed above.

Authoritative discipline styles are beneficial to the school community because they get beyond mere compliance in the classroom, where the primary aim is to achieve compliance with the teacher's instructions. While teachers may prefer mere compliance, the research suggests that when the focus is on compliance over learning, the learning outcomes are poorer for children. Kohn (1996) has argued this form of compliance is dangerous for a number of reasons: (a) children can be put at risk when they are taught to simply obey an adult authority; (b) children can model this form of domination of others, and put other children at risk, as is typical of school bullying; and (c) it is an ineffective model of what a good society should be. The goal of a humanist (or authoritative) approach is to educate the student in a holistic sense, so as to nurture the development of both individual and social responsibility.

Humanists also argue against the rewards and punishment approach of behaviourists because of the focus on the external sanctioning system. Behaviourists focus on external processes and sanctioning systems, presuming that these feed the development of a healthy internal sanctioning system. For humanists, the preference is to focus on the development of a healthy and responsible internal sanctioning system. Thus, the essence of the debate between behaviourists and humanists is the emphasis on, and understanding of, internal and external motivation, and the sanctioning systems that regulate them. For many behaviourist these days, given the building research on the ill effects of negative sanctioning systems, the focus has shifted to establishing the appropriate reward structure, or positive sanctioning system, for young people.

Louise Porter (2001) puts a strong case against both rewards and punishment. She outlines a number of problems with this approach, including: (a) an emphasis on an external, as opposed to an internal, locus of control; (b) the goal of discipline is compliance and obedience, rather than the development of consideration and self-discipline; (c) the ethos is to expect the worst behaviour from children, so positive and negative coercion is used to coax out the right behaviour; and (d) behavioural disruptions are viewed as naughty and inappropriate, rather than an opportunity to teach new behaviours. Particular to rewards, she cites a number of further problems. For instance, children's self-esteem might suffer from the implication that they are approved of only when they meet our ideals and are rewarded. Thus, children might not learn to value what they achieve but work only to earn rewards. Furthermore, external rewards do not teach children to monitor and evaluate their own actions, and children may become discouraged, and disruptive, at being unable to meet high standards. Also, rewards are difficult to deliver in a manner that is fair and consistent to all, and therefore they can increase competitiveness and can breed resentment at being manipulated. Porter (2001) advocates the development of internal sanctioning systems, over external sanctioning systems, making a compelling case on why external sanctioning systems fail. Indeed, we can fail students as much by bribing them, as punishing them. Further, because the focus is on behaviour, and not the systems that regulate behaviour, we fail to build knowledge of the development of internal sanctioning systems.

Kohn (1996) has also made strong arguments against authoritarian theories, such as behaviourism. He argues that these theories are based on a negative view of children (and people more generally) and that they see children as egocentric, acting in their own self-interest, and only acting pro-socially when they are rewarded or punished for their behaviour. This is the typical Hobbesian view of life. In contrast, Kohn believes that children are capable of both acting in their own interest and acting in the interest of others. What is important is the development of the internal sanctioning system. As was argued in Chapter 2, students have a need to develop both autonomy and a sense of belonging with others, so that they are fully capable of acting in their own individual self-interest and in the interests of others. Kohn (1996) argues that when students act disruptively, they are often reacting to a denial of autonomy.

Many now argue that autonomy can only be secured through first securing a sense of belonging, through strong emotional attachments to others. As argued in Chapter 2, individuals, and their behaviour, need to be understood in the context of social relations, and in particular, within the emotional milieu that has the power to bind people together with shared interest and excitement, or tear them apart through shame and rage. Desmond Tutu, in writing about the truth and reconciliation process in South Africa in his book, *No Future Without Forgiveness*, makes this point:

> In one way or another, as a supporter, as a perpetrator, as a victim, or one who opposed the ghastly system, something happened to our humanity. All of us South Africans were less whole … Those who were privileged lost out as they became more uncaring, less compassionate, less humane, and therefore less human … Our humanity is caught up in that of all

others. We are human because we belong. We are made for community, for togetherness, for family, to exist in a delicate network of interdependence ... We are sisters and brothers of one another whether we like it or not, and each one of us is a precious individual. (1999, p 196)

It is the process of marrying a sense of autonomy with a sense of belonging that is the key issue in tailoring programs and practices to restore safe school communities. The tension between acknowledging individual uniqueness, and developing cohesion and solidarity, parallels the tensions that Durkheim wrestled with in his work.

Durkheim – Balancing the "I" and the "we"

Briefly, Durkheim (1893) argued that social solidarity and integration involved both elements of individualism and collectivism. He favoured functionalism and made a distinction between healthy and pathological forms of social organisation, believing that the generality of a phenomenon is bound up with the general conditions of collective life. Thus in the context of school violence, the phenomenon is a function of wider social processes. In one of his most well-known works, *Suicide* (1897), he sought to demonstrate that suicide is a social phenomenon, rather than a purely individual one. While he differentiated between different types of suicide, resulting from different social conditions, the main argument was bound up in the balance between autonomy and belonging, or the "I" and the "We". Recall in Chapter 2 that Scheff used Durkheim's work to build his analysis of shame and alienation. The figure below helps to see the pattern of alienation and integration within a matrix of high and low levels of autonomy and belonging. Recall also that alienation had two forms: isolation and engulfment. Isolation results when individuals are high on autonomy (I), but low on belonging (We); engulfment results when individual are high on belonging (We) but low on autonomy (I); and solidarity results when individuals are both high on autonomy (I) and belonging (We).

Responding to violence in schools – Finding a balance

When we respond to school violence, we can ask the question: when they get it wrong, do we get it right? (Blood, 2000). What are schools' options when responding to violence? The matrix above can be used to map out an analysis of responses to violence in school. Conceptually, when we address school violence two broad outcomes are sought: (a) safe school communities; and (b) behavioural change for individuals. Depending on the approach, these two outcomes can be at odds with each other.

Figure 3.1. A typology of belonging and autonomy

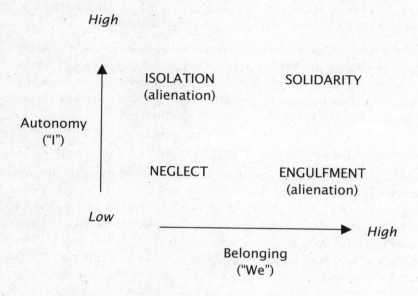

Sometimes interventions focus on the welfare of the individual, while putting the community at greater risk; other times, interventions focus on the welfare of the community, putting the individual at greater risk. And, at times, nothing is done, in the hope that the problem will resolve itself. When the focus is on the welfare of the community, this approach is typically driven by conservative ideals that promote social control through limit-setting, and endorse punishment as the response. When the focus is on the welfare of the individual, this approach is typically driven by libertarian ideals that promote compassion, and endorse rehabilitation as the response. The former values accountability, while the latter values social support. Restorative justice, however, values both. Restorative justice offers an opportunity to jump off the see-saw between legalistic punitive approaches and moralistic indoctrination approaches (Zehr, 1990).

The social discipline window is a useful model in differentiating restorative justice from other forms of social regulation (Wachtel & McCold, 2001; see Figure 3.2). As outlined, a punitive approach is typically high on accountability but low on support, while a permissive therapeutic approach is high on support but low on accountability. When the approach is low on both, it can be neglectful, but when the approach is high on both accountability and support, the approach can be restorative.

Figure 3.2. Social discipline window

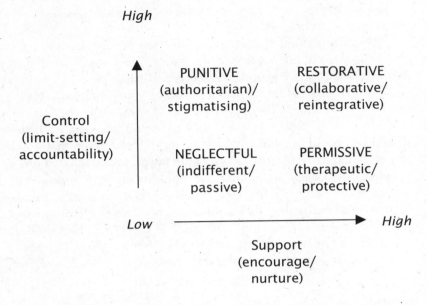

Wachtel & McCold, 2001, adapted from Glasser, 1969

If we map the above matrix (Figure 3.2) onto the previous matrix (Figure 3.1), we can see that when there is too much emphasis on the "we" (or belonging) the response tends to become therapeutic; when there is too much emphasis on the "I" (or autonomy) the response tends to become punitive. What is interesting here is that both responses could make the problem worse. In the case of students alienated through isolation, punishment could further isolate the individual. In the case of students alienated through engulfment, therapy could focus too much on the individual, and fail to acknowledge the individual in the context of their social relations at school. In both cases, restorative interventions aim to work with students in the context of their social relations at school, while including other members of a student's community of care, including parents and other family members, as well as adults and peers within the school community.

Interestingly, the x and y axes of this matrix can be defined in a range of different ways, each making a different point. Whichever way one looks at the matrix, the four cells of the matrix remain the same. Substituting the individual for Durkheim's "I", and the community for the "we", a model for building social capital and human capital is established, with punishment eroding social capital, and permissive approaches eroding human capital. Thus, when we value human capital over social capital we tend to be punitive, when we value social capital over human capital we tend to be permissive.

We can extend this analysis one step further by looking at the matrix in terms of our value systems. Values are goals in life and ways of behaving that transcend specific objects and situations, and that serve as standards or principles to guide our actions. Values belong to the domain of what we should do, as opposed to what we want to do or have to do (Rokeach, 1973). Not only are values the standards that we believe we should live by in our daily lives, they are the standards that we believe others should live by (Scott, 1965). Values are part of our shared conception of what our society should be like (Braithwaite & Blamey, 1998). Yet values are not purely social phenomena. Values are internalised beliefs, deeply held and remarkably stable, which we use to evaluate our own actions and those of others (Braithwaite & Law, 1985; Blamey & Braithwaite, 1997; Feather, 1975; Rokeach, 1973; Smith, 1963). In some sense, they reflect an individual's internal sanctioning systems.

Figure 3.3. The human and social capital window

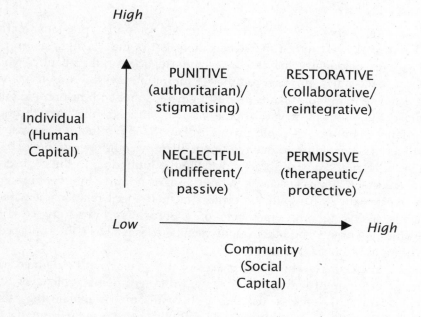

Adapted from Wachtel & McCold, 2001

Many academics have drawn a distinction between values that guide the competitive struggle for finite or scarce resources in a community, and values that guide the sharing of resources and the quest for wisdom and social harmony (Fromm, 1949; Hogan, 1973; Sorokin, 1962; Weber, 1946). Researchers have been tracking values of these kinds in Australia over a 20-year period (1975–1995) (Braithwaite, 1994; Braithwaite & Blamey, 1998; Blamey & Braithwaite, 1997), defining two broad categories: security values and harmony values. In terms of the matrix, the analysis is extended through juxtaposing security values (along the y axis) with harmony values (along the x axis).

The security values brings together guiding principles that ensure that one is well positioned to protect one's interests and to further them within the existing social order. Security values guide us in deciding how we divide up limited resources, what kinds of competition between groups and individuals is legitimate, and how we define winners and losers. The security value system encompasses values such as the rule of law, authority, social recognition, economic prosperity, and competitiveness.

In contrast, the harmony values brings together ideals for furthering peaceful coexistence through a social order that shares resources, communicates mutual respect, and cooperates to allow individuals to develop their potential to the full. Harmony values orient us toward

Figure 3.4. The social values window

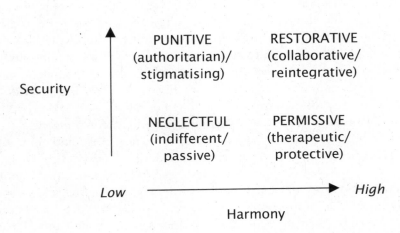

Adapted from Wachtel & McCold, 2001

establishing connections with others, transcending our individual grievances and dissatisfactions, and finding peace within ourselves and with our world. Harmony values include a good life for others, rule by the people, the pursuit of knowledge and wisdom, as well as tolerance, generosity and forgiveness.

The security and harmony systems are stable, enduring, and valued at some level by the vast majority of the population (Braithwaite & Blamey, 1998). While some people prioritise one value system over the other (for example, advocates of traditional versus liberal education systems), the majority strives for ways of maximising both. Restorative practices aim to maximise both security and harmony values.

Hence, the point across each of these figures is that restorative justice values: accountability and support, the individual and the community, human capital and social capital, and harmony and security. The challenge for schools is to find the balance between each. The idea is not to hand out accountability with one hand, and support with another; the idea is to marry them. The aim is to acknowledge that schools are made up of both individuals and communities, each of which value harmony and security in the development of human and social capital. The challenge for schools is to find this balance.

A simple way to think of the matrix is described by Wachtel and McCold (1999; see also Morrison, 2003). They argue that the punitive approach values the community over the individual, with the community handing down punishment *to* the individual. The permissive therapeutic approach values the individual over the community, with the community focusing on doing something *for* the individual. The neglectful approach values neither the community nor the individual; it is about *not* doing anything. The restorative approach values both the individual and the community; the focus is on the individuals affected within the community working *with* each other to address the concerns of the community most affected, be it the school community as a whole or only a small number of the school community. In other words the choice of response varies from *not* doing anything, to doing something *to* someone or *for* someone, with the collaborative approach being doing something *with* someone.

Typically each of these four responses does not stand alone. Often as school communities struggle with ongoing behavioural problems, the response quickly flips from one of these four approaches to another, sometimes in a haphazard manner. It is not uncommon for schools to first respond through support and then quickly flip to punishment. Increasingly, many school administrations are adopting punitive approaches in line with zero-tolerance policies for violent incidents. Overall, the approach to violence in schools is no different than the approach to violence in other jurisdictions. It is the approach that defines our judicial system.

Violence, within this system, is most often addressed in moral and legal terms; asking how evil is this action and how much punishment does it deserve? (Gilligan, 2001). This approach has become the normative paradigm across a range of institutions and behaviours. For example, Rigby (1996) has shown how this approach has been used to address school bullying. Moralistic and legalistic approaches now dominate our bureaucracies' responses to violence leaving us with little understanding of its causes and effects. We need to build understanding about these causes and effects, so that we can better understand and meet the needs of individuals and communities; thus, enabling all affected to move on from the injustice surrounding the violence.

Restorative justice offers such an approach. It provides us with the building blocks to be more responsive and more restorative. Restorative justice empowers us to be more responsive to both the needs of the individual and the community, through taking participants through a process that values both accountability and support. It is the process by which we marry accountability and support that is key to processes that restore individuals to communities.

This approach enables us to move beyond the predominant paradigm of regulatory formalism, where institutional representatives make a moral judgment about the "evilness" of the action and a legal judgment about the appropriate punishment. Regulatory formalism requires us to define the rules and the responses in advance. The aim is to maximise consistency. Restorative justice allows us to be more responsive because it entails giving back the harm, or wrongdoing, to the community most affected and creates a process for the community to address the harm.

Moving beyond harmful behaviour and harmful responses

Part 1 of this book examined the harmful behaviours that students experience in schools, through bullying, violence and alienation, and looked at these behaviours through the lens of shame and humiliation. This chapter looked at the way that many of our responses, as teachers and administrators, contribute to further harm. While there are no clear-cut and simple answers to addressing violence in schools, restorative justice offers one way forward, beyond ignorance, band aids and zero-tolerance options. A restorative approach challenges us to face our fears and accept responsibility, whether it be the fears and responsibilities we hold as administrators and teachers, or the fears and responsibilities we hold as those affected by violence in our school community. As Gilligan (2001, p 118) concludes: "we will have to renounce our own urge to engage in violence – that is, punishment – and decide that we want to engage instead, so as to facilitate maturation, development, and healing". The challenge to get beyond band aids, zero tolerance, and the under-lying assumption that punishment (and rewards) works, is an important challenge for schools to embrace. Restorative justice and responsive regulation give us the tools and framework to take up that challenge.

Chapter 4

Restorative justice

Where, after all, do universal human rights begin? In small places, close to home – so close and so small that they can not be seen on any map of the world. Yet they are the world of the individual person: the neighborhood he lives in; the school or college he attends; the factory, farm or office where he works. Such are the places where every man, woman and child seek equal justice, equal opportunity, equal dignity without discrimination. Unless these rights have meaning there, they have little meaning anywhere. Without concerted citizen action to uphold them close to home, we shall look in vain for progress in the larger world.

Eleanor Roosevelt (1953)

Cowardice asks the question: is it safe? Expediency asks the question: is it politic? Vanity asks the question: is it popular? But conscience asks the question: is it right? And there comes a time when one must take a position that is neither safe, nor politic, nor popular – but one must take it because it's right.

Martin Luther King (1968)

Restorative justice: A humanistic approach

Restorative justice is about addressing basic social and emotional needs of individuals and communities; particularly in the context of responding to harmful behaviour to oneself and others. The practice of restorative justice offers all participants – victim(s), perpetrator(s) and other members of the community who are involved and affected by harmful behaviour – an opportunity to participate in a dialogue that builds understanding. Through a respectful dialogue, empathy and responsibility are nurtured as each person contributes their story of what happened and how they were affected. This process enables participants to connect at an emotional level. Instead of promoting reason over emotion, as many institutional practices encourage us to do, restorative justice finds reason for emotions, recognising that there is a need for greater emotional intelligence within our social systems, particularly justice and education (see also Sherman, 2003). Restorative justice, in this sense, addresses basic human needs through engaging both reason and emotion, and offers respect and a sense of belonging to all individuals within a community affected by harmful behaviour. It is closely tided to the Indigenous South African idea of Ubuntu:

> Ubuntu is very difficult to render in Western language. It speaks of the very essence of being human. When we want to give high praise to someone we say "*yu, u nobuntu*"; "*hey, so-and so has ubuntu*". Then you are generous, you are hospitable, you are friendly, caring and compassionate. You share what you have. It is to say, "My humanity is caught up, inextricably bound up, in yours". We belong to a bundle of life. We say, "A person is a person through other persons". (Tutu, 1999, p 31)

As with restorative justice, Ubuntu is also linked to the idea of forgiveness – forgiveness for one's own sake, as much as for others'.

> To forgive is not just to be altruistic. It is the best form of self-interest. What dehumanizes you, inexorably dehumanizes me. Forgiveness gives people resilience, enabling them to survive and emerge still human despite all efforts to dehumanize them. Ubuntu means that in a real sense even the supporters of apartheid were victims of the vicious system which they implemented and which they supported so enthusiastically. Our humanity was intertwined. (Tutu, 1999, p 31)

In this vein, restorative justice, in the context of school communities, recognises that harmful behaviour affects everyone. When individuals and administrations dehumanise those who offend, they become victims themselves, and the cycle of violence deepens. So when children get it wrong, and harm others, the response to the harm must not dehumanise those involved, but open a path to reintegration, wherein each person is offered dignity, respect and an opportunity to be heard. Through giving each person the opportunity to tell their story of how they were affected by the harmful incident, important learning and healing can occur. Unlike other approaches, there is no rigid predetermined consequence for harmful behaviour; instead, the focus is to repair the harm done, and the fulfilment of this obligation is best understood from the perspective of those most deeply affected.

Restorative justice offers a framework that gets beyond simplistic and deterministic answers to complex social and emotional problems. For members of the school community, the practice opens a pathway into the hidden social and emotional curriculum of school life. The process enables school communities to be directly responsive to the physical, social and emotional needs of the school community. The aim is to engage participants in a process that maximises their ability to address individual and collective needs, particularly in the aftermath of harmful behaviour. The structured and carefully managed process enables school communities to move beyond the predominant paradigm of regulatory formalism, where institutional representatives make moral and legal judgments about the wrongness of the action and hand down the appropriate punishment – a response that largely fixates on perpetrators and ignores victims.

Restorative justice provides a way for school communities to be more responsive to harmful behaviour, and the subsequent impact, by empowering the affected community to address the harm, through *resolution, restoration* and *reconciliation.* Through *resolution,* individuals and communities take on the responsibility to address (and hopefully reduce) the risk of the harm reoccurring by taking responsibility for themselves, through *restoration* the harm is repaired, particularly to relationships; and through *reconciliation* comes emotional healing. Each one of these is closely tied to the other, and each underlies the reintegration process. This conceptualisation is aligned with Zehr's (2002) view on the outcomes restorative justice encourages: responsibility (*resolution*); reparation (*restoration*); and healing for all (*reconciliation*).[1]

Defining restorative justice

Restorative justice has been defined both as a process and as a set of values. In terms of a process, it has been described as "a process whereby all the parties with a stake in a particular offence come together to resolve collectively how to deal with the aftermath of the offence and its implication for the future" (Marshall, in McCold, 1997). The parties are typically victims, offenders, and the affected community; the aftermath is whatever the stakeholders see as needing to be restored (Braithwaite, 1999). In terms of values, restorative justice is "about healing rather than hurting, moral learning, community participation and community caring, respectful dialogue, forgiveness, responsibility, apology, and making amends" (Nicholl, 1998). Braithwaite has defined three sets of values:

- *constraining values* that define essential values for the process to be restorative;

- *maximising values* that define the outcomes that are valued;

- *emergent values* that define the healing values of restorative justice.

---

1   This chapter offers initial insights into the growing and rich field of restorative justice. The following texts extend, and may help clarify, many of the ideas within this chapter: *Shame Management through Reintegration* (Ahmed, Harris, Braithwaite & Braithwaite, 2001); *Restorative Justice and Responsive Regulation* (Braithwaite, 2002); *Restorative Justice Reader: Texts, Sources and Contexts* (Johnstone, 2003); *Restorative Justice and Civil Society* (Strang & Braithwaite, 2001); *Repositioning Restorative Justice* (Walgrave, 2003); and *The Little Book of Restorative Justice* (Zehr, 2002), which offers a wonderful little snapshot of restorative justice; *Restorative Justice: Healing the Foundation of our Everyday Lives* (Sullivan & Tifft, 2005); *The Handbook of Restorative Justice* (Sullivan & Tifft, 2006); *Handbook of Restorative Justice* (Johnstone & VanNess, 2006).

The constraining values being: non-domination; empowerment; enforce-able upper limits on sanctions; respectful listening; equal concern for all stakeholders; accountability; appealability; and respect for fundamental human rights. The maximising values being: restoration of property; emotional restoration; restoration of dignity; and compassion and social support. The emergent values being: forgiveness; remorse; mercy; censure. The values and process are equally important, one informs the other at all times, but in certain instances one may trump the other (see Braithwaite, 2002, p 12). Zehr (2002, p 25) brings the values and process together in this way: "Restorative justice requires, at a minimum, that we address victims' harms and needs, hold offenders accountable to put right those harms, and involve victims, offenders, and communities in this process". In other words, harmful behaviour creates obligations, which are best met through engaging those most directly affected by the harmful behaviour.

Restorative justice has been conceived as a third model, or a new "lens" (Zehr, 1990, p 95): a way of getting off the seesaw between welfare and punishment, incorporating virtues of both. Like the welfare model, restorative justice is strong on support; like the punishment model, restorative justice is strong on accountability. It is the process of marrying support and accountability (as described in Chapter 3), along with the values underpinning the process that differentiates restorative justice from other models. Non-domination, dignity and respect typify the pro-cess and the values, which bring the affected parties together. Zehr (2002) differentiates restorative justice from retributive justice (see Table 4.1).

While the table above helps to clarify the distinction between retri-butive justice and restorative justice, Zehr (2002, p 58) now contends:

> I have come to believe that this polarization may be somewhat misleading. Although charts that highlight contrasting characteristics illuminate some important elements differentiating the two approaches, they also mislead and hide important similarities and areas of collaboration.

In the broadest sense, restorative justice is based on the philosophy that productive citizenship is upheld when judicious processes are about restoring victims, restoring offenders, and restoring communities as a result of a participatory process that involves those stakeholders affected by the situation at hand (Braithwaite, 1999). The philosophy of restorative justice grounds and enhances our notions of freedom, democracy and community – it is the heart of responsible citizenship. When a process is truly restora-tive, cooperative relations will ensue between the parties affected and individual dignity and autonomy will be upheld. The aim is to take partici-pants through a process that repairs the harm done and reduces the likelihood of further harm. The emphasis shifts from the traditional approach of guilt and punishment to one of responsibility and restoration.

Table 4.1. Retributive justice versus restorative justice

Retributive Justice	Restorative Justice
Crime is a violation of the law and the state.	Crime is a violation of people and relationships.
Violations create guilt.	Violations create obligations.
Justice requires the state to determine blame (guilt) and impose pain (punishment).	Justice involves victims, offenders, and community members in an effort to put things right.
Central focus:	*Central focus:*
Offender getting what they deserve.	Victim's needs and offender's responsibility for repairing the harm
Central questions:	*Central questions:*
What laws [rules] have been broken?	Who has been hurt?
Who did it?	What are their needs?
What do they deserve?	Whose obligations are these?

Zehr 2002, p 21

A short history

Restorative justice is new in theory but old in practice. It can be found in ancient traditions of justice in Arab, Greek and Roman civilisations (Van Ness, 1986, pp 64–8) and in other traditional cultures as diverse as the Indian Hindu, Buddhist, and Taoist religious cultures as well as the indigenous cultures of North America and New Zealand (see Braithwaite, 1999, 2002).

Historically there has been a long decline in the practice of restorative justice in Western developed countries, with the decisive shift coming with the Norman Conquest of much of Europe around 1180 (Van Ness 1986; Weitekamp, 1998). A central aspect of the Norman monarch's program of domination was transforming wrongdoing against another person to wrongdoing against the crown (or state). In the 1600s the Hobbesian ideals of human nature became influential. Hobbes (1651, p 61) argued that individuals are involved in a struggle against all others, each having "a perpetual and restless desire of Power after power, that ceaseth only in Death". He deduced a universal, irreconcilable conflict that, if not controlled, would lead to "the war of all against all", arguing for the necessity of obedience to a sovereign state to control the ultimate destructive nature of individuals.

Thus, the role of the state was to impose power to oppress the inherent greed of individuals. This mind-set further magnified the institution of state-dominated power. And in the 1900s reason and emotion became polar forces, as Reddy (2001, pp 216–17) explains:

> In the late eighteenth century, reason and emotion were not seen as opposed forces; in the early nineteenth they were. In the late eighteenth century, natural sentiment was viewed as the ground out of which virtue grew. In the early nineteenth, virtue was regarded as an outgrowth of the exercise of the will, guided by reason, aimed at disciplining passions – much as it had been from ancient times up to the seventh century. In the late eighteenth century, political reform was deemed best guided by natural feelings of benevolence and generosity. In the early nineteenth century, while some would have continued to grant benevolence and generosity a role in politics, much more importance was attached to personal qualities such as commitment to principle, soldiery courage, a willingness, if necessary, to resort to violence, and, above all, a proper understanding of justice and right.

We are still navigating the fact that these institutional mind-sets and tensions are embedded in our justice systems. However, in recent years, as dissatisfaction with traditional state-focused punishment system has mounted, there has been a resurgence of the growth of restorative ideals (see Zehr, 1990; Roche, 2003).

One of the first experimental victim–offender reconciliation programs began in 1974 in Kitchener, Ontario (Peachey, 1989; Wright, 1996). A probation officer, who was also a member of a local Mennonite group, proposed that rather than impose a fine and probation on two young men who had vandalised 22 properties, the young men should meet with the victims and discuss repairing the damage, or compensate the victims for costs. The success of this initial proposal led to the first Victim–Offender Reconciliation Project (VORP) in 1975. The 1980s and 1990s saw the rise of activists calling for reforms to the juvenile and criminal justice systems in New Zealand, Australia, North America and Britain, which lead to a huge influx of programs in the 1990s (see Braithwaite, 2002). By the mid-1990s, Umbreit (1998) reported that there were at least 300 programs in North American and 500 in Europe. It was at this time that these programs, which aimed to "repair the harm done" or be "restorative" for victims, offenders and communities, came to be conceptualised as restorative justice.

The researchers and practitioners who work in the field of restorative justice struggled and deliberated on defining the field and agreeing on the name, and healthy debate continues today (see Braithwaite, 2002; Johnston, 2002). The field now embraces a number of often disparate strands of research and practice that initially grew from dissatisfaction with the justice system. While the roots of restorative justice grew from frustrations with conventional criminal and juvenile justice systems, based on the retributive model, these same ideals have been successfully applied to a growing number of jurisdictions: policing; family welfare; community building; workplaces; diplomacy and peacekeeping; and schools (see Johnstone & VanNess, 2006; Morrison & Ahmed, 2006; Sullivan & Tifft, 2006). This growth reflects a shift of thinking about restorative reforms within criminal and juvenile justice to broader justice reforms, in the context of growing understanding of the relevance of such reforms to personal and collective well-being.

Emergence of restorative justice in schools

As people struggled with defining the field of restorative justice, the role of schools in promoting restorative justice was seen as central to developing a more restorative society as a whole. For instance, Marshall (1997, np) argues:

> Even more crucial is the work just beginning in schools – anti-bullying systems, the prevention of truancy and exclusions, class circles, conflict resolution training, peer mediation. In schools we have society in miniature and persons in the process of learning to become citizens. It is not simply a milieu for job-training. How well we manage our schools will determine how well our society works a generation later.

In parallel with the rise of restorative justice, was the rise of peace education or Conflict Resolution Education (CRE) in schools, responding largely to social justice concerns. For instance, the work of the Association for Conflict Resolution demonstrates clear similarities with restorative justice. Jones and Compton (2003, p 19) argue:

> [CRE] models and teaches, in culturally meaningful ways, a variety of processes, practices and skills that help address individual, interpersonal, and institutional conflicts, and create safe and welcoming communities. These processes, practices and skills help individuals understand conflict processes and empower them to use communication and creative thinking to build relationships and manage and resolve conflicts fairly and peacefully.

There are now numerous programs and practices that aim to build students' skills in conflict resolution and create safe and welcoming school communities (see Jones & Compton, 2003). Some of these early programs, such as Discipline that Restores (Claassen, 1993) and Restitution: Restructuring School Discipline (Gossen, 1992), are notable examples of practices that offer clear alternatives to punitive forms of discipline in schools.

More recently, within this same movement, there has been the rise of programs in schools aimed at building social and emotional intelligence, based on Daniel Goleman's (1995) work on emotional intelligence. As the term gained currency, the definition of emotional intelligence evolved, Mayer, Caruso and Salovey's put forward this popular definition:

Emotional intelligence refers to an ability to recognize the meanings of emotions and their relationships, and to reason and problem-solve on the basis of them. Emotional intelligence is involved in the capacity to perceive emotions, assimilate emotion-related feelings, understand the information of those emotions, and manage them. (1999, p 267)

Goleman (1995) proposed five domains of emotional intelligence: knowing one's emotions, managing emotions, motivating oneself, recognising emotions in others and handling relationships. In recognising that social and emotional learning was an essential aspect of education (from preschool through to high school) Goleman co-founded the Collaborative for Academic Social and Emotional Learning (CASEL; see their website <www.CASEL.org>) in 1994. Goleman (1995, p 279) believes that schools are "the one place communities can turn to for correctives to children's deficiencies in emotional and social competence". Expanding the notion of emotional intelligence to what it means to be educated, Maurice Elias (2001, p 133), another strong contributor to this field, answers:

The current view is that to be educated involves being knowledgeable, responsible, and caring, and many would add, nonviolent. It means that the traditional focus on intellectual skills – IQ – must be supplemented by a strong concern with social and emotional skills – "EQ", the skills of emotional intelligence (EI). The reasons for this are many, but none are more compelling than what we have learnt about brain functioning, human memory, and the difference between learning for test performance and learning for the purpose of living one's everyday life. For the latter, social and emotional factors are paramount.

There are now hundreds of programs, internationally, involved in developing social and emotional intelligence in schools, which fits very well with Lawrence Sherman's (2003) conceptualisation of restorative justice as emotionally intelligent justice. Thus, in many ways the practice of restorative justice in schools has been developing in schools for some time now.

Having said this, the practice of restorative justice in schools, per se, had its genesis in the mid 1990s in Australia, through the leadership of a number of people, notably Margaret Thorsborne, Terry O'Connell, David Moore and John McDonald. It was Margaret Thorsborne (Cameron & Thorsborne, 2001, p 181) who introduced restorative justice into Queensland schools in 1994, as a result of her:

[S]earch for a non-punitive intervention for serious misconduct ... In particular, an intervention for serious cases of bullying which did not put the victim at further risk and also involved parents of both the offender and the victim ... [C]onferencing seemed to fit the bill of the ultimate intervention which increased empathy and lowered impulsivity on the part of the bully.

Margaret Thorsborne was working as a school-based guidance officer (school counsellor) in a large high school (1600 students) in south-east Queensland, when she heard about this new approach. The police in New South Wales were adopting Community Conferencing to divert young offenders from court. These conferences were modelled on the Family Group Conference, developed in New Zealand through invest-ment in Maori culture (see Maxwell & Morris, 2003). After hearing about the process she ran the first restorative justice conference in a school, following a serious assault at a school dance. These initial steps quickly lead to the first large pilot study of restorative justice in schools (see Chapter 6).

Restorative justice conferencing, in the context of schools, has now been used to address a range of harmful behaviours, including bullying, drug use, property damage and theft, as well as carrying guns at school. The case study below highlights how bullying can lead to more serious events, such as bringing a gun to school, and how restorative justice was used to address the escalating violence.

Restorative justice in practice:
Bullying escalates to bringing a gun to school

Source: Margaret Thorsborne

Location: Queensland, Australia

Facilitator: School guidance officer, who had only just completed her training

The original incident occurred at school after a birthday party to which a number of Year 8 and 9 students had been invited. The birthday girl, Anna, a Year 9 student, formed an attachment during the evening with one of the invited boys, Jack, a Year 8 student. They held hands and cuddled under a blanket while watching videos.

The next day, Jack told his mates that Anna was a "slurry dog". Anna heard of his comment from the school gossips and was deeply hurt. In the two weeks which followed this incident, her grandfather died and she and her mother cleaned out his house. They found an old handgun from the war which had belonged to him. Anna wrapped it in a t-shirt and brought it to school the next day in her school bag. It was seen by a number of girls that morning on the way to school, and at school she showed it to more friends.

A Year 9 boy, Daniel, well known in the school for lies, exaggerations and stirring up trouble, told Jack that Anna had the gun and that he had better be careful.

At some point in the lunch hour she found Jack and showed him the gun (by lifting her shirt) which was tucked into the waistband of her school skirt. She then returned the gun to her bag, and was seen doing so by several students including Daniel. He reported to administration that she had threatened Jack, and that he had definitely heard her click the gun twice (he said it sounded like she was putting bullets in it) when she was putting it back in her bag. She was called up imme- diately to the deputy's office. She flatly denied having the gun. When her bag was demanded and subsequently opened by the deputy she grabbed the gun and ran out into the school grounds, yelling at the top of her voice, "they're going to get the pigs onto me, someone please take the gun". Two boys eventually took the gun from her and hid it in some bushes in the grounds.

The school principal was called back to the school to deal with the crisis, and called Anna's mother in. The gun was found and Anna's mother was able to identify it as the grandfather's. She also assured the school that the gun was sealed with lead and inoperable. She asked to take it home immediately and the principal handed it over. Anna was suspended for 14 days.

That same day there were an extraordinary number of other inci- dents which the administration struggled to deal with, including some which also warranted suspensions. In the confusion of managing a number of crises, the school principal neglected to phone Jack's mother to inform her that he had been involved in the incident with the gun. She was extremely angry about that and also violently disagreed with the principal's decision to allow Anna's mother to take the gun home. She felt it should have been handed to police and that they ought to have been involved. She reported the principal to regional office for his "mishandling" of the incident.

When Anna returned to school after her 14 day suspension, she discovered that Jack was now involved with another girl. Anna and a friend then wrote and circulated a letter about Jack's new girlfriend. The letter was sexually explicit and very abusive. It was seen by Jack who showed it to a teacher.

The conference

The conference dealt with all issues: Anna's hurt by Jack's comments; her inappropriate response with the gun and subsequent behaviour when called to the office; Daniel's lies and "pot stirring"; the school's (and particularly the principal's) handling of the incident; the roles of other friends; the abusive letter and the extent of the distress suffered by all parties.

The conference agreement reflected the group's feelings that it was the lies and gossip which had incited the conflict to the point of crisis. Undertakings were made to put the whole incident behind them and there would be no further vendettas. Rumours and gossip were to be discouraged and "squashed".

Afterwards

The conference facilitator, who had a major role in following up with parents and students, reported that again, calm descended and there was no further trouble from any of those involved.

As this case study reveals, understanding behaviour is never about a simple black-and-white analysis; there are many layers of grey, just as there are many victims, many offenders and many layers of responsibility. Restorative justice allows us into the grey areas of school life – shaped by the hidden social and emotional curriculum that members of the school community experience each day.

Restorative justice and responsive interventions

As highlighted in Chapter 3, interventions can be responsive without being restorative; however, regardless of the differences in approaches, three aims are widely held: (a) to stop, or minimise, the potential for future harmful behaviour; (b) to minimise the harm done; and (c) to support those affected by the harmful behaviour within the school community. Within the context of zero-tolerance policies, this is often managed through accountability sanctions that typically involve sanctions placed on the offender(s); and, when the resources are in place, support mechanisms for the victim(s). In other words, accountability and support work through different mechanisms, for different people. Within the context of restorative justice, accountability and support work hand-in-hand for all community members affected by the harmful behaviour. The three main aims to be addressed are as follows: through *resolution*, individuals and communities take on responsibility to address (and hopefully reduce) the significance of the harmful behaviour for themselves and others; through *restoration* the harm is repaired; and through *reconciliation* comes emotional healing through the support and care of others.

These outcomes are achieved in many ways, and depending on the lens used the essential elements of restorative interventions can be defined in different ways. The two below are highlighted not for the sake of comparison but to offer different perspectives on restorative justice.

Restorative justice as opportunity

Early in the development of restorative justice, O'Connell (1995) suggested the following list as important elements in successful intervention processes:

1. Opportunity for the offender to gain insight into the consequences of their actions.
2. Opportunity to learn from his or her experience.
3. Opportunity of accepting responsibility for the harm done and to self-regulate behaviour in accordance with this responsibility.
4. Opportunity for the victim to be involved in the process and for their needs to be addressed.
5. Opportunity for the offender's and victim's families to participate in the reconciliation and reintegration, and to take responsibility where needed and to provide a supporting role for the victim and offender.
6. Opportunity for the collateral harm in the school community to be addressed.

Restorative justice as emotionally intelligent justice

More recently, Sherman (2003) defined restorative justice as "emotionally intelligent" justice, outlining a number of defining elements within the current field of practice:

Purpose: To repair the harm of the [wrongdoing] under discussion, and prevent further [wrongdoing] by the offenders, victims, or supporters of either.

Responsibility: Offenders must first accept responsibility for having caused harm and not dispute the factual claim that they are guilty, regardless of whether they formally plead guilty.

Method: Any means that can produce reconciliation between victims, offenders and their supporters, minimising anger and leave all satisfied that they have been treated fairly while justice has been done.

Decisions: To the extent possible, decisions about what should happen next to repair the harm and prevent future [wrongdoing] are made collectively and consensually by all individual participants in the process who were closest to the [harm done].

Emotional power: The power of the process comes from the engine of emotional engagement of the participants, in contrast to the suppression of participants' emotions in [legal] determinations of guilt.

Emotions to engage: Remorse, guilt, shame, empathy, hope.

Emotions to avoid: Anger, humiliation, fear, disgust.

Outcome: Offenders repair the harm as feasible, given the nature of the [wrongdoing]. (2003, pp 10-11)

Taken together, the former perspective emphasises the social dynamic while the later emphasises the emotional dynamic – both are important. Only when the full range of these elements is present will the process maximise the opportunity for the key outcomes of effective intervention: *resolution, restitution* and *reconciliation*.

In the context of schools, all members of the school community must work to create the space that fosters opportunities for emotional engagement in building and maintaining safe school communities. Because the social and emotional curriculum of school life touches every aspect of life at school, the framework for building safe school communities must also touch every aspect of school life.

Conceptual framework of restorative justice

When schools develop safe school policies and frameworks, they are typically derived from both formal and lay theories of human behaviour; restorative justice is no different. In the field of restorative justice, practice has driven theory, as much as, if not more than, theory has driven practice. However, restorative justice has also linked theory and practice through the building of rigorous empirical evidence (see Ahmed et al, 2002; Sherman, 2003). While this is true, there is no causal theory that describes the exact mechanisms by which restorative justice is intended to work. However, there are strong theoretical connections to Braithwaite's reintegrative shaming theory (1989; Ahmed, Harris, Braithwaite & Braithwaite, 2001), Tyler's procedural justice theory (see Tyler and Balder, 2000), Sherman's defiance theory (1993), and Turner et al's (1987) self categorisation theory. These theories form the broad theoretical basis for an "optimistic" vision of restorative justice (see Braithwaite, 2002).

For example, Tyler's work shows that individuals care about justice because of concern over social status, in that justice communicates a message about status. Building on his model of procedural justice, high levels of cooperative relations within institutions have been found when individuals feel a high level of pride in being a member of the collective and have a high level of respect within the collective (see also Chapter 2). Thus, status is important to understanding the social dynamics of conflict and cooperation within institutions such as schools. These findings resonate with the conclusions of the National Research Council's (2002) examination of the school rampage shootings in the United States. The council concluded that concerns over social status are central to understanding, and preventing, school violence:

> One message that comes through loud and clear in the [school rampage] cases is that adolescents are intensely concerned about their social standing in their school and among their peers. For some, their concern is so great that threats to their status are treated as threats to their very lives and their status as something to be defended at all costs. (2002, p 336)

The council recommended:

> It is important for siblings, parents, teachers, guidance counselors, youth workers, and employers to be vigilant in noticing when these threats to an adolescent's status occur and to be active in helping them deal with their status anxieties ... Young people need some places where they feel valued and powerful and needed – this is part of the journey from child-hood to adulthood. If they cannot find paths that make them feel this way, or they find the paths blocked by major threats, they will either retreat or, in the case of lethal shooting and rampages, strike back against those who seem not to value them, or are threatening them, or are blocking their way. Holding spaces and pathways open for them may be an important way of preventing violence. (2002, p 336)

Restorative justice is about creating spaces where the pathways that define a young person's life can be re-opened, through addressing the social and emotional status imbalances that affect young people, parti-cularly in the aftermath of violence. This resonates with Zehr's under-standing of restorative justice as a journey to belonging, which:

> [I]mplies that alienation as well as its opposite – belonging – are central issues for both those who offend and those who are offended against. The journey metaphor also suggests that the goal – belonging – requires a search or a process and that belonging is not simply binary – you do or you don't – but rather might fall on a continuum. Paradoxically, per-haps, the journey to belonging often involves a journey to identity – the two are deeply intertwined, like a double helix. (2000, p 1)

The challenge of restorative justice is to create these spaces throughout the developmental stages of a young person's life as they navigate their journey to belonging. This is particularly important for a young person who may have lost their way and is beginning to take on an identity that may be harmful to themselves or others. In this instance, the safe place that school communities create allow young people to re-invent themselves in a way that is not harmful to themselves and others. Thus, this space must be one where young people can be heard and participate in safety; one where the respect and dignity of all members of the school community is valued and considered.

John Braithwaite's (1987; see also Ahmed et al, 2002) reintegrative shaming theory offers important conceptual cornerstones in creating this space. He argues that reintegration is maximised through *participatory* processes that address wrongdoing while offering *respect* to each of the parties involved, through *consideration* of the story each person tells of what happened, how they were affected, and what they need to feel safe again. While this framework grounds a process that had its origins in addressing harmful behaviour, the framework can equally be applied to community building and fostering personal growth. For example, Braithwaite (2001) has shown how the restorative justice conferencing model can be used to foster personal growth, through what he calls Youth Development Circles. These circles involve teachers, parents, peers and others involved in the development of a young person's life, and they are structured much like a conference. They can be used to address concerns, as well as build strengths. These circles offer collaborative spaces where young people "feel valued and powerful and needed", as recommended in the NRC's report (2002, p 336). They are not only important to preventing violence and other harmful behaviour, they are also important to the development of human capital and growth. This fits with the conclusions of researchers involved with CASEL, whose president was invited to provide testimony to a hearing being held by the United States Senate Committee on Health, Education, Labor, and Pensions:

> There is growing evidence that school-based SEL [Social and Emotional Learning] programming can successfully enhance students' academic performance as well as reduce substance use and address other problem behaviors (Greenberg et al, 2003; Zins, Weissberg, Wang & Walberg, 2004). In spite of the fact that most schools' mission statements embrace the notion of the whole child, most schools do not make systematic efforts to institutionalize promotion of social and emotional competencies and creation of environments supporting their development. (Weissberg, 2004, p 6)

Restorative justice in schools seeks to create the safe spaces in schools where the whole child is nurtured and developed.

While the building of emotional intelligence across a range of emotional experiences is important, Braithwaite's (1987) theory of reintegration argues that one emotion, in particular, is central to this process: the emotion of shame. The Maori people of New Zealand have a saying about shame that offers an interesting perspective when one is juxtaposing punitive and restorative measures as a response to wrongdoing. Maoris say "ma te whakama e patu", or, by way of translation, "leave him alone he is punished by shame". For Maoris, it is the wedge of shame resulting from disappointing family or community that is at the heart of the process that builds safe and productive communities. It is the shame associated with the integrity of social relationships that must be healed for the individual to be reintegrated back into the community. As with Braithwaite and colleagues (see Ahmed et al, 2001), the shame/guilt associated with the act is only one part of this shame equation. At the same time, the shame/guilt associated with the act is central to the dynamic of the reintegration process. Building on Braithwaite's (1989) argument that it is important to conceptually separate the act from the person, it is the shaming of the act, but not the person, in the company of a community of support and care that allows the shame associated with the integrity of the social bonds to be repaired.

It may be helpful to visualise this conceptual framework in terms of the circle process that structures the practice of restorative justice. When a restorative justice conference is convened, all members of the community affected by the harmful behaviour sit in a circle. This includes the victim(s) and the offender(s), together with their respective supporters, who typically have also being deeply affected by the harmful behaviour. At the centre of the circle is the behaviour, which becomes the focus of attention for all participants. The offender is not sitting in the centre of the circle, and thus, is not the centre of attention. Instead, the offender is sitting in the circle with the other members of community, each of whom has been affected by the harmful behaviour. The circle, which is made up of community members sitting side by side, symbolically represents the social and emotional ties each member has with the others. These emotional ties are repaired through the discharging of the shame associated with the act that is the focus of attention for all participants and which sits in the centre of the circle. A sense of collective vulnerability arises when participants come to realise that they have all been deeply affected by this single event. Collective shame comes to the fore and is discharged through the common resolve to repair the harm done. Symbolically, through separating the person from the behaviour, the process reintegrates, and does not further stigmatise, the offender. It is important to note that while we commonly associate shame with the person who has committed the harmful act, hence the phrase *shame on you*; the victim(s) and other participants also experience shame associated with the harmful behaviour, and this process assists in repairing their ties with the community as well. (See Harris et al, 2004, for a fuller description of the emotional dynamics in restorative conferencing).

Creating safe spaces in schools

The challenge for schools is to create safe spaces that maximise the opportunities for reintegration when harm has occurred within the school community. Five key elements, seem central to the effectiveness of the process:

1. All members of the school community, offenders and victims alike, are valued members of the school community whose supportive ties with others should be strengthened through participation in communities of care (Bazemore & Umbreit, 1994).

2. Regulation of harmful behaviour concerns actions and should not involve the denigration of the whole person; expect the best from the person without condoning the behaviour (Moore & O'Connell, 1994).

3. Each individual must take responsibility for their behaviour to move forward (Heimer, 1998).

4. The emotional, social and physical harm done must be acknowledged (Scheff & Retzinger, 1995).

5. Reparation for the harm done is essential (Retzinger & Scheff, 1996).

These elements guide the core sequence of a restorative process, with the first two elements setting the stage for the intervention:

1. It is important to create and nurture relationships of care and concern around all people affected by harmful behaviour; thus upholding the value and dignity of all members of the school community.

2. It is important to create a context where it is the behaviour, and not the person, that is the focus of the process. The aim is to shift behaviour through expecting the best from participants, valuing their inherent dignity and their relationship with members of the school community. The key to shifting behaviour is through building the relevant and appropriate community of care around the persons involved.

The next three elements guide the questions that are asked of all participants involved in the conference; in other words, they guide the dialogue of the intervention:

3. Taking responsibility for behaviour is established through asking: What happened?

4. Acknowledging the harm done is established through asking: Who has been affected and how?

5.   Repairing the harm done is established through asking: What do we need to do to repair the harm done?

Each of these three elements is important and each has benefits in its own right, but together they lay the basis for a potentially powerful intervention.

What happened? The storytelling phase

Kay Pranis (2001, p 7), who has a long and respected history as an advocate and practitioner of restorative justice, tells us:

> Storytelling is fundamental for healthy social relationships. To feel connected and respected we need to tell our own stories and have others listen. For others to feel respected and connected to us, they need to tell their stories and have us listen. Having others listen to your story is a function of power in our culture. The more power you have, the more people will listen respectfully to your story. Consequently, listening to someone's story is a way of empowering them, of validating their intrinsic worth as a human being.

Listening and responding to the story of someone who has been victimised helps to integrate that person back into the community. In the same way, listening to the story of someone who has offended helps that person become more accountable for their actions, and to become reintegrated back into the community. Stories create a way to share pain, as well as joy. Ronnie Earle, District Attorney of Travis County, Texas, defines community as a place where both joy and pain are shared. Sharing stories of pain and joy, then, become a way of building community, of strengthening our connections and commitments to one another. It is difficult to maintain distance from a person if you have truly heard their story.

Storytelling is also a powerful teaching tool at the societal level. Stories express societal values, fears, and our expectations of life and of one another. The stories we choose to tell and listen to create the culture we live in and the lens through which we view the world. In order to create safe places to address bullying, violence and alienation, students' stories of pain and joy need to be affirmed, as do their stories of hope and resilience.

Who was affected and how? The emotional engagement phase

Restorative justice seeks not to judge others or their behaviour, but to seek understanding. The process simply asks: How were you affected? Individuals involved need only to speak for themselves. There is no value attached to coming up with the "right" answer. By way of an example, have you ever asked a young child, or an adult for that matter, *why* they did something, particularly when they know you are not happy about what happened? The emotional medium of the message is what they quickly understand over the message itself. The answer is typically curt, as rational defensive thought patterns go into high alert to make reasoned sense of the situation. Often when children (and adults) are involved in harmful behaviour, reason is better addressed through our emotions: How were you feeling when that happened? How have you been feeling since? How do you think others are feeling? How do you think we can make everyone feel better? It is this phase of restorative justice that enables negative feelings, such as shame, to be discharged, and positive feelings, such as interest and enjoyment, to be built. This is the heart of processes that heal. Formalised legal and rule-based judgments, on their own, can keep people righteous and defensive, whereas the emotional engagement of restorative justice allows people to touch each other's humanity.

What needs to be done to repair the harm? The restitution phase

True restitution occurs through offenders taking on the responsibility and obligation to repair the harm done as much as possible for those affected. Through bringing together all those affected by harmful behaviour, and their supporters, restorative justice enables a holistic and active form of responsibility that uncovers the many layers of the issues to be resolved. Through the traditional adversarial approach, where the offender(s) are singularly held in the accountability spotlight, others can tacitly declare their innocence (see Harmon, 1995). The distinction between innocence and responsibility is often much greyer than that proposed by a strictly legal framework. The aim in restorative justice is to create a context in which offenders can willingly take on responsibility for their harmful behaviour. This often occurs when others also take on responsibility and become emotionally engaged in the process. For example, bystanders of the bullying process can take responsibility for having observed the bullying but for failing to get involved or to bring the matter to the attention of another member of the school community, particularly a senior member, and also by understanding the impact this inaction has had on the victim. Braithwaite (2002) refers to these individuals as "soft targets", highlighting how they are effective, and important, instilling responsibility and shifting behaviour.

Through the taking on of responsibility, the full extent of the harm and injustice that has occurred is more fully established and recognised. This process of taking on responsibility has a very different tone and feel than that which is imposed by deterministic judgments of responsibility and accountability. It is the emotional engagement that enables the active shift to responsibility. As Heimer (1998, p 369) puts it: "It is the humanity of other people that inspires responsibility". In other words, responsibility is a function of human connectedness; that is, engagement with others at an emotional level.

Our best evidence shows that communicating the full extent of the harm caused is best fulfilled when the victim is present. Hand-in-hand with this, the offender is more likely to take on responsibility, when the full extent of the harm caused has been communicated directly from those most affected. Zehr (2002) argues that, at a minimum, restorative justice requires offenders to fulfil their obligation to address the harm experienced by victims. It is important for the victim to have a voice in the process, or at least, to have an opportunity to have a voice in the process. As Nils Christie (1977) has argued, it has been the lack of a voice from victims that has been a central problem of criminal justice institutions, which he describes as "stealing conflict" from those affected. This depersonalises the conflict as the offence is against the state, rather than the person or people involved. Through administrations stealing conflict from those most affected, we are less likely to foster active responsibility from offenders for harms caused and less likely to repair the harm. Likewise, Strang and Sherman argue:

> One of the leading arguments for restorative justice is the abandonment of victims' interests by the jurisprudence of retribution. That jurisprudence is arguably based on false assumptions about the facts and limited imagination about possibilities. (2003, p 15)

In Strang's (2002) book, *Repair or Revenge*, she asked the question: what do victims want out of justice? Her research reveals that victims want: a less formal process where their views count; more information about the processing and outcome of their cases; participation in their cases; fair and respectful treatment; material restoration; and emotional restoration, including an apology. While this research was conducted in the context of juvenile and criminal justice, these points are equally relevant to school communities, where schools typically endeavour to keep the victim safe by removing them from the process, and sometimes the school. The involvement of the victim seems central to active responsibility by the offender and repairing the harm done. This is important for addressing the emotional impact of harmful behaviour. The evidence shows that: "Conference victims reported that their feelings of fear, anger, and anxiety fell markedly after the conference while feelings of sympathy and security rose ... [They] also reported that their treatment most often had a beneficial effect on feelings of dignity, self-respect, and self-confidence" (Strang, 2002, p 198). Revenge by the victims was also much less likely following a restorative justice conference, compared to court. Specifically, almost 50 per cent of victims of violent crime who went to court wanted revenge, while only 9 per cent of victims who participated in a restorative justice conference wanted revenge, given the opportunity.

This last point is an important one, especially in the context of the school rampage shootings, where the young men responsible wanted revenge following their own experiences of bullying and alienation. The importance of victim satisfaction and empowerment is clearly relevant to schools, as feelings of estrangement from the school community raise potential risks to the individual and the community. Further, recent evidence from studies in England has shown that victims of crime who participated in a restorative justice conference, compared to those who did not, decreased their levels of post-traumatic stress disorder (Sherman & Strang, 2004). Given that some victims of bullying experience post-traumatic stress (Mynard, Joseph & Alexander, 2000), with one symptom being absences from school, it seems that participation in a restorative justice conference may be a healthy and productive approach for school communities to consider.

At an institutional level, through not addressing victims' needs in preventing and addressing harmful behaviours, schools are opening themselves up to legal action through failure to uphold a duty of care (see Slee & Ford, 1999; Varnham, 2001). This is particularly apparent in the context of the harmful effects of school bullying. In Australia, and elsewhere, unprecedented cases are being presented to the Supreme Court, with more being settled out of court (*Sydney Morning Herald*, 9 April 2005). Clearly there is a lot at risk here, not only for individuals, but for school themselves.

It seems that by focusing on the central obligation of repairing the harm done, and the needs of the victims, both offenders and communities benefit, as evidenced by reduced recidivism rates, particularly for violent crime (see Braithwaite, 2003). As Strang and Sherman conclude:

> [Through restorative dialogue] it seems victims and offenders are more able to understand an event whose by-products are haunting them, and can then try to move on with their lives. With the storytelling and sense of feeling heard that is typical of [restorative dialogue] victims and offenders are able to meet their needs in an emotionally-validating way. (2003, p 55)

The evidence suggests that emotional restitution is equally as important as, if not more important than, material restitution, because with this comes emotional healing. While the participation of the victim in a conference can be perceived to be emotionally risky, when these risks are safeguarded through careful planning and structure, participation in the process offers clear benefits for all involved. Some of these benefits will not be immediately apparent, as some benefits do not necessarily translate into outward reconciliation between the parties involved.

In the end, the most important reconciliation process is within each participant, because the emotional trauma has secured a place in each of them. The emotional trauma becomes the internal enemy, the "other" that can hold an individual hostage. Without an opportunity to express deep hurt, the trauma can define and stigmatise an individual. An internalised status of "victim", "offender", "nerd" or "other" can erode an individual's self-worth. Burying the emotional trauma can potentially destroy an individual, along with their communities. Restorative justice offers an opportunity for the "emotional trauma" to be healed, through creating a safe space for dialogue where participants can voice and build understanding around the trauma. Through this internal reconciliation process participants are enabled to find a new way forward. The process offers hope.

Moving beyond a zero-sum analysis

At the end of Chapter 3, it was argued that sometimes school administrations favour the individual over the community, putting the community at risk through hope of a rehabilitative process for the individual. At other times, the individual is put at risk, through valuing the community over the individual, often excluding the individual from the community. Managing this balance is seen as a zero-sum game; that is, if one party wins, the other loses (see also Strang, 2002), in the context of juvenile and criminal justice). Restorative justice, through valuing and engaging all members of the school community in the process of nurturing and securing safe schools offers greater emotional synergy for a win–win solution.

The rise of research within the areas of restorative justice, conflict resolution, emotional intelligence and social and emotional learning, as well as in a host of other areas, has shown the adaptive value of emotions (see Katz, 1999). It seems that dualistic, win–lose mentalities come out of an over-emphasis on rationality. But, as the research has shown, by allowing reason and emotion to work together, we can instil emotional intelligence in our school communities, and in doing so, build safer and stronger school communities. Larry Sherman (2002), in his presidential address to the American Society of Criminology, argued that research and development on restorative justice can help modify both theory and innovations as a basis for democratic institutions to work towards a new paradigm of emotionally intelligent systems that focus on the role of emotions in the "causation and regulation of human behaviour". We see this as our agenda in the development of safe school frameworks. The following chapter, on responsive regulation, explores a range of innovative responses schools can develop that aim to restore safe school communities.

Chapter 5

Responsive regulation

Functioning institutions, along with functioning families, are central to a community's capacity to uphold a certain code of non-violent behaviour. Individual citizens alone cannot successfully demand of each other and their children behaviour that is legal and morally acceptable. Non-violence must be a community standard, supported and reinforced by all institutions and groups within the society.

Prothrow-Stith (1993, p 76)

[H]e that will not apply new remedies must expect new evils: for time is the greatest innovator, and if time of course alter things to the worse, and wisdom and counsel shall not alter them to the better, what shall be the end?

Francis Bacon (Of Innovations, 1625)

It's not the strongest species that survive, nor the most intelligent, but the most responsive to change.

Charles Darwin

Restorative justice and responsive regulation

Restoring safe school communities goes hand-in-hand with regulating safe school communities. In other words, the mechanisms through which safety and behaviour are regulated within schools are closely tied to the behaviours that schools seek to foster in restoring and maintaining safe communities. The predominant approach to regulating safety across many jurisdictions, from schools to courts, has been regulatory formalism, where institutional representatives make a moral judgment about the wrongfulness of an action, and a legal judgment about the appropriate punishment or consequence. Within this framework, regulatory formalism requires rules and responses to be defined in advance. The aim is to maximise consistency. Within the jurisdiction of schools, zero-tolerance policies are a prime example of regulatory formalism, typically specifying the behaviour and the formal response within detailed student codes of conduct. These responses, while seemingly clear and consistent, actually enable authorities to act on their worst prejudices, often discriminating against those who are worse off and who bring added challenges to an already burdened system (see Chapter 3).

The reality is that students bring a wide range of learning challenges and opportunities to schools. Students' behavioural repertoires make school life intriguing and challenging at the same time. On both sides, opportunities for learning, problem-solving and growth are required when compliance falls short of behavioural standards, particularly when school safety is compromised. Simply put, when it comes to harmful behaviour in schools, mechanisms need to be in place to build understanding between those affected by the wrongdoing and those responsible for the wrongdoing. Further, when schools fail to address the emotional needs of those affected by harmful behaviour, feelings of helplessness within the school community are heightened because members of the school community are not given the opportunity to take on responsibility for safety. Safety is seldom a third party's problem – it is always a community problem that needs to be addressed as such. Thus, while formalised approaches to regulating safe school communities appear responsive, especially when a higher authority steps in, they may actually be working against the very thing that schools seek – safe and healthy communities that foster learning and growth.

The practice of restorative justice allows school communities to be more responsive because the process entails giving back the harm, or wrongdoing, to the community most affected. This enables the community to address the harm, through *resolution*, *restitution*, and *reconciliation*. As discussed in Chapter 4, through *resolution* the community takes responsibility to address and reduce the risk of harm reoccurring, through *restitution* harm is repaired, and through *reconciliation* comes emotional healing. It is through this approach that collective responsibility for school safety is achieved. In contrast, the formalised regulatory platform of zero tolerance denies the school community an opportunity to foster growth, resilience and responsibility. These formalised processes become numbing, rather than nurturing. Zero-tolerance policies, while seemingly responsive, are in fact not responsive to the needs of the school community and diminish emotional resilience and responsibility. This chapter examines the use and structure of responsive regulation within school communities, beginning with the development of an institutional framework to think about the role of conflict, and hope, in the development and emancipation of young people. This is followed by the development of a whole school approach to responsive regulation based on the practice of restorative justice. A number of approaches to this form of responsive regulation are outlined and a number of case studies provided.

Social institutions and social regulation: A school perspective

Social institutions formally and informally regulate patterns of inter-action and behaviour; in other words, they frame our behavioural choices. Embedded in institutions are beliefs, ideals, and possibilities. Institutions hold the capacity to create hope, as well as the capacity to erode hope, through mechanisms that either nourish or disenfranchise the community. Schools, as our primary developmental institution, play a vital role in this regard. Schools have traditionally been associated with developing students' human capital; that is, developing skills, such as reading, writing and arithmetic which build students' skills base for the job market. Yet school life teaches students many more lessons that go beyond the traditional three R's. In particular, schools also play an important function in developing students' social capital (Morrison, 2001). The development of social capital shifts the focus from academic skills development to the nurturing of strong relational foundations within the school community, through developing social skills for interacting with others. Instead of human capital laying the groundwork for developing social capital, social capital lays the groundwork for enhancing the development of human capital. As Robert Putman states in his influential book, *Bowling Alone*:

> Child development is powerfully shaped by social capital. A considerable body of research dating back at least fifty years has demonstrated that trust, networks, and norms of reciprocity within a child's family, school, peer group, and larger community have wide-ranging effects on the child's opportunities and choices and, hence, on his behavior and development. Although the presence of social capital has been linked to various positive outcomes, particularly in education, most research is focused on the bad things that happen to kids who live and learn in areas where there is a deficit of social capital. The implication is clear: Social capital keeps bad things from happening to good kids. (2000, p 296)

More recently, Putnam (2003) has differentiated between the bonding and bridging aspects of social capital. Bonding social capital characterises connections within homogenous groups; bridging social capital charac-terises connections across heterogeneous groups. While both bonding and bridging promote civility, the difference highlights what could be called "emotional capital". Emotional capital, it seems, provides the social glue that binds us to another and thus reflects bonding, more so than bridging. The building of all forms of capital – human, social and emotional – is the hard work that we entrust to the institutions of schools, as well as families. And when deficits arise, in that families fall short in their endowment of human, social and/or emotional capital, we rely on schools to compensate for this deficit. Generation after generation, schools build hope for students through each of these forms of capital, each of which helps to provide the foundations of productive skills, social engagement and emotional resilience. To build hope, schools, formally and informally, must be responsive to the needs of all students, and build a strong foundation across all forms of capital. This is particularly important, and challenging, where human, social or emotional endowments are in deficit. Deficits must be addressed at both the institutional and individual levels, and hope must be an institutional value, as well as an individual value, to be effective.

Simply put, schools hold an important place in regulating hope for the next generation. As McGeer concludes, responsive hope, like responsive regulation, is the hope of care, in both its individual and communal dimensions:

> [T]he most surprising conclusion … is the extent to which an individual's capacity for hoping well depends on that individual's being responsive to the hopes of others and, beyond that, participating in or even building a community of others who are likewise responsive to hopeful lives beyond their own. If this analysis is right, it shows that our success as individual hopers has an irreducibly communal dimension: we cannot hope well without taking a hopeful interest in the hopes of others and visa versa. (2004, p 125)

This analysis, along with the recognition that the hopes of one generation do not necessarily match the hopes of the next generation, highlights the interconnectedness, and associated tensions, of both individual life and group life. An ongoing dialogue that builds bonding and bridging social capital is essential to address the reciprocal needs and tensions of individuals and groups. As social forces emerge and recede, hope takes on different agendas; thus, schools, as a microcosm of society and our primary developmental institution, cannot be static and deterministic in responding to the needs of the school community and wider society. Schools, as well as students, must be active engagers and learners, in concert with governments, other institutions, and the wider school community, and at the centre must be the students, the future generation, whose hopes these institutions regulate. The challenge for schools is large and the challenge exists at all levels of the school community: schools must, as outlined by Schumacher (1997, p 142), balance the opposites of stability and change, tradition and innovation, public interest and private interest, planning and laissez-faire, order and freedom, and growth and decay. Only thoughtful deliberation and wisdom will reconcile these forces.

Schools are institutions that build hope through a journey of emancipation, such that, students become strong individuals through the building of social, emotional and human capital. Through these endowments, domination at an individual and collective level can be overcome. As Braithwaite (2004, p 191) argues, society needs to invest in institutions that foster the reciprocal development of emancipation through hope and hope through emancipation. Building on McGeer's analysis, Braithwaite (2004, p 88) argues that the "art of good hope is responsive hope – a way of hoping animated by care and interdependence. Responsive hope might be institutionalised by the creation of spaces where young people expect compassion, where care for the self is nurtured by experiencing care from others".

Braithwaite (2004) argues that the practice of Youth Development Circles, which applies the principles of restorative justice to general learning, offers emancipation for all young people. The practice of restorative justice also offers a platform for schools to regulate the building of human, social and emotional capital. When schools capitalise on the social and emotional curriculum of school life, through the practice of restorative justice, they nurture human growth and development in the broadest sense. If schools fail to capitalise on the development of the social and emotional curriculum, alongside the standard skills-based curriculum, students' growth will be stymied and their life opportunities dampened. Restorative justice is not only a journey to belonging, it is a journey of emancipation and of hope.

Engaging with conflict

Some students will gain the endowments of positive youth development through a range of formal and informal life experiences, for others deficits will be revealed through unresolved conflict or disharmony. Conflict, individual and collective, provides the opportunity for growth and development. However, this will only be realised through engagement with conflict rather than being avoided, trumped or denied. These approaches to conflict can be characterised by the four approaches to managing safe school communities outlined in the social discipline window; specifically, the *not, to, for* and *with* analysis (see Wachtel and McCold (2001), in Chapter 3). Trumping conflict is aligned to doing something *to* someone, through domination and punishment. Denying conflict is aligned to doing something *for* someone, through rescuing or excusing. Avoiding conflict is aligned to *not* doing anything, or ignoring the conflict. While there can be a greyness in the distinctiveness of these three categories, all three of these strategies disempower. Restorative justice seeks to empower; it is aligned to a *with* strategy, through harnessing conflict as a point of growth and empowerment. Most school communities engage in each of these strategies.

Johnson and Johnson (1995) have acknowledged the failure of many schools to deal with conflict head on. They differentiated between "conflict negative" schools, those that manage conflict destructively, and "conflict positive" schools, those that manage conflict constructively. They note that most schools today are conflict negative, where conflict is dealt with through denial, suppression or avoidance. They advocate a cultural change to conflict positive schools, where conflict is addressed openly. Through using restorative justice practices, students will have the opportunity to learn productively from their experiences of conflict.

As Weissberg (2004) testifies, lessons in conflict resolution are seldom systematically introduced and developed in schools. If anything, conflict resolution is learnt in an informal manner, through the implicit curriculum of schools, as situations arise and teachers assist students in resolving their differences. Sometimes the situation is resolved in a manner that meets the needs and concerns of the members of the school community involved, however in many cases the stage is set for further conflict. One study found that in schools where staff and students had no formal training in conflict resolution, 90 per cent of the conflicts resulted in one or both parties being injured physically or psychologically (Johnson & Johnson, 1995). In general, conflict resolution is learnt through informal channels, at home and at school. Children can also get conflicting messages about the best way to resolve conflicts: parents may model conflict avoidance, denial and suppression when managing conflict, which may clash with what is deemed appropriate at school. There may also be chronic family disharmony, with family members managing conflict in mutually damaging ways. Further, the media often models violence and aggression as legitimate ways to manage conflict successfully. Students will be influenced through many different channels, and be offered many different scripts on how best to resolve conflict. Schools can make a difference but their commitment to addressing the problem must be solid and consistent.

The results have been hit and miss when it comes to addressing violence and conflict in schools. A number of schools have made a difference in providing a safe and productive learning environment for students, while others have failed. For the most part, we don't know how effective efforts are in addressing everyday conflicts, given that evaluation is often the lowest priority when programs are implemented (Weissberg, 2004). For example, in the context of school bullying, some peer mediation and conflict resolution programs have been found to give students important skills in reducing bullying (Cunningham, 1997; Fine, Lacy & Baer, 1995). However, meta-evaluations have generally found that peer mediation programs that simply trained students to resolve disputes when conflicts arose showed weak or non-significant effects on observable aggressive behaviour (Gottfredson, 1997; Brewer et al, 1995). The evidence suggests that conflict resolution programs must fit within the ethos of a wider safe school framework. As Braithwaite puts it:

> It appears a whole school approach is needed that not just tackles individual incidents but also links incidents to a change program for the culture of the school, in particular to how seriously members of the school community take rules about bullying. Put another way, the school not only must resolve the bullying incident; but must also use it as a resource to affirm the disapproval of bullying in the culture of the school. (2002, p 60)

Herein lies the strength of restorative justice, which capitalises on the conflict and harnesses it to enable growth and development, both at an individual level and a community level. Restorative justice not only aims to harness the conflict, it also aims to harness its preventative capacity by engaging soft targets when addressing the problem. Soft targets are those students who fail to intervene before the bullying (or other act of violence) gets out of hand. This could be why whole school approaches to bullying have been found to be effective, while those who merely target the bully, and not the web of relationships sustaining the behaviour, by and large, fail. Indeed, the path of influence to the hard target could well be through the soft targets. From a prevention point of view, the idea is that bystanders have preventative capabilities within the school, yet are softer targets than the offenders themselves. The sanctions that can be most effectively harnessed are the social and emotional sanctions of disapproval directed at and harnessed by the soft targets. Thus, the practice of restorative justice within a whole school approach heightens the responsibility of all members of the school community to intervene and provides students with skills to do so in safe and effective ways. Soft targets are also an important resource when an incident of bullying, or wrongdoing, must be addressed through a restorative justice conference. Soft targets are essential to effective interventions, and need to be included in the process of addressing the harm and wrongdoing.

How does a restorative justice conflict resolution program differ from other programs?

Within schools there are a range of programs that aim to address issues relating to safe schools (see Jimeson & Furlong, 2006), behavioural management (see Evertson & Weinstein, 2006), conflict (see Jones &

Compton, 2003) and bullying (see McGrath and Noble, 2006). As high-lighted in Chapter 4, a key facet of restorative justice is the role of emotional intelligence in preventing and reducing conflict. Interestingly, a review of the many conflict resolution programs currently being imp-lemented in schools reveals that many fail to acknowledge the emotional aspects and barriers that are inherent to many forms of conflict. If the role of emotions is acknowledged, it is seen as a secondary issue rather than a primary component that needs to be addressed. Typically, the emphasis is on changing or stopping behaviours rather than addressing the obliga-tions raised by the harm caused. Repairing the harm done, emotional and otherwise, is a key element of restorative practices. Failure to address this element, invites further conflict and harm.

The previous chapter also highlights the importance of the emotion of shame in understanding children who bully and who are victims of bullying. As such, shame management provides an important link in furthering our understanding of conflict resolution, particularly for those students who fall outside the range of current programs. A framework based on restorative justice and responsive regulation brings together three important aspects of regulating safe school communities – conflict resolution, social and emotional intelligence, and shame management – under one conceptual umbrella. Students need to learn effective conflict resolution skills that focus on resolving the situation at the overt beha-vioural level, as many conflict resolution programs do, but they also need to resolve the wrongdoing at an emotional level. It is at this level that restorative justice makes a difference.

How conflicts are managed and what is learnt from them, deter-mine whether the conflict has been constructive or destructive for those involved. Constructive conflict resolution brings those affected back into what can be characterised as communities of care; that is, communities that foster mutual respect. The process aims to be restorative to those involved through building emotionally supportive relationships for them. In essence, the focus aims to build hope and security for students, through building foundations of social and emotional intelligence and resilience. Constructive conflict resolution restores social bonds and fos-ters responsible citizenship; in contrast, destructive conflict resolution breaks down social bonds and leaves those affected feeling estranged from the communities within which they live.

Conflict is always a difficult issue to address. However, when there is a power imbalance, conflict can be particularly harmful as it implies domination of a weaker party by a stronger party. Restorative justice values non-domination. This value enables productive and responsible citizenship. Bullying is more than a conflict of interest with another party, it is domination of one party over another. Restorative justice prioritises not only settling conflict, but justice without domination. Justice is then served through self-regulation rather than by pressure imposed through the further imposition of power. It aims to transform conflict into cooperation, through addressing the power imbalances that underpin the conflict. These processes lie at the heart of how schools nurture and balance the reciprocal forces of cooperation and competition, with cooperation being defined as working together and competition being defined as striving together (see May & Doob, 1937). These behaviours reflect the reciprocal forces of autonomy and belonging which are at work in schools every day, promoting positive youth development.

Cooperative and competitive frameworks

Schools, as developmental institutions, instil the virtues of cooperation and competition within students. Sometimes competitive frameworks provide the best environment to challenge individual and team development. A simple example would be participating in academic and sporting competitions. Sometimes a cooperative framework has the capacity to produce the best results, for example, when learning new material and adapting to change. These frameworks drive change and development in different ways. For example, competition, through *striving* together, drives innovation while cooperation, through *working* together, drives adaptation. When performance skills operate in a competitive institutional framework, one cannot afford to take risks; conversely, risk-taking, which involves making mistakes and trying new things, is associated with cooperative frameworks. When things go wrong, as schools navigate the development process that challenges students to strive and grow, cooperative systems allow behaviour to be evaluated and adapted within the support of the community. Striving together (competition), and working together (cooperation), go hand-in-hand within the school community. The hard work of school is to balance the competitive and cooperative frameworks. The challenge is to balance these systems in a way that maximises the ability of schools to be inclusive, such that hope and emancipation are developed for a diverse student body.

Pressure to enhance performance outcomes, as with growing standardised curricula, strengthens the competitive system, often to the detriment of the cooperative system. Schools must enhance a student's capacity to work within both cooperative and competitive frameworks. We need policy and curricula that strengthen both systems, and to sustain and strengthen both systems we need effective ways of dealing with conflict. Restorative justice and responsive regulation frame how this is possible. High performing schools go hand-in-hand with safe schools. These schools nurture both the academic curriculum as well as the social and emotional curriculum of school life.

Dewey (1899) long ago recognised and emphasised the public function of education. Drawing on the ancient Greeks' conceptualisation of education, he discussed the relationship between social order and education. As he (1899, p 36) stated, "[The Greeks] regarded education as the chief, if not the only fundamentally important instrument of social progress". Dewey (1899) also recognised that an individual's self-worth is developed in the context of their social relationships. When we fail to offer respect to students, when we fail to allow children to respond to and learn from their own experiences, particularly when a harmful incident has occurred in our schools, we fail ourselves. We fail ourselves because each of our lives rests on our interdependencies with others. By not approaching the problem of bullying, and other harmful acts, and not engaging with those affected, the seed is sewn for the breakdown of social relationships. Students will then fail to self-regulate in ways that are appropriate and productive. Dewey conceptualises the problem as follows:

> The reason that they are social wreckage or failures, or burdens, is simply, at least partly, in the fact that they never have been educated to habits of self-control and self-adjustment, they never have been rendered flexible, capable of using good judgement during their school years, and the result is that they are not adjusted. (1899, p 92)

Well-adjusted students capitalise on effective cooperative and competitive frameworks, and they learn to meet both individual and collective goals. We must create the right environment for students, a place that fosters collective pride as well as respect for individuals. A first step that needs to be taken is to transform schools from exclusionary environments, those that capitalise on difference and domination, to inclusive environments that are characterised by participative democracies that acknowledge the homogenous and heterogeneous nature of school communities.

Indeed many schools recognise these elements when building their school cultures. At the same time, this analysis does not go far enough. Creating cooperative and positive school cultures will go a long way but only to the extent that we embrace our differences, and with that our individual (and collective) histories. Children who chronically bully others, and children who are endlessly bullied, are carrying a lot of alienation and anger with them. We need to develop, model and teach processes that allow us to work through our differences more effectively and productively. We need to create safe inclusive spaces that allow all members of the school community to relinquish shame and re-connect with others. This is the heart of democratic citizenship. How schools can do this, in the context of restorative justice and responsive regulation, is the topic of the following section.

A whole school approach to responsive regulation: A continuum of restorative practices

Within any school there is often a continuum of interventions that aim to keep schools safe. Some are reactive and some are proactive. Responsive regulation involves not only developing a range of appropriate responses in reaction to incidents of harm and wrongdoing, but also involves developing proactive strategies that support reactive responses. It is important to develop a synergy between proactive and reactive strategies that will unite programs across a continuum of practices. If this synergy is not developed and maintained, programs will become less effective, no matter where they sit on the continuum. A clear message from the early evaluations of restorative justice conferencing in schools was that the take-up rate for schools, across a range of incidents, was slow and uneven – for a variety of reasons. The evidence suggested that what was needed was a broader institutional approach that supported the practice across all levels of behaviour (see Cameron & Thorsborne, 2001; Morrison, 2001; O'Connell & Ritchie, 2001). In other words, restorative justice must touch the culture of the school as a whole. For example, the Responsible Citizenship Program, a proactive program based on the principles of restorative justice, aims to create a space and a process for this cultural transformation to occur (see Appendix 2). At the same time, it is only one part of a continuum of practices. Taken together this continuum of responses, from proactive to reactive, must sit within a comprehensive institutional framework that supports a range of responsive regulatory practices based on the principles of restorative justice.

Guided by Braithwaite's (2002) work on responsive regulation, a whole school model of restorative justice has been developed based on three levels of regulatory intervention: *primary, secondary* and *tertiary* (see Morrison, 2003, 2005). This is consistent with a number of other approaches, including that of the National Research Council's (Moore et al, 2002) report, *Deadly Lessons,* and Gilligan's (2001) model of violence prevention. The building consensus is that school safety be regulated in line with public health regulation; that is, along three different levels of preventative efforts that form a continuum of responses based on common principles. By way of analogy to a health care model, interventions range from immunisation strategies to targeted and intensive strategies for specific groups and individuals:

- The *primary* (or universal) level involves all members of the school community in an "immunisation" or "defense" strategy so that conflict does not escalate into violence when differences first arise. The aim is to develop and affirm students' social and emotional competencies and skills, particularly in the area of conflict resolution, so that students are able to resolve differences in respectful and caring ways. While there are many programs that provide this for schools, the Responsible Citizenship Program (see Appendix 2) is one example that is explicitly based on principles of restorative justice.

- The *secondary* (or targeted) level often involves a small to medium sized group of the school community (eg, a mediation team or a class), as a conflict situation has become protracted or involves (and affects) a large number of people. In these situations a third party is often required to facilitate the resolution. The use of problem-solving and healing circles, as a regular practice within classrooms, are examples, and are described in Chapter 6.

- The *tertiary* (or intensive) level involves the participation of an even wider cross-section of the school community, including parents, guardians, social workers, and others who have been affected, when serious incidents occur within the school. A face-to-face restorative justice conference (see Chapters 2, 4 and 6), is proposed at this level.

Taken together, these practices move from proactive to reactive, along a continuum of responses. Movement from one end of the continuum to the other also involves widening the circle of care around participants. The emphasis is on early intervention through building a strong base at the primary level, which grounds a continuum of responsive regulation across the school community (see also Morrison, 2003, 2005). Across all levels, restorative practices aim to develop inclusive and respectful dialogues that focus on the development and safety of the whole school community. This is consistent with the conclusion of the National Research Council's (2002, p 8) report which states: "Specifically, there is a need to develop a strategy for drawing adults and youth closer together in constructing a normative social climate that is committed to keeping the schools safe from lethal incidents".

Supporting the emerging consensus on three-level models of school safety, when Russell Skiba and Gil Noam (2001) asked contributors to their special issue of *New Directions for Youth Development* to offer alternative models to zero-tolerance approaches, the contributors were remarkably consistent in their recommendation of tri-level models of prevention (see Gagnon & Leone, 2001; Noam et al, 2001; Osher et al, 2001), much to the surprise of the editors who made no specification along these lines. Thus, there is converging evidence of the utility of this approach. As Skiba and Noam conclude:

> [O]ur best knowledge suggests that there is no single answer to the complex problems of school violence and school discipline. Rather, our efforts must address a variety of levels and include universal interventions that teach all students alternatives to violence, procedures to identify and reintegrate students who may be at risk for violence, and interventions specifically designed for students already exhibiting disruptive or aggressive behavior. (2001, p 4)

Their review of the data consistently shows that the most promising programs and practices emphasised inclusion over exclusion within a comprehensive whole school approach. The inference is that when schools have a policy of exclusion for certain behaviours, this puts the entire school at risk. Effective interventions work precisely because they are inclusive.

Within a whole school restorative justice approach, primary, secondary and tertiary practices come together as follows: The primary, or universal, level targets all members of the school community, with the aim of developing a strong normative climate of respect, a sense of belonging within the school community, procedural fairness and the development of strong social and emotional skills. The secondary, or targeted, level focuses on a small percentage of the school community who are becoming a risk for the development of chronic behaviour problems or have been involved in an incident in the classroom or schools and that has affected themselves or others and they cannot resolve themselves. Finally, the tertiary, or intensive, level targets students who have already developed chronic and intense behaviour problems or have been involved in serious incident at school. Within this conceptual model, students who are involved in intensive interventions typically have also been involved in targeted interventions, and all students, including those at the targeted and intensive levels, are involved in universal interventions. Further, while the recommendation is to model violence prevention on a health care model, the model is much more dynamic. Instead of a one-shot inoculation at the universal level, the intervention must be reaffirmed in the everyday practice of school life. At the targeted level, while particular students or groups of students are targeted, the inclusive practice of restorative justice necessarily involves students not at risk. This participatory strategy is about reconnecting these students with the school community, through repairing relationships, and thus necessarily involves students not at risk. The behaviour of some students may keep them involved with targeted interventions for an ongoing period of time, others may drift to this level

Figure 5.1. A whole school model of restorative justice

1–5% of population

Tertiary or Intensive

REBUILDING RELATIONSHIPS
through intensive facilitated dialogue that includes a broad social network

Secondary or Targeted

REPAIRING RELATIONSHIPS
through facilitated and supported dialogue

Whole School

Primary or Universal

RE-AFFIRMING RELATIONSHIPS
through developing social and emotional skills

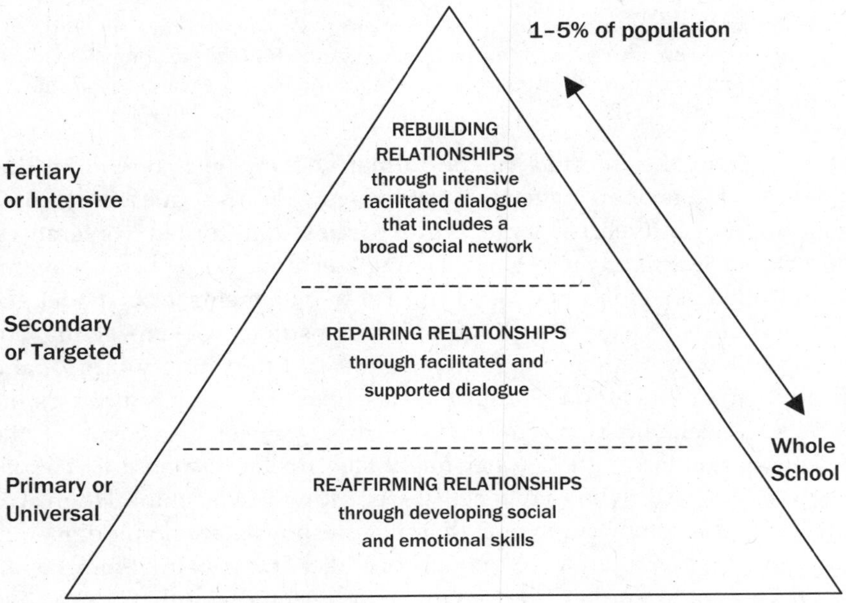

only a few times, and others not at all. At the intensive level, these students will have participated in previous levels of intervention but because of the seriousness or ongoing nature of a behavioural problem an intensive focus on rebuilding relationships is the aim of this level of intervention. In summary, the universal level is about re-affirming relationships, the targeted level is about repairing relationships, and the intensive level is about repairing and re-building relationships.

Models of restorative practices

There are many different ways to develop a range of restorative justice initiatives within a whole school approach. A number of continuums of restorative practices have evolved, and are described below. These examples are not prescriptive nor definitive but are included as illustrations of how the language and practice of restorative justice has developed in schools.

A continuum of practices: From the informal to formal

Wachtel and McCold (2001) have developed a continuum of responses that move from the informal to the formal range of restorative practices.

Wachtel and McCold argue that as one moves from the informal to the formal:

> [T]he restorative interventions ... involve more people, more planning, more time, are more complex in dealing with the offence, more structured, and due to all those factors, may have more impact on the offender. (1999, p 2)

Moving from the informal to the formal end of their continuum, the practices outlined are: affective statements; affective questions; small impromptu conferences; large group circles and formal conferences. *Affective statements* express to the wrongdoer how his or her behaviour has affected an individual or class. These statements also model the appropriate expression of feelings and demonstrate problem-solving. For example, a staff member might say: "Claudia, I find it very hurtful and disappointing when you disrupt the class like that. And it surprises me because I feel you don't mean to hurt anyone on purpose". If the behaviour continues, the teacher might step up the response to *affective questioning*: "Fred, what happened there? How do you think Hugh was affected?" It is important to note that these responses are non-judgmental and they offer an alternative to questions like: "How many times have I asked you not to do that?" Or "Why do you keep doing that?" Affective questions mirror the same questions that are used in a formal restorative justice conference: what happened; who was affected and how; and what needs to happen to repair the harm done? This same process is used in *small impromptu conferences*, or corridor conferences. Small impromptu conferences tend to involve just those involved and affected, but can also involve supporters. The following is an example of a small impromptu conference held in a court building, while people gathered awaiting a placement hearing. The grandmother of the 14 -year-old boy to be placed, told the director of the residential placement:

> [H]ow on Christmas Eve, several days before, her grandson had gone over to a cousin's house without permission and without letting her know. He did not come back until the next morning, just barely in time for them to catch a bus to her sister's house for Christmas dinner. The director got the grandmother talking about how that incident had affected her and how worried she was about her grandson. The boy was surprised by how deeply his behaviour had affected his grandmother. He readily apologised. (Wachtel & McCold, 2001, pp 125-126)

The next stage is a *large group conference* which involves members of the school community coming together to discuss how they were affected by an act of harmful behaviour. Wachtel provides the following example:

> Two boys got into a fistfight recently, an unusual event at our [alternative] schools. After the fight was stopped, their parents were called to

come and pick them up. If the boys wanted to return to our school, each boy had to phone and ask for an opportunity to convince the staff and his fellow students that he should be allowed back. Both boys called and came to school. One refused to take responsibility and had a defiant attitude. He was not re-admitted. The other was humble, even tearful. He listened attentively while staff and students told him how he had affected them, willingly took responsibility for his behavior, and got a lot of compliments about how he handled the meeting. He was re-admitted and no further action was taken. The other boy was put in the juvenile detention center by his probation officer. Ideally, he will be a candidate for a formal conference. (1999, p 3)

A *formal conference* defines the formal end of the continuum and involves bringing together victims and offenders along with their families and communities of care. But as Wachtel states: "we rarely hold formal conferences. We have found that the more we rely on informal restorative practices in everyday life, the less we need formal restorative rituals" (1999, p 3). Conferencing is used for significant issues of harm. It is a formal process that involves time to prepare and time to facilitate. If a school only ever ran formal conferences, the recommendation would be to introduce primary and secondary practices, to prevent or de-escalate the problem earlier.

A jigsaw approach to creating a "just" school

Belinda Hopkins (2004) describes her whole school approach to restorative justice as a framework that pieces together the jigsaw of life at school. She describes a continuum of restorative processes of increasing complexity, with more and more people becoming involved in the process (see Hopkins (2004), p 32–7 for these descriptions). The continuum of practices she describes, increasing in complexity, are:

- *Restorative enquiry* describes a way of listening that enables the listener to draw out the speaker's story as well as acknowledging their thoughts, feelings and needs in a given situation.

- *Restorative discussions in challenging situations* are used when there might be a power imbalance, and are intended to keep communication flowing so that both sides can express their feelings and needs and achieve mutually acceptable outcomes.

- *Mediation* is a process involving a neutral third party or parties, whose role is to support those in conflict to come to a mutually acceptable resolution, or at least to find a way of moving forward.

- *Victim/offender mediation* is used when one person has accepted responsibility, at least to some degree, for the harm caused to the other.

- *Community conferences and problem-solving circles* are used when there is a problem to be discussed as a group, a conflict that needs addressing or an event that has caused distress to a whole group.

- *Restorative conferences* bring together the person causing the harm with the person who has been harmed, together with their respective communities of care.

- *Family group conferences* bring together families with a trained professional to assist a young person and their family to make some changes to behaviour.

Hopkins (2004) grounds these processes in a range of skills and values. She defines a pyramid with the values at the base which support the skills, which in turn support the processes at the tip of the pyramid. The values, which are at the foundation, include "respect, openness, empowerment, inclusion, tolerance, integrity and congruence" (Hopkins, 2004, p 38). The skills that build from these include: "remaining impartial and non-judgmental; respecting the perspective of all involved; actively and empathically listening; developing rapport amongst participants; empowering participants to come up with solutions rather than suggesting or imposing ideas; creative questioning; warmth; compassion; patience" (Hopkins, 2004, p 37–38). The processes are the restorative interventions and practices outlined above. Together, Hopkins (2004, p 38) argues, these processes, skills and values "inspire many different initiatives that seek to involve more of the school community in making decisions about how the community is to run. What makes [Hopkins's approach] unique is that it considers how all of these initiatives can fit together, like the pieces of a jigsaw, to make a coherent, congruent whole".

Congruence is the key to bringing the jigsaw of school life together. Hopkins (2004, p 38) stresses that it is important for schools to address the question: "Is everything we do here at this school informed by this ethos, these values and a philosophy which gives central importance to building, maintaining and, when necessary, repairing relationships and community?" Like other approaches, the emphasis is on building and strengthening healthy relationships. The following case study illustrates how the negative effects of bullying and exclusion can be transformed through the process of restorative conferencing:

> Leanne, a year 7 girl, had been on the receiving end of some bullying behaviour since starting at her new secondary school. Present at the conference were Leanne and her mother; Sharon, who had been causing Leanne's distress (also in year 7); Sharon's father; the police officer to whom the matter had been reported; and [the facilitator]. The conference went well. It became clear to the "victim" and her mother that their own loving, supportive, relatively affluent family was what both the "bully"

and her father did not have. The father was struggling to make ends meet and raise the family and, feeling let down by life, took things out on his daughter for whom he did not have a single kind word. When Sharon found herself in a supportive, non-judgmental environment, and felt that her own story had been heard, she was able to appreciate the distress her behavior had caused Leanne and her family. She made a genuine apology and plans for future friendship support were made. The police officer offered Sharon's father information on local support available for single parents. In the final closing "go-round" [the facilitator] asked if anyone had anything else they wanted to say and the jubilant original "victim", clearly visibly relieved and elated, said: "Whoopee!" (Hopkins, 2004, p 130)

Conferencing: A multi-level continuum approach

Thorsborne and Vinegrad (2003) have developed an approach that divides conference processes into two types: (a) proactive processes that enhance teaching and learning; and (b) reactive processes for responding to harm and wrongdoing.

- *Proactive classroom conferences* provide a robust process to enhance teaching and learning outcomes while being explicit about limits and boundaries, and emphasising the importance of relationships. They aim to provide a process that links curriculum, pedagogy, and behaviour management. They can be used for establishing class rules, curriculum topics, teaching strategies, peer tutoring and support, working styles, learning tasks, project and assignment work (as well as providing a forum for experiential and research-based learning), cooperative learning and independent study, and student and teacher feedback.

- *Reactive classroom conferences* can range from: an individual conference involving a teacher and a student; a small group conference involving a teacher and several students; a whole class conference involving a teacher and a class of students; to a large group conference involving a teacher and an entire level, grade or year of students.

- *Reactive community conferences* are used when the community affected by harmful behaviour extends beyond the classroom and others are invited to participate in the conferencing process. Depending on the situation, these people may include parents, siblings, grandparents, uncles and aunts, other students and teachers, members of the wider community, or other school communities and professionals.

These conferencing processes can complement a range of protective and preventative programs that schools currently use, where relationships and community problem-solving are central guiding principles. The aim is to develop a restorative culture, and conferencing can provide the foci

and links to other aspects of school life, be it within the formal or informal curriculum of school life. As Thorsborne and Vinegrad, argue:

> The use of conferencing as a major restorative intervention provides the
> interpersonal and disciplinary link between proactive student manage-
> ment policies and the life of the classroom. The benefit in the long term
> is that the staff and student population undergo fundamental behaviour
> and cultural change. The focus on more open and transformative dia-
> logue impacts positively on the daily operations of the school. (2003,
> p 56)

The following case studies provided by Thorsborne (2004) illustrate the
many different situations and groups that are amenable to conference
processes.

Case Study: The Pub

Location: Tasmania

The following incident was resolved and managed by the community
conference process. Of significance is the role played by this school in
a community that was the last broad acre housing commission development implemented in Tasmania, which, at one point in time, was famous
for having the worst levels of community health in Australia.

During a usual school day several students truanted and returned to
the school intoxicated. These students disrupted many classes, assaul-
ted a male teacher and then left the school grounds followed by a trail
of administrators and onlookers. The school was keen to limit the
damage from this incident and to sort it out with the best interests of
all in mind.

The list of defined "offenders" for this conference included a female
student who was responsible for purchasing the alcohol, two male and
one female student who consumed the alcohol and the manager of the
hotel who was liable for selling the alcohol. Of interest was the
manager of the hotel who was visibly tired of the ongoing community
backlash about his pub providing alcohol to their kids. He was keen to
view the school as an ally with all this trouble.

The conference was a success. The school, once again, received
feedback about its boring, ad hoc and irrelevant curriculum. The
offending students were reintegrated back into their school community
and their parents and guardians were pleased with the process and
outcomes. The male teacher was able to speak about his shock and
surprise from the assault and disclosed later that he felt comfortable
talking about his distress rather than keeping up his masculine front.

The local pub came out of the conference with a new sense of community understanding and support. After speaking about the ongoing battle with adults purchasing alcohol for youngsters, false identification cards, under age parties around the community and difficulty obtaining staff who could follow strict guidelines resulted in the community gaining valuable insight into just how "OK" the pub was. Another result of this conference was an agreement by the manager to review all the operations of the hotel with a focus on underage drinking. In acknowledgement of the school's work the manager donated a perpetual trophy to recognise student success. The key to this conference was the offenders' understanding of the impact of their behaviour on the people who worked at the pub, where previously they felt that the pub was just a place and a building.

Case study: The sports program

Location: Tasmania

Two long standing rival private schools had for many years conducted their battles on the sporting field. Unfortunately one of the schools included a very lewd ditty in their sporting program for the upcoming athletics carnival. The ditty concerned the rival school and caused an uproar which made the front page of the local newspaper. For several days the controversy raged without any solution in sight. I contacted both schools and suggested that we could all meet at my school and participate in a community conference. Being a government school, it could be considered neutral territory. Both parties were hesitant at first, but agreed to trying this new process of sorting out difficult issues. The conference went really well with several highlights. Staff from the school which had produced the offensive document could not understand what all the fuss was about. They had been printing programs like this for years. Offended staff from the other school had not done their research into past practice, as many of the senior administrators had left or changed jobs, hence there had been a change in culture. Symbolic reparation was made with promises of meeting "like this" more regularly to build more bridges and to resolve other issues. Of significance was the changed impressions regarding the status of government schools like ours. We really could make an impact and a difference in our community.

A responsive and restorative pyramid: An integrated approach

Figure 5.2. Whole school model of restorative practices: An integrated approach

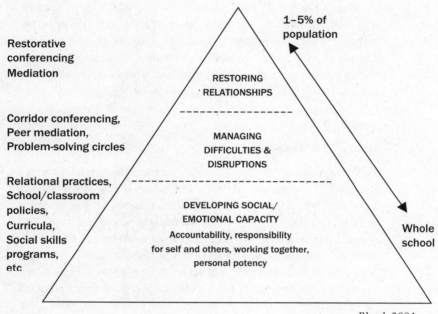

Blood, 2004

Blood (2004) had defined her whole school approach to restorative practices as an integrated approach, drawing on a range of relational practices.

* *Whole school relational practices* are emphasised at the base of the pyramid, with particular emphasis on developing the social and emotional capacities within the school, to prevent incidents from occurring and to strengthen relationships. Following Porter (2002), who argues that consideration is the most important skill children need to develop, Blood (2004) focuses on: (a) accountability; (b) responsibility for self and others; (c) working together; and (d) personal potency. These are put into practice within the school and classroom through policies, curriculum and social skills programs. In many ways, what is put in place at this level becomes the values base of the school.

- *Managing difficulties and disruptions* in the school and classroom through corridor conferencing, mediation, and problem-solving circles are at the next level of intervention. The aim is to develop a skills base for teachers, administrators, students and parents such that issues can be addressed in the everyday life of schools. These interventions develop the capacity for problem-solving. The aim is to create a culture where problem-solving is modelled and treated as an opportunity to learn and to make a difference, and where empathy, responsibility, and accountability are fostered.

- *Restoring relationships,* at the tip of the pyramid, involve processes that aim to repair and rebuild relationships when significant disruption and harm occurs. These processes hold people to account, encourage responsibility, and help to develop empathy and an understanding of how individuals' behaviour has affected others. The aim is to bring out the participants' common humanity, hence the process, above all other considerations, seeks to be humane. The focus is on being both firm and fair.

With the emphasis on building a strong base to the pyramid, Blood (2004) has used the Help Increase the Peace Program (HIPP) (Liss, 2004) to develop a restorative culture within schools. HIPP was developed by the American Friends Service Committee (AFSC), a Quaker organisation which sought "to change patterns of behaviour that keep young people in conflict ... and to train students and teachers in conflict resolution skills and through this experience to knit the school into a caring community" (Blood, 2004, p 3). HIPP works across age groups, gender, class, race and behaviour. Typically in a small group of 15 to 18, two to three students with behavioural issues will be selected to participate in the program alongside a diverse range of students, with the aim of maximising the diversity of the group. (HIPP is reviewed further in Chapter 6.) While HIPP is seen as a useful initiative to help build social and emotional capacities within the school community and to shift relational dynamics, restorative practices add rigour to the process. Just as a successful HIPP group cannot proceed without the foundations of community, conflict resolution, trust and negotiation, the group will not function without responsibility and accountability for self and others, as the following case study illustrates:

> In a HIP group once, two young lads arrived late for the second day of a three day program. It was the second time this group had come together, after the first attempt had folded some 12 months earlier. As the group had started, we stopped to ask the two boys what had happened? In the course of this discussion, it emerged that the trouble

had started when they went onto a building site near their home (without permission) which had started a serious chain of events, that included stealing from the building site and joy riding in a shopping trolley on their way to the group. The dialogue quickly moved into a full scale conference as we not only dealt with the impact on the group, but also of the stealing and their dangerous behaviour on the main road. Both boys in the end really got the impact on the group, their parents, the builders and the leaders. They acknowledged the impact on the group and made arrangements to take the stolen item back to the building site and explain their actions to the builders. The group was stronger for the real life interruption and intrusion that could have been skipped over, had they not been held to account for their disruption to the group by their lateness. (Blood, 2004, np)

HIPP principles have also been successfully applied as a framework for classroom management practices, especially when used in conjunction with restorative practices. Restorative questions are used as a simple but effective debriefing tool within HIPP and for debriefing for classroom or group activities: *What happened? What was the hardest part?* and *What would you do differently next time?* If something happens, the group or class might form a conference to explore and repair the harm. New agreements and ways of behaving might be agreed to or the teaching method may be challenged.

Blood also illustrates how these questions can be used outside a school context:

A boy was seen outside the school grounds yelling obscenities at 2 other boys in the play ground. Concerned about the young person's obvious level of distress, the teacher stopped to ask if he was okay and what happened? The boy angrily told his story of how the other two boys had locked him in a cage near the school grounds. He said he was OK and going home. As he proceeded he yelled more obscenities back at the boys and on seeing a Police car drive by, attempted to wave them down – to no avail. Seeing this was enough for the teacher to reverse up the driveway and seek out the other two boys. The first boy joined them and dialogue was facilitated between them.

To the two boys: What happened? (Lots of justifications were offered at this point). What were you thinking at the time you did that? Both responded that they were just having fun. Not withstanding what happened, how do you think your mate felt when he realized he was locked in the cage? Both boys in turn offered how they guess he must have got real scared. To the young person that had been locked in the cage: What was it like when you realized that you were locked in?

118

"I was scared and all I wanted to do was get out. When I got out I was so angry that I just threw whatever I could at them". To the 2 young "offenders": Is there anything you would like to say at this stage? Both turned to the young person and said they were sorry, they didn't realize and didn't mean to hurt him. He then spontaneously said he was sorry for throwing rocks at them. All three boys then said thank you and walked off together, once more mates and hopefully the wiser for the experience. Without this, one wonders how they would have dealt with this. Most probably the most aggrieved would have walked home, trashed a few fences along the way and angrily told his story at home. The other two (shamed by the experience and concerned about getting into trouble) would have more than likely denied the experience or stated that it wasn't as bad as it was. Had the police car stopped, the aggrieved young person may have even been cautioned about his language and unceremoniously taken home, 3 mates split by a thoughtless act. (2004, np)

Conclusion: Working towards a just society

Restorative justice, developed within a framework of responsive regulation, offers an opportunity for schools to invest in justice, broadening the range of institutional mechanisms that work towards a just society. Within this framework, restorative justice is transformed from a simple "one-off" disciplinary opportunity to one that embraces the ongoing and emerging complexities of school life.

Restorative justice seeks social and emotionally intelligent justice. Responsive regulation takes a problem-solving approach that aims to be more institutionally responsive to the concerns of all members of the school community, offering an alternative to the structured regulatory formalism of zero tolerance. Working hand-in-hand, responsive regulation provides a framework for locating restorative justice in institutional space (Braithwaite, 2002). Simply put, responsive regulation and restorative justice is about responding to behaviour and restoring relationships, along a continuum of institutional practices. More to the point, restoring safe and healthy school communities goes hand-and-hand with how safe and healthy schools are regulated.

A responsive regulatory framework, which capitalises on Braithwaite's (1989) notion of separating the behaviour from the person, is an important policy distinction. Too many policies and practices that seeks to regulate safe school communities focus on behaviour, and emphasise the rules of behaviour, while failing to address the relational needs of the school community and the web of relationships that sustain the school community's health and safety. By way of analogy, when we focus too much on behaviour, we fail to see the forest for the trees. We must understand behaviour in the context of the relationships that regulate that behaviour.

Fully realised, restorative justice and responsive regulation is not about adding another program, or set of practices, to the tool bag of school life, it is about institutionalising a process that facilitates micro-institutional change that is responsive to the ongoing and emergent needs of individuals and communities in working towards a just society. The following chapter will examine the evidence base in achieving these aims.

Chapter 6

Practising restorative justice in schools: The evidence

> It is not uncommon for educators to work from the premise that achievement and mastery rather than belonging are the primary, if not sole, precursors of self esteem ... The current education system, in fact, has dissected and inverted Maslow's hierarchy of needs so that belonging has been transformed from unconditional need and right of all people into something that must be earned, something that can be achieved only by the "best of us".
>
> *Kunc* (1992, p 381)

> If civilization is to survive, we must cultivate the science of human relationships – the ability of all peoples, of all kinds, to live together, in the same world at peace.
>
> *Franklin D Roosevelt, 1945* (in Lasch, 1972, p 210)

In different ways, and to different levels and standards, restorative justice has probably always been practised in schools: good schooling, like good parenting, typically has restorative elements, where respectful relationships are valued and behaviour is held to high standards. This chapter reviews the different ways restorative justice has been practised in schools and the evidence backing the effectiveness of these practices. This review does not aim to be definitive but draws upon the best evidence we have to date, while acknowledging that good research is currently underway and that much more is needed. Drawing on the three levels of responsive regulation developed in Chapter 5, current practice and evidence is presented for intensive (tertiary), targeted (secondary) and universal (primary) practices. The decision to review the evidence in this particular order is intentional, as the practice of restorative justice in schools, per se, began with restorative justice conferencing at the intensive level; however, the importance of developing a strong base of restorative practices at the universal level is now well recognised. With this evolution, restorative justice is now practised at all levels of the pyramid, with the broad aim of developing a climate of fairness, dignity and safety for all members of the school community, where those affected by harmful behaviour have

121

the opportunity to participate in deliberative learning processes that aim to affirm, repair and rebuild relationships.

Intensive restorative interventions

Recall, it was Margaret Thorsborne's (Cameron & Thorsborne, 2001, p 181) "search for a non-punitive intervention for serious misconduct" that put restorative justice on the behavioural map in Australian schools. As such, restorative justice was first used to address serious behavioural incidents within schools using a community accountability conferencing model in a similar manner to how it was used in a juvenile justice context. This initiative quickly lead, in 1995 and 1997, to the first evaluations of the restorative justice conferencing model in schools (Education Queensland, 1996, 1998). The aim of these intensive restorative interventions is to create a circle of care to support those involved, so that an open, honest and respectful dialogue can develop, where individuals can acknowledge how the incident has affected them and allow each participant to take responsibility for how best to repair the harm done. This circle of care is made up of those who care most about those involved, and can support them in different aspects of their life. Typically these people include parents, other care givers, coaches, teachers, professionals, peers, and brothers and sisters.

This process has worked under a range of names: "community accountability conferences" (Education Queensland, Australia), "school forums" (New South Wales Department of Education and Training, Australia); "community group conferencing" (Colorado School Mediation Center, United States); "community conferencing" (Calgary Community Conferencing, Canada), and "restorative conferencing" (Home Office, England). Beyond these semantic preferences, large circle processes also exist in a variety of forms, each having unique features. For example, peacemaking or healing circles use rituals associated with the Native Indians of North America, such as a talking piece (see Pranis, Stuart & Wedge, 2002); and family group conferences, influenced by the Maori culture in New Zealand, involve private time for immediate and extended family members to work through concerns (see Maxwell & Morris, 2006). In the context of face-to-face community conferences, there are also a number of distinctive variations that relate to the use of: a scripted or non-scripted model; one or two facilitators; a refreshment break; and a follow-up conference (see Barton, 2003; Hopkins, 2004; Sharpe, 2003; Thorsborne & Vinegrad, 2003, 2004; O'Connell, Wachtel & Wachtel, 1999). There is no empirical evidence that shows that any one of these models is any better than the others. In choosing a model, it is important to choose one that best meets the concerns and needs at stake, and is culturally appropriate.

Indeed, there is little empirical evidence on the use of restorative justice conferencing in schools. Only a handful of evaluations have currently been conducted, with none being carried out at a rigorous experimental level, largely due to lack of funding and political will for such activities. Evaluations are typically carried out post-conference only, and with no comparison group. To date, across a range of countries – including Australia, Canada, England and the United States (see Calhoun, 2000; Hudson & Pring, 2000; Ierley & Ivker, 2002; Shaw & Wierenga, 2002) – results generally replicate those of the initial evaluation of community accountability conferences in Queensland, which remains important in term of outcomes and lessons learnt (Cameron & Thorsborne, 2001).

Within these initial two pilot studies in Queensland a total of 89 (56 and 33 respectively) school-based conferences were convened, in response to: serious assaults (43); serious victimisation (25); truanting, class disruption, damage to school reputation, and bullying (18); property damage and theft (12); drugs (2); and a bomb threat (1). Overall, outcomes across all participants were positive, reporting they: had a say in the process (96 per cent); were satisfied with the way the agreement was reached (87 per cent); were treated with respect (95 per cent); felt understood by others (99 per cent); and felt agreement terms were fair (91 per cent). Specific to victims, they reported that they got what they needed out of the conference (89 per cent) and felt safer (94 per cent). Offenders reported they felt: cared about during conference (98 per cent); loved by those closest to them (95 per cent); able to make a fresh start (80 per cent); forgiven (70 per cent); and closer to those involved (87 per cent). Further, offenders complied with most or all of the agreement (84 per cent) and did not re-offend within the trial period (83 per cent). School personnel reported that the process reinforced school values (100%) and that they had changed their thinking about managing behaviour from a punitive to a more restorative approach (92 per cent). As for family members who participated, they expressed positive perceptions of the school and comfort in approaching the school on other matters (94 per cent).

The positive early results of community conferencing in Queensland, concur with the experience of Ierley and Claassen-Wilson (2003), who wrote a chapter called "Making things right: Restorative justice for school communities". This chapter includes a number of insightful case studies, some of which address the issue of bullying in schools. Here are the words of one student who works on the High School's Student Conflict Hearing Board (in Colorado, in the United States) a student-driven restorative justice program that facilitates restorative justice circles:

I think absolutely having programs like this around the nation would be good because people need options and need to know more than just zero-tolerance policy, and that is pretty much across the board with how our nation's schools are run at the moment and it doesn't work, I don't think … The offenders keep offending. They don't ever learn why it was really wrong. They are punished … But sitting down with us and actually learning what they did that was wrong and actually apologizing. I mean, apologizing is such a big thing, especially if it is meaningful. I think people actually learn to be better people through this. (2003, p 217)

Likewise, teachers report how the process is not only beneficial for students, but beneficial for them as well. An Education Assistant in Calgary recounts a powerful story titled, "Heart of the Matter", in Calgary Community Conferencing's book, *Beyond the Comfort Zone* (Sharpe, 2003). The Assistant had built a strong relationship with a student through her work, but when work demanded that another student needed support, the former student became angry and started to bully the latter student, physically and mentally. The student also spread rumours about the Assistant, which quickly grew, and lead to a formal investigation by the school. For the Assistant (Sharpe, 2003, p 4):

My whole world started to fall down around me. I started to wonder what new career path I could take – if I'd be allowed to work with children again – how it would affect my own children and so on. The investigation was quickly dropped but I was changed as a result. I began feeling "afraid" to get close to children. I didn't look forward to going to work and I felt as if parents and colleagues were still questioning the truth behind the allegations.

The following year the Assistant continued to worry about how these events were affecting the student and others. One day the opportunity to participate in a community conference was presented, and in due time was convened:

By the end of the conference there was not a dry eye in the room. I can easily say that it was one of the most powerful events of my life. It moved me and inspired me. Needless to say our conference ended in a lot of hugging, a lot of resolved feelings. I know that it brought closure to the events for me and I know in my heart that the student learnt from her mistakes, matured and was truly held accountable for her actions. (Sharpe, 2003, p 4)

These results are encouraging: when community conferences are presented as an option, and are thoughtfully planned and carried out, the outcomes can be very positive.

At the same time, evaluations of conferencing trials to date highlight tensions between traditional philosophies and practices in controlling behaviour, which are typically characterised by punitive measures emphasising accountability over support, and restorative philosophies and practices, such as conferencing. This is particularly problematic when restorative conferencing is implemented as a "one-off" intervention for serious incidents and not supported by other restorative measures within the school. By way of illustration, 227 school personnel from 75 schools were trained for the first Queensland trial, but only 56 conferences were conducted within the 12 months of the trial (Department of Education Queensland, 1996). The overriding lesson: broader institutional professional development and support is required to implement, develop and sustain the practice of restorative justice within schools.

Based on the lessons of the Queensland study, the State of Victoria conducted a smaller pilot study of restorative justice conferencing, involving 69 school personnel, from 23 schools within four regional clusters, which met three to four times during the year through the support of regional staff (Shaw & Wierenga, 2002). Over the nine-month trial, 14 conferences and 23 mini-conferences were recorded in eight (of the 23) schools. The key recommendations (Shaw & Wierenga, 2002) from the pilot study were:

- *A whole school approach* is needed, given ongoing tensions with traditional methods of discipline.
- *Involvement of school leadership* is essential; that is, principals and their deputies must be committed to the process of implementation.
- *Collegiate support* is necessary to sustain and develop practice.
- *Time* needs to be made available for training and implementation of restorative justice, as well as the facilitation of conferences.

This evaluation concluded that the process of conferencing:

> [E]xtended school staff beyond their "comfort zones", and they have needed the support of regional staff and networks. The information collected through this evaluation affirms that if a conference is selected well, approached thoroughly by a team who are prepared to do the groundwork, and carried out within the spirit of Restorative Practices, it can be a powerful tool for exploring and managing school discipline issues. (Shaw & Wierenga, 2002, p 15)

The building of the emotional economy of the school seems a core feature of the process of implementing and sustaining effective behavioural management programs. Reflecting on the Queensland trials, Cameron and Thorsborne put it this way:

> The lesson for our education system is to introduce restorative measures as early as preschool, and build on creating a climate where relational values are translated into prosocial behavior by all members of the

school community. The teaching and modelling of emotional intelligence and relationship skills becomes part of the daily business in classrooms. Children are taught to understand what they are feeling and how to deal with difficult situations. Situations and their consequent emotions, which, when unacknowledged, feed the need for interpersonal violence, are dealt with openly. (2001, p 208)

According to Shaw and Wierenga the importance of social and emotional learning was also highlighted in the Victorian pilot study, where some participants in the community conferencing process:

[R]eferred to their inability to express themselves clearly, or to do so without becoming emotional. As adults, we may reassure adolescents that emotionality is legitimate. However, emotionality which results in disadvantage to the young person is humiliation. (2002, p 48)

The recommendation for schools is that it is important for students to develop the skills to identify and articulate feelings. Not only will this be helpful in curbing conflict as it arises, it also reduces a sense of disadvantage for some conference participants. Thus, developing students' social and emotional skills is an important aspect of the empowerment process.

These trials of conferencing highlighted two points: (a) for conferencing to be effective, it needs to be supported by other practices and proactive measures; and (b) all practices need to be congruent within a wider framework, substantiated through integrated policy. In other words, restorative practices, to be effective, must contribute to all aspects of the school discipline system. The development of restorative processes at the targeted level, supports, and helps curb, the need for higher level intensive practices.

Targeted restorative interventions

As conferencing began to be established in schools, some schools recognised that a full conference process was not needed for all behavioural concerns. Some schools paired peer mediation with conferencing, others added corridor (or informal) conferencing, while others developed restorative circle processes as part of normal classroom activities to address problems at a classroom level. What is common across each of these practices is that while the level of harmful behaviour has not reached a level that requires intensive resources, the level of harmful behaviour has reached a point where a third person is needed to help develop safe, productive and honest dialogue between those affected. Sometimes this person is a fellow student, sometimes it is a teacher, administrator, or other member of the school community. Of these practices, peer mediation programs have been evaluated to a far greater extent than other practices; hence, these programs provide the greatest insights for the development of the field. Along with peer mediation, a quasi-experimental study or problem-solving circle is also reviewed in this section.

Problem-solving circles

Problem-solving circles can be developed and run in many different ways. The program presented aims to builds students' capacity for collective problem-solving through a process that addresses everyday concerns within the classroom and school. This classroom practice was built from initial workshops that developed a normative climate of healthy social and emotional skills, but then took the process one step further through introducing the students to the three stages of a restorative justice conference using role play and discussion. Once the students felt confident with the process, they were encouraged to bring problems and concerns within the classroom to the circle. Circles then became a regular feature of the classroom.

This program was evaluated in an Australian elementary school (Morrison & Martinez, 2001). All students in three mixed classes (of grades four, five and six) took part in the study. The intervention was tested in one classroom (n=12), while the other two classrooms acted as quasi-control groups. Problems brought to the circle included annoying behaviour, teasing, feeling left out, aggressive behaviour and stealing. The teacher reported a number of benefits to the classroom, including that it: "Gave us a safe place to share problems face to face; modelled effective conflict resolution; encouraged the open expression of emotion; allowed us to move beyond niggling behaviours; and contributed to a 'way of being' based on respect, communication and support". She also reported a number of significant breakthroughs: a boy, who would shut down during conflict at the start of the year, was asking for open communication by the end of the year; another boy evolved naturally from the role of aggressor to supporter; another boy with extreme learning difficulties found a voice for his strength in providing positive solutions; another boy's modelling of open expression broke the taboo on shedding tears; a girl who was a strong learner convened two of the circles independently; and a boy integrated from the behaviour support unit, willingly contributed and found another tool for managing his relationships.

This program was also evaluated against a same-age control group within the same school. A number of significant differences were found, including that students in the intervention class reported: (a) higher levels of emotional intelligence; (b) greater use of productive conflict resolution techniques; (c) that the teacher was more interested in stopping bullying; (d) that the teacher held bullies and victims more accountable for behaviour; (e) less use of maladaptive shame management strategies; and (f) less involvement in bullying (Morrison & Martinez, 2001).

Peer mediation

Mediation has been defined as a "structured method of conflict resolution in which trained individuals (the mediators) assist people in dispute (the parties) by listening to their concerns and helping them negotiate" (Cohen, 2003). After the mediator clarifies the structure of the process and allows the parties to explain their thoughts and feelings, participants are encouraged to talk directly, develop options, and reach a consensual settlement that will accommodate their needs. In the context of peer mediation, the neutral person is a fellow student (or students), who has been trained in mediation. These students support other students to take responsibility for decisions that affect their lives and the lives of their fellow students. The broader aim is for this self-regulating process to become part of the ethos of the school. This, of course, takes time. The emphasis is on developing students' skills in conflict resolution. As Maxwell states:

> It is the self-empowering aspect of mediation – the fact that disputants actively participate and make decisions about issues and problems that are central to their own lives – that establishes mediation as an important tool in the fostering of self-regulation, self-esteem and self-discipline. (1989, p 154)

Bagshaw (1994) has outlined a number of reasons this might be the case: (a) discipline is less time-consuming and studies have found as much as an 80 per cent drop in the number of disputes reported to teachers; (b) family relationships, particularly among siblings, are also improved through developing communication and conflict resolutions skills (see Gentry & Benenson,1993; Johnson, Johnson, Cotton, Harris & Louison, 1995); (c) a safe place for children to learn about conflict resolution is created (Miller, 1994); and (d) schools that are proactive about conflict resolution usually have a more cooperative climate on the whole. There is an overall feeling of improved social relationships. This is attributed to the fact that the social skills of effective conflict resolution are modelled amongst peers (Walker, Colvin & Ramsey, 1995; Wilkins, 1993) and that students learn about rights and responsibilities, as well as choices and consequences (Trevaskis, 1994).

In New South Wales, Australia, a study of peer mediation programs by Soutter and McKenzie (1998) found that 15 schools involved in the Dispute Resolution Project, compared to others who were not, reported a lower incidence of: (a) reported fighting; (b) students believing that avoiding the person/problem was a good way to resolve disputes; and (c) disputes being resolved through a disciplinary warning. The study also found a higher incidence of: (a) teachers discussing disputes with affected parties; and (b) students talking with teachers/counsellors. For the schools that did not participate in the Dispute Resolution Project the problems associated with behavioural management increased. There were significant increases in: (a) suspensions; (b) the number of students being sent to the executive by their teachers; (c) the belief that disputes could not be resolved through discussion; (d) the belief that disputes could be resolved through fighting/arguing; and (e) the belief that avoiding the person/problem was a good way to resolve disputes.

The evidence suggests that peer mediation needs to permeate the school culture to be most effective. Many schools have reported that peer mediation has contributed positively to their school culture (see Jones & Compton, 2002). The program must be positively positioned within the student welfare framework so that when responsibility is given to students to resolve their own disputes it is aligned with the school's philosophy and culture about student responsibility in general. In other words, a program's effectiveness rests on its ability to develop effective citizenship in schools through a self-regulating process that becomes self-empowering.

Programs that are self-empowering can be effective in addressing bullying, given that bullying erodes an individual's power base. Once domination of others sets into social relationships the pattern cements itself in further protracted conflict, for as Johnson and Johnson (1995, p 67) have shown: "anything that allows students to fail, remain apart from classmates, be socially inept and have low self-esteem increases the probability of destructive conflict strategies". Thus the earlier this damaging pattern is broken the better and there is evidence that peer mediation programs have been found effective in managing bullying (Soutter & McKenzie, 2000).

Peer mediation programs are now an extremely popular means of resolving conflict in schools, with literally thousands of programs in existence, in many different countries, and grounded in different mediation models (see Cohen, 2003). However, while some programs have been found to be effective, systematic reviews of peer mediation programs show non-significant or weak effects (Gottfredson, 1997). One reason for this could be that peer mediation alone is not a strong enough intervention to address serious or extended conflict.

Indeed, this was the experience of the New South Wales Department of School Education, where a Community Forums Program (1999) was launched to complement the Dispute Resolution Project. As well as complementing the peer mediation program, the aim was to reduce the number and length of suspensions in schools through engaging students at risk in a supportive network where they could learn from their experiences in school. Of the 20 conferences carried out in the initial trial: 12 addressed bullying and harassment; six addressed disruptive and aggressive behaviour; and two addressed other disputes, one involving money and the other a dispute between a student, teacher, and family. Of these, 16 had a successful outcome. The results were particularly strong for bullying, where 11 of the 12 conferences were successful. A successful outcome was defined as a significant reduction in the target behaviour (for example, bullying) and no further suspensions.

McKenzie (1999, pp 7–8) made a number of observations regarding the trial. For instance, she observed that forums provided a clear process and opportunity for parents and other significant people to get involved in behaviour management issues and to use the resources of the community to resolve the problem. Furthermore, schools with peer mediation programs saw it as a dispute resolution process on a continuum where mediation was an early intervention tool and forums were a strategy for serious discipline incidents which could not be resolved by suspension. McKenzie (1999, p 8) concluded that "school community forums work best when used as an anti-bullying and harassment intervention ... The forum process confronts the bully with the consequences of their anti-social behaviour more powerfully than do many other forms of intervention". In line with Olweus (1993), who argues that empathy raising is an important element of anti-bullying programs, the forum process was found to be a powerful empathy builder. Further, through inviting the offending subjects' peer group and friends, they became an important link in sustaining the behavioural change that was hoped for. The process was also found to be satisfying for the victims; in particular because it gave them the opportunity to express their feelings and have some say in the negotiations and outcomes. Moreover, forums were found to address the power imbalances inherent in bullying better than peer mediation.

The report (McKenzie, 1999, p 10) concludes that effective behavioural management systems "will not only manage student behaviour but will also encourage the growth of self-discipline within the individual and respect for others. Suspensions deal with violation of school rules, forums deal with violation of a person's rights. This study shows that the two strategies may co-exist in a school's behaviour management plan to provide both consequences and restitution". This is in line with a responsive regulation approach which upholds the meshing of a number of strategies in building safe schools (Ayres & Braithwaite, 1992; Braithwaite, 2002). In others words, what is needed in schools is a range of responsive strategies that work together to keep the school community a safe and respectful place to learn. Braithwaite concurs with the New South Wales experience:

> It appears a whole-school approach is needed that not just tackles individual incidents but also links incidents to a change program for the culture of the school, in particular to how seriously members of the school community take rules about bullying. Put another way, the school not only must resolve the bullying incident; but also must use it as a resource to affirm the disapproval of bullying in the culture of the school. (2002, p 60)

To this end, a whole school approach to restorative justice must not only include intensive and targeted interventions, but must also include universal interventions that ground the practice of restorative justice in schools.

Universal restorative interventions

It is now recognised that the practice of restorative justice must be grounded in a whole school framework that outlines how behaviour and relationships are managed in schools. This begins with how behavioural expectations are introduced and modelled within schools, as well as developing the skills for managing relationships within the school community as a whole. Each of the programs reviewed below emphasises the importance of social and emotional intelligence to build strong social relationships that underpin social capital. There is increasing evidence that these skills are just as important as those associated with academic intelligence and human capital (Weissberg, 2004). Indeed, as has been argued, the development of human capital and social capital go hand-in-hand.

A number of different programs have been used as primary or universal interventions. See the CASEL website <www.casel.org> for an excellent review of many of these programs. The three programs highlighted below emphasise the importance of building strong relationships and resolving conflict: creatively (Resolving Conflict Creatively Program; Lantieri & Patti, 1996); peacefully (Help Increase the Peace Project; Anderson, 1999) and productively (Responsible Citizenship Program; Morrison, 2002). Each aims to create a diverse culture of social relationships, which affirms and regulates healthy and responsible behaviour.

Resolving Conflict Creatively Program (RCCP)

This comprehensive K–12 program supports school communities in the development of the social and emotional skills necessary to resolve conflict, decrease violence and prejudice, and build strong relationships and healthy lives. The program aims to develop the skills of active listening, empathy and perspective taking, cooperation, negotiation and the appreciation of diversity. Workshops involve all members of the school community: students, teachers, administrators, support staff, and parents. For students, the program offers 51 different developmentally appropriate lesson plans, which are introduced over the course of four years, with schools moving through the following stages of implementation: beginning; consolidation; saturation; and full model.

A large evaluation (involving 5000 students, 300 teachers, and 15 public elementary schools) of this program was carried out in New York City over a two-year period (Aber, Brown & Henrich, 1999). The social and emotional skills developed reduced crime, antisocial behaviour and conduct problems. However, there were fewer positive effects for boys, younger students, and students in high-risk classrooms and neighbourhoods. Students who received a higher number of lessons (on average 25 over the course of a school year) benefited the most. Interestingly, the students who received only a few workshops, compared to those who received none at all, had poorer overall outcomes, signalling the importance of consistency. The workshops were often complemented with peer mediation training for a select group of students to enable them to mediate conflict amongst their peers. Interestingly, the research showed that when there was more emphasis on developing a normative climate, through the introduction of more workshops with only a few peer mediators, those classrooms experienced significantly less hostility compared to classrooms that had more peer mediators and less workshops. This highlights the importance of building a strong base at the primary, or universal, level of intervention. Further, in addition to curbing anti-social, and building pro-social, behaviour patterns, students who received substantial RCCP instruction also performed better on standardised academic achievement tests.

Help Increase the Peace Program (HIPP)

The Help Increase the Peace Project was developed in the United States in the 1990s and grew from a concern for the increasing violence in society, particularly in schools. There was a conviction that a school-based non-violent conflict resolution program could be an effective point of intervention. HIPP, according to Anderson (1999, p 11), is based on two assumptions: "first, that conflict, while natural to all human interaction, does not have to be destructive, but can instead instigate positive change and growth. The second assumption is that societal injustice lies at the root of a great deal of violent conflict". The aim is to develop a community of care and trust so that participants feel significant and recognised, with the students' interests becoming the basis for the learning. The process also includes role plays so that students can implement the skills they have developed. The program now has roots in many different countries, including Canada, New Zealand and Australia, where it has been used to complement other restorative practices in schools (see Blood, 1998).

In practice, HIPP brings together a cross-section of the school community or classroom and takes participants through a series of workshops that aims to build skills for: (a) responding to conflict without violence; (b) analysing the impact of societal injustice on themselves and others; and (c) working on taking action for positive, non-violent personal and social change. The program is more about process than content, in that it is the process of involving the students in the program that is the cornerstone of its effectiveness. Further, learning occurs at a process level through active modelling by facilitators and other group members. As the program develops the facilitators find that the groups become self-regulating so that the students take on the responsibility of regulating their peers. As such, regulatory "rules" are not handed down from a higher authority (such as a teacher or principal) but become everyday practice for all members of the school community. As such, the aim is to shift from a paradigm of power and control, to a paradigm of mutual respect and understanding.

A pre–post evaluation of HIPP (Woehrle, 2000, p 14) was conducted in the United States in the 1998–1999 school year. The results showed that students who completed HIPP workshops were significantly more likely to utilise constructive responses to conflict and to exhibit problem-solving behaviour rather than responding with destructive or conflict-escalating behaviour. Students who participated in a HIP focus group suggested the program: (a) broke down student cliques; (b) "humanised" their relationship with their teachers; and (c) helped them be more proactive in dealing with violence in the school. One inner city high school student, after participating in a HIPP group, said:

> With all the high school shootings, I think if it is not required but everybody goes to it, at least one day of it, and open up to people and they don't feel alienated and they feel like they have friends, people they can talk to, then we wouldn't have the violence around here ... I hate to say it but I'm surprised we haven't had a school shooting already, I mean there are so many people around here that feel like they are left out of everything, and you try your hardest to get them involved but you know they've been outcast so long that they'll just kind of push you away ... But I think HIPP would definitely help if everybody goes to it. They can find out they can be friends and don't have to alienate somebody because they're different. (Woehrle, 2000, p 16)

Teachers who participated in a HIPP focus group suggested that the program: (a) teaches important life skills; (b) changes the student–staff relationship; and (c) changes the school climate. One teacher commented:

> HIPP has allowed me to get much deeper with students – more than can be done in a regular class! The training always gives me a sense of hope and awe as I see students catch the glimmer and spark of positive power and as barriers between students begin to thaw. Working with student trainees as colleagues has helped me let go of "in-chargeness" and has provided immense growth for the students in their confidence and self-esteem. (Woehrle, 2000, p 16)

Responsible Citizenship Program (RCP)

This program aims to develop a range of related processes that support the maintenance of healthy relationships: community building, conflict resolution, emotional intelligence, and adaptive shame-management. The program is based on a number of principles of restorative justice. One set of principles grounds the community building process and a second set grounds the conflict resolution process. The first set of principles plays on the program acronym (RCP), in that the program seeks to build community through promoting and facilitating: respect (R), consideration (C), and participation (P). These principles are relevant in that restorative justice is a *participatory* process that addresses wrongdoing through offering *respect* to the parties involved, and by *consideration* of the story each person tells of how they were affected by the harmful incident. While these core principles remain relevant throughout the program, a second set of principles is used to develop students' strategies on how to *resolve conflicts productively* (a further play on RCP). These principles are introduced to the students as the REACT keys: Repair the harm done; Expect the best; Acknowledge feelings; Care for others; and Take responsibility.

This program was piloted in an Australian elementary school (age: 10–11 years; n = 30; see Morrison 2001). The pre–post evaluation showed that: (a) students' feelings of safety within the school community increased significantly; and (b) students' use of adaptive shame management strategies (that is, shame acknowledgement) increased and maladaptive shame management strategies (that is, shame displacement and internalised feelings of rejection) decreased. In other words, post-intervention, the students' use of strategies became less characteristic of victims (who typically feel they would be rejected by others following wrongdoing), and less characteristic of offenders (who typically displace their shame and anger onto others). The levels of respect, consideration and participation reported by the students also increased. The school principal noted the real-life relevance of the program, as did the class-room teacher who commented that she had noticed the use of particular jargon associated with the program being used in everyday situations. The students felt the program taught them: (a) to understand how other people felt; (b) what to do if they hurt someone or someone hurt them; and (c) to respect other people, consider them, and let them participate proudly. In summary, the most important conclusion to draw from this pilot study is that programs such as RCP, and no doubt others, are effective in developing students' adaptive shame management strategies and decreasing students' use of maladaptive strategies. This is an impor-tant research and development agenda to pursue.

There are other intervention programs that are explicitly based on restorative justice principles and these include the Conversation Peace program (Fraser Region Community Justice Initiatives, 2004) and Resto-rative Discipline (Claassen, 2002).

Whole school restorative justice

Some evaluations have not been carried out on individual-level programs and practices, but as part of a whole school approach. Initially most of these whole school programs developed as a response to rising sus-pension rates and zero-tolerance polices (for example, the Minnesota model outlined below). More recently they are being developed to curb insidious violence, such as bullying and to build a culture of care and respect in schools (for example, the MacKillop model, outlined below).

Good Beginnings Project at Lewisham Primary

One of the earliest trials of a whole school approach to restorative justice occurred at Lewisham Primary School, a small inner city school in Syd-ney, Australia. It was classified as a "disadvantaged school", with 80 per cent of students having non-English speaking parents and 10 per cent representing Aboriginal and Pacific Island communities (see Ritchie & O'Connell, 2002). The Lewisham project began at the beginning of the school year in 1998, when the school implemented a "Conflict Resolution and Behaviour Management Program" assisted by the (former) Resto-rative Justice Group of the New South Wales Police and the Port Jackson Behaviour Team for the New South Wales Department of Education. The aim was to develop a supportive, relevant and safe learning environment for students and their families within the wider community. As a mea-sure of success, the project aimed to reduce suspension rates and police attendance at the school.

The staff received training in the theory and practice of restorative justice. Through this process teachers made the commitment to incorporate restorative justice principles into their classrooms on a day-to-day basis. This involved their interaction with all members of the school community including students, teachers and parents. They also developed and standardised a continuum of restorative practices so that each student had the opportunity to learn from his or her experiences. To help teachers with this shift in culture within the school, the teachers designed a pocket-sized checklist of key questions to be employed in disciplinary interactions. These questions emphasised "relationships" in the context of harmful behaviour and strived to build understanding of how others were affected. HIPP workshops were also introduced within the school. These workshops drew together a cross-section of the school community representing different age ranges, learning styles, and behavioural issues. By the end of the school year, the results were encouraging. For instance, suspensions dropped to 20 per cent of those given the previous year and when a suspension did result, the harm done was addressed through a restorative justice conference. Also, incidents reported in the discipline register dropped from 20 to 30 a week to only two to three a week, and incidents reported to the district office dropped from four to five per week to one in a 10-week period. Finally, staff felt more confident about handling serious incidents in the school without relying on police involvement and thus police attendance was reduced (Blood 1999).

Minnesota Restorative Schools Program

The Minnesota Department of Children, Family and Learning (2002), which supports long-standing projects using restorative justice in schools in the United States, has shown how the use of restorative practices across a range of levels is an effective alternative to the use of suspensions and expulsions. This whole school initiative was "spurred by concerns about zero-tolerance policies that produced a three-fold rise in expulsions over a two-year period" (Riestenberg, 2000, p 1). The Department supported the schools involved through a range of outreach activities, including technical assistance, referrals to community or law enforcement restorative justice programs, workshops, week-long seminars, and grants for training, implementation, and evaluation. Two rounds of grants were issued. In the first round (1998 to 2001) four school districts were selected, with some applying all the funds to one school (elementary or high school) and some distributing the money over three schools (elementary and high schools). Rather than be prescriptive, schools developed their own training and development packages, and implemented programs and practices of their choice. The teachers also extended ideas from the training into other classroom practices. Schools implemented a continuum of practices from universal (*Restitution* or *Judicious Discipline*, anti-bullying programs, *Second Step*, community circles) to targeted (peer mediation and conflict management) to intensive (victim/offender dialogues, group conferencing and circles to repair harm).

Circles were used in a variety of circumstances, as described below:

> A tenth-grade student was referred to circle for attendance issues. In addition he had also been in trouble for smoking. During the second circle he told a story about how he had not felt comfortable in school since he had been expelled in the fall of his eight-grade year. No one at the high school had any idea how traumatic the experience had been for him until both he and his mother talked about it in the circle. He told the members that this was the first time since the eighth grade that he thought anyone at school had really tried to understand where he was coming from.
>
> *Princeton Grant Report, 1999*

> A third grade boy made a derogatory comment to three other boys about their race. The restorative justice planner facilitated a circle of understanding. Through the circle process the victims explained that the comment reminded them of: an uncle being shot by a white man who called him the same name as he was shooting him, a movie that has "those people dressed in white doing mean things to us", and a victim said, "It hurt my heart badly and I needed to do something about it". The offender/applicant explained that he then understood what he said was wrong. The students became friends and play together daily.
>
> *South St Paul Grant Report, 2000*

> A teacher requested a circle with a student after he yelled at the student for not completing his homework. The teacher wanted to repair the harm done to the student out of anger and frustration. In the circle, the student's mother said, "welcome to being human". The student said, "We all can do better and I'm ready to do my part". The teacher had the courage to admit his mistake and seek help in repairing the harm through the circle.
>
> *See Riestenberg, 2000*

The following describes an interesting unintended outcome in Minnesota that supports the use of early intervention:

> The junior high staff perceived the junior high students, 90% of which came from South St Paul elementary schools, as good and easy to teach. The staff was so pleased with the manners of the students, that at the recommendation of the high school principal, they voted to give

their staff development money to the two elementary schools, so that the adults there could continue to do their good work and send them good students.

South St Paul Grant Report, 2001

The aim of the evaluation was to track suspensions, expulsions, attendance, academics and school climate. However, obtaining consistent baseline data proved difficult, and the evaluation's focus shifted to only a few measures – suspensions, office referrals and attendance – within each school. Of particular note, out-of-school suspensions, over a three-year period, decreased in one junior high school from 110 to 55, and in a senior high school from 132 to 95. One elementary school found that office referrals for acts of physical aggression dropped from 773 to 153 over the three years. Given the success in reducing suspensions and aggression, a second round of grants was offered, with the learning from the first round applied to the second. From the first round of grants, Riestenberg (2000) noted three key learning outcomes: (a) restorative practices, such as circles to repair harm, were viable alternatives to suspensions; (b) restorative philosophy and practices had classroom management and teaching applications; and (c) staff hired on grant money inevitably leave a district when the grant money is spent. It was found that while schools who hired specialists in restorative practices got up and running quicker, the model was less sustainable, as school personnel tended to defer to the specialist. On the other hand, it was found that schools who invested in staff training and development were investing in sustained program development; thus, the second round of grants (2002 to 2003) adopted this model. As Riestenberg states:

> Given the uncertainty of grant awards and general funding for education, as well as the natural mobility of teaching staff, it seemed to be more cost effective to teach a lot of people "how to fish", rather than have them depend on a guide with a good boat for a limited amount of time. (2003, p 1)

Five grants were awarded in the second round, varying in geography, scale and plan (see Riestenberg, 2003). Below are a few examples of the results achieved from schools that participated in the second evaluation.

Cass Lake-Bena (K–4) Elementary School

This school focused on building school-wide learning opportunities for teachers and students. The teachers participated in a week-long training in Responsive Classrooms, with follow-up at each grade level. The teachers then held morning circles to teach social skills and create a sense of belonging. In the second year they introduced a problem-solving intervention, Take-a-Break for Small Things, and increased the use of their Buddy Room to resolve conflicts. The results included: (a) discipline referrals and in-school suspensions decreased from 335 to 153 (57 per cent); (b) out of school suspensions decreased from 57 to 13 (77 per cent); (c) expulsions decreased from seven to one; and (d) 69 per cent of students reported that they were better able to resolve conflicts. The evaluator attributed the outcomes to: (a) an emphasis on early intervention; (b) a sense of belonging established by morning meetings; (c) staff buy-in; (d) ongoing staff development with the consultant; and (e) effective administrative leadership.

Nellie Stone Johnson (K–8) Elementary School

This school chose to immerse the staff in the circle process, and began the school year with a four-day circle training with three facilitators, who then mentored teachers over the rest of the school year. The circle process was used within classrooms and by administrators to address more challenging issues in the school. The result over one year was that suspensions decreased from 800 to 292 (63 per cent).

Ramsey Fine Arts (K–8) Elementary School

This school had been developing their use of restorative practices for six years and developed an innovative community-building activity, Stop Everything and Dialogue (SEAD) that provided staff with a structure and reason to practise the circle process with students once a month. They also developed their use of restorative practices to address issues related to cultural differences. The result over one year was that suspensions dropped from 272 to 149 (45 per cent).

Continued support for Minnesota schools

The above examples illustrate the range of ways restorative practices are developed in schools and while the State no longer funds the grants, the Minnesota Department of Education continues to support schools with ongoing training opportunities. The onus is on the schools but when schools take the learning on board they continue to develop innovative ideas. For example, one administrator organises re-entry meetings following a suspension. The meetings focus on four important aspects of a student's life at school: physical safety, academics, social wellbeing and emotional wellbeing. At the re-entry conference, the young person, and typically his or her parents or guardians, are asked to respond to a set of questions, with the young person speaking first. Riestenberg argues that the circle process allows:

[A]dults and students to be connected to each other through that pro-
found invisible web woven of talking and listening to words and to
silence. The restorative idea of doing things with students rather than
to them or for them or simply ignoring them, can, be squeezed into the
regular order of the day. (2005, p 2)

The innovation of working with students is now being adopted in many
areas of school life, with the ideas of restorative justice evolving to focus
on positive youth development.

The MacKillop model

At Mary MacKillop Primary School in Penrith, Australia, the principal
and her leadership team were becoming concerned that their safe and
caring environment was being stretched through the changes being
experienced by families and society in today's world. While the problem
was not endemic in the school, the issues that were raised consistently
pointed to deeper hurt and underlying tensions. The leadership team
went looking for a new safe school framework that would assist them in
re-weaving the fabric of school life, based on their knowledge that building strong and healthy relationships was the key to creating a safer
school, as well as a solid foundation for learning. They knew what they
needed, but were struggling with how to do it.

Out of their search, the school embraced a restorative practices
framework, and began building a common language and understanding
of the practices, as well as agreed strategies for their implementation. One
of the distinctive aspects of the MacKillop model was the full and explicit
involvement of three sectors of the school community: school staff,
parents and students. Each of these groups participated in workshops on
restorative justice. To infuse the culture with a common language, understanding and practice, students and teachers were provided with cards
that spelt out two sets of restorative questions. One set of questions
focused on those who had caused harm, while the other set focused on
those who had suffered the harm.

These questions were also displayed on signs and posters in
classrooms and the playground.

As part of the implementation and development process, quali-
tative and quantitative data were collected from each of these three
groups (O'Callaghan, 2004). Staff were asked to define their classroom
climate, with the great majority describing it as "relational" (rather than
punitive, authoritarian, neglectful, permissive, or restorative). When
using circles, staff mostly used circles for prayer and learning more than
pastoral care; and used small restorative circles much more than large
circles processes. The circles were mostly used when required, but were

also used quite regularly by some teachers on a weekly basis. The teachers reported that restorative practices had been effective for them as teachers, with the average response being eight (on a 10-point scale), and effective for the students, with the average response being seven or eight (on a 10-point scale). The greatest challenge for teachers was having time when an incident occurred. The staff also made comments such as (O'Callaghan, 2004): "I've become a better listener. I have discovered bigger issues behind the behaviours"; "The children are beginning to trust themselves"; "My relationships with the children have matured"; "For the children who could not verbalise, I ask them to draw what they were trying to say. I also ask them to draw what they wanted to be different"(O'Callaghan, 2004).

Parents were asked to respond to a number of questions on a 10-point scale. Most indicated that their children had a good ability to manage relationships (average seven); that they thought restorative practices were effective (average seven to eight); and that the practices improved their child's capacity to manage challenges in their relationships (average seven to eight). Parents also said (O'Callaghan, 2004): "Restorative practices has changed my life"; "Thank you for making sure we were a part of this new way of working with our children"; "Restorative Practices should be reinforced at all times and at all levels at school" (O'Callaghan, 2004).

Students were also asked to respond to a number of questions on a 10-point scale. Most indicated that restorative practices were an effective way to build and maintain friendships (average eight) and were effective at resolving conflict (average eight). The students particularly found the restorative questions to be helpful, with many indicating that they helped them work out differences with friends. Students also said: "At home when I had a fight with my sister then I went to my room and read these questions to myself and it really helped"; "It has helped me when I have had a fight with a boy in our class. A teacher asked us those questions and after we had answered them and listened to both sides of the story I felt better"; "I was outside and had a fight with some of my friends and I was angry and sat in front of the sign with the questions on it and the questions helped me a lot" (O'Callaghan, 2004).

The development of restorative practices across staff, parents and students continues to be developed at Mary MacKillop Primary School, with data collection remaining an integral part of their development process.

Schools within schools

In Minnesota, Tartan High School has a school within a school program (SWAS), based on restorative practices. It offers an alternative program for students who are struggling academically and behaviourally. The six staff members provide instruction and support for the students and use circles and conferences to address issues that arise. They also conduct a circle each Monday morning to enhance community and connection with the students. Likewise, Palisades High School in Pennsylvania established a school within a school, called the Academy, for students who did not feel connected to school and were struggling with behaviour or academic performance. Referring to the development of the Academy, the principal noted (Mirsky, 2003, pp 2–3) that: "We made a critical error: we addressed the content of the program, not relationships between teachers and students. And from the first day, the program was as close to a disaster as you can imagine. ... [As a result, the staff at the International Institute of Restorative Practices (IIRP) were given] an opportunity to test their theory in our most difficult setting".

The IIRP trained Academy staff in the use of a continuum of restorative practices, ranging from affective statements and questions to large group restorative circles (as described in Chapter 5). They also used circles to set goals and expectations during their check-in and check-out time of class periods. The result: "Word soon spread throughout the school that the Academy had been successful with students no one had been able to reach before" (Mirsky, 2003, p 3). Over the next three years, restorative practices were introduced into the entire high school. The first year the "believers" were trained, the following year "believers" and "fence sitters" were trained in mixed groups, the third year, those requiring the hard evidence that the program worked, the "critics", were trained. The carry-on effect then spread to Palisades Middle School, when the principal noted the warm relationships between students and administrators at the high school graduation. The middle school principal then trained all staff and support staff in his school. He describes his experience:

> I had an epiphany, a metamorphosis ... I use to be one of these black and white, law and order guys. Kids had to be held accountable and the only way to do that was to kick them out of school – to show the other kids that you're the boss. That doesn't work. I didn't solve problems; I just postponed them until they got to high school and then somebody else had to deal with them. Restorative practices work. We now fix and solve problems. (Mirsky, 2003, p 4-5)

When the principal of Palisades High School was transferred to another school the learning continued. The demographic of this new school was different, more urban and street smart, but the results were similar. Again, the principal started with an eager small group and then expanded the training. The results again were positive, as reported in the tables across the three schools below.

Table 6.1. Disciplinary data for three schools after the introduction of restorative practices

	1998–1999	1999–2000	2000–2001	2001–2002
Palisades High School				
Disciplinary referrals	1752	1426	1410	1154
Administrative detentions	716	585	529	282
Teacher detentions	128	145	70	50
Incidents of disruption	273	256	162	153
Out of school suspensions	105	96	60	65
Palisades Middle School				
Disciplinary referrals	–	–	913	516
Incidents of fighting	–	27	23	1
Springfield Township High School				
Incidents of inappropriate behaviour	–	–	99	32
Incidents of disrespect to teachers	–	–	71	21
Incidents of classroom disruption	–	–	90	26

Source: <www.restorativepractices.org/library/ssspilots.html>

What is evident in the data from these three schools is the steady trend of decreases in behavioural issues over time. Without a control group or any further analysis, however, it is impossible to attribute this trend solely to the implementation of restorative practices. But, if you combine this data with the stories of the staff and students at the schools, there is certainly a trend worthy of further understanding.

Alternative schools

The Peers Enjoying a Sober Education (PEASE) Academy, the first "recovery" high school in the United States, is located in Minneapolis,

Minnesota. The school takes students who are committed to working on recovery from chemical dependency while also becoming successful students. Safety in this environment is a priority concern for staff, parents and students. The PEASE Academy held an initial three-day training in circles and restorative practices for 14 people: teachers, administrators, a local community liaison, and a special education teacher. Additional follow-up training was also provided. Circles are now used in many aspects of school life, for example, as part of in-depth learning and community-building. While the use of circles is important, the staff and students feel the circles have made their strongest impact as part of the students' recovery process. Every Monday and Friday circles are used for students to check in about the highs and lows in their sobriety. Circles are also used in times of crisis. If a student uses and immediately asks for help, they are allowed to stay in the school, on the condition that they agree to learn from the experience through sharing their story with the entire student body within a circle process. These processes have helped this school "create a truly respectful, student-centred program" (Riestenberg, 2004, p 1).

Likewise, the Community Service Foundation and Buxmont Academy operate eight school-day treatment programs. These alternative schools operate within a "restorative milieu" – termed "because the culture is comprised of many formal and informal restorative techniques and processes, not just isolated formal restorative justice interventions" (McCold, 2005, p 1). A study of the effectiveness of these schools found a significant reduction in re-offending for youths participating in these restorative programs three months or longer, with these results being extended and replicated in a follow up study by McCold (2005).

Evidence from criminal and juvenile justice

The most rigorous evidence to date on restorative justice is largely carried out through the Jerry Lee Program on Randomised Control Trials in Restorative Justice. While these trials have not been carried out explicitly in the context of schools, the results are still relevant. These trials have been carried out in Australia and England, and involved post-intervention interviews with participants, victims and offenders that were randomly assigned to the restorative justice intervention or the traditional court intervention. The most consistent effects across all trials are for the victims of crime, where (compared to traditional court proceedings) victims suffered less post-traumatic stress symptoms (including the ability to go to work), as well as less anxiety and anger and they were less inclined to seek revenge for the crime (Strang et al, 2006; see also Sherman et al, 2005).

These authors conclude:

> Crime victims consistently say they are better off after joining in a civil society institution of face-to-face RJ [restorative justice] than they were before. Regardless of the kind of crime they have suffered, the kind of community they live in, the point in the criminal justice process, or the physical location of the conferences, victims who have done RJ report very positive experience. This conclusion applies to almost every criterion on which data are available. This evidence ... builds a firmer evidence base for supporting a policy of RJ. (Strang et al, 2005, p 304)

The most variable effects within these trials were for repeat offending. For example, in Australia the most positive effects were found for violent crime, where 50 per cent less re-offending was found after two years (in comparison to court), while for property crime, there was substantial re-offending after three years. Strang (1999) examined 10 school-based offences, involving 20 individuals within this larger study, which showed that the rate of re-offending was 6.5 times higher for court, over conferences. While it is not possible to draw a strong conclusion from this finding, given the small sample size, the results support restorative justice conferencing over court. One other randomised control trial was carried out in the United States, with juveniles between seven and 14 years of age. The study found that the effects for victims were again positive, as were the effects for offenders, who re-offended significantly less following a family group conference, across a range of offences (McGarrell & Hipple, 2005).

While there are encouraging results, the disaggregated data from the randomised control trials in Australia showed that for Aboriginal offenders the conferencing process did not reduce re-offending. In England, the effect for females under the age of 18 was encouraging (in comparison to final warnings, in this trial), with less re-offending, but this did not hold true for males, where there was more re-offending. However, for both males and female under the age of 18 in England, the effect was encouraging for non-violent and property crimes. The authors concluded:

> The point is to be sensitive to the possibility of differential reactions within large groups, and to proceed with care in implementing new restorative justice programs so that the possibility of adverse reactions can be measured. (Sherman et al, 2004, p 6)

This is a very important point; schools must heed this advice when implementing restorative justice practices, be they at the universal, targeted or intensive levels. Restorative justice is not a panacea. Thoughtful research and development processes that includes ongoing evaluation must be put into place.

Comprehensive evaluation

The most comprehensive study of whole school practices of restorative justice to date was carried out by the Youth Justice Board for England and Wales (YJB 2004). They conducted a national evaluation of the "Restorative Justice in Schools Programme", involving 26 schools (20 secondary and six primary) in nine boroughs across England and Wales. The practice of restorative justice in the schools varied widely, and included practices such as active listening, restorative inquiry, circle time, peer mediation, mediation and restorative justice conferences.

Restorative justice conferences were convened in response to a number of behavioural concerns (in declining rank order): bullying; assault/violent behaviour; name-calling; verbal abuse; family feuds; friendship/relationship breakdowns; incidents involving teachers; gossip; incidents outside school; theft. Almost a quarter (24%) of the conferences were used to resolve long-term disputes, with boys being twice as likely as girls to be involved in physical violence and girls being three times as likely to be involved in social and emotional violence, such as name-calling and gossip. Agreements were reached in 92 per cent of conferences, with only 4 per cent of agreements being broken within the three month follow-up time. Students reported satisfaction with the process (89%) and that the process was fair (93%).

The conferences were most likely to be facilitated by a school staff member (49%) or by a member of the Youth Offending Team (37%), followed by police officers (8%), staff from local mediation service (3%) and trained volunteer (3%). Interestingly, less than a fifth of the conferences involved a parent (19%), reflecting the wide variety of processes defined as a conference. Different schools coded for conferences using different criteria; for example, some included short informal conferences, others did not; some used a scripted conference model, others used a more open-ended model. In secondary schools (Years 7–10) participation in conferencing peaked in Year 7, then declined. In primary schools participation in a conference peaked in Year 6, and began in Year 3.

Schools using restorative practices were compared with schools not using restorative practices. A survey of 5,986 students examined students self-reports of levels of bullying and overall safety. Significant differences were only found for the three schools that had been using restorative practices for the full three years of the evaluation, supporting the claim that effecting behavioural change takes time. For the schools that had been using restorative practices for three years, students reported (in comparison to schools not using restorative practices): their school was doing "a good job" at stopping bullying (10% higher); bullying was less of a serious problem at their school (23% lower); less incidents of being called racist names (11% lower). The teacher/staff questionnaires (n = 949) also indicated that behaviour had improved since the introduction of restorative approaches.

The study concludes: "Restorative justice is not a panacea for problems in schools but, if implemented correctly, it can improve the school environment, enhance learning and encourage young people to become more responsible and empathetic" (YJB, 2005, p 65). However, the study did highlight a number of issues:

- given that the intervention was initiated by the YJB, and not the Department for Education and Skills (DES), there was consensus that the latter needed to be involved in the sponsorship of the initiative to make it more relevant to the agenda of schools and education;

- successful implementation was characterised by leadership and vision, integration into the school behaviour policy, and adequate staff training;

- follow-up is needed to monitor that conference participants are adhering to agreements made in a conference;

- there was lack of consensus, and definition of, what defines a restorative justice conference;

- the language of restorative justice (for example, "victim", "offender") did not transfer easily to the school setting, in particular the term "justice" itself.

The recommendations mirror these concerns with the addition of one further point:

- implementation of restorative practices is an excellent vehicle for improving interagency partnerships.

The Youth Justice Board's report sets a number of guidelines for implementing restorative justice in schools, which are largely consistent with past reviews. Broadly, these recommendations can be collapsed into two points: (1) restorative practices need to be institutionally relevant to schools; and (2) the implementation of restorative practices must be framed within a broad agenda of institutional reform.

Conclusion: More evidence

While these developments and evaluations are encouraging, it is too early to make any strong conclusions about the effectiveness of restorative justice in schools, as to date, there has been no rigorous evaluation. The process of youth development and socialisation is a complex process. What works for one student, may not work for the next; and what works for one group of students, may not work for all groups of students. We need rigorous tests of restorative justice in schools, as has been done in criminal and juvenile justice. Schools, as part of their own research and development process, also need to track their own local data, as many of the schools described above are currently–doing, as part of their own research and development processes. Schools also need to disaggregate their data; we need to know when restorative justice works and when it doesn't. In the words of Zehr (2004), we need to know about and share our bullfrogs (stories of caution), as well as our butterflies (stories of hope). The bullfrogs provide powerful insights, while the butterflies provide encouragement.

We need to get beyond the question – does restorative justice work in schools? We need to ask: When didn't it work? For whom? And where? Under what circumstance? And we need to know more about the process itself. Who should facilitate? When do we need to bring in other professions? What is the best way to include fellow professionals? Are there better ways to include families? And there are many more questions that need to be answered. These are important questions because optimising the relational context of a restorative practice is crucial. For example, the outcomes for Aborigines who participated in conferences in Canberra, Australia, could be very different if perhaps: a different facilitators were used, in a different location, or with a different model. In the context of the trial, the facilitators were typically white Australian police officers and the conference was held in the police station. These small differences are significant in a relational context, wherein the focus is repairing the harm done. The important point to remember is that the focus is on relationships; hence, who participates and why will influence the outcome of the process. This highlights the importance of the preliminary work involved in facilitating a face-to-face restorative justice conference.

Given that the most consistently encouraging results to date are for victims who participate in restorative conferences, and given we know the debilitating effects of bullying and other acts of harmful behaviour towards students, responding to school safety from a victim's perspective seems paramount. Just as in the criminal and juvenile justice systems, too often the focus is on the offender over the victim. Given the findings that restorative justice relieves the symptoms of post-traumatic stress disorder for victims of crime and they feel more able to go to work (Angel, 2006), the practice of restorative justice in schools may be able to relieve the same symptoms for students who are victimised, potentially addressing the health risks for these students, as well as the possibility that these students will seek revenge. This too requires much more careful and thoughtful research and development.

Research questions need to develop our understanding of how to best support victims at all levels of restorative practices: universal, targeted and intensive. The questions also need to address how to best support victims in the pre-conference and post-conference stages, particularly since schools are face-to-face communities and the parties are likely to come into daily contact, and to ask what will address the established power imbalances inherent to bullying behaviour. Finally, the research questions should ask how this can all come together within a whole school approach.

Above all, it seems that it is vital to create safe spaces within school communities for victims of harmful behaviour, as well as those who have harmed. Indeed, allowing all members of the school community to be listened to and heard (and to just "be") is an important step for schools to take. These safe spaces must be public and private. It takes a lot of courage for victims to come forward, some will be more ready to come forward than others, so creating safe spaces supports victims through a culture shift where students are empowered through the success of others. Upholding the dignity of the individuals involved must be at the heart of these safe spaces.

While in the context of juvenile and criminal justice the effects of restorative justice across offence types varies considerably, these need to be tested carefully in the context of schools. There may not only be differences across the type of harmful behaviour, gender and race, but there may also be developmental differences across ages. Having said this, if a whole school approach is taken, with restorative practices embedded across the three different levels and supported with adequate follow-up, schools may be in a much stronger position to address the underlying issues associated with harmful behaviour, than a single face-to-face restorative justice conference as is typical in the criminal and juvenile justice systems. On the other hand, because schools are face-to-face communities, where "offenders" and "victims" typically know each other and see each other, and where relationship patterns are both highly dynamic but also culturally embedded within this tightly woven community, careful consideration of this aspect of restorative justice in schools must also be considered.

Given that the evidence to date from different school communities is encouraging – both in terms of the quantitative data and anecdotes – there is good reason to move forward and learn more about what works, what doesn't and what's promising from school communities. The broad aim must be to be responsive and restorative to the needs of all members of the school community. At the same time we must proceed with care, keeping the first principle of restorative justice in mind: do no harm. In order to carry out this developmental process with integrity we must proceed with care when implementing restorative justice in schools, using the evidence at hand, while empowering the school community, staff, parents and students, to also proceed with integrity. Thoughtful long-term implementation that produces sustained culture change is the key to success. Given this, implementing, developing and sustaining restorative justice and responsive regulation in schools is the topic of the next chapter.

Chapter 7

Responsive implementation, sustainability and development: A restorative framework

Gandhi ... demonstrated that a powerful human following can be assembled not only through the cunning game of the usual political manoeuvres and trickeries but through the cogent example of a morally superior conduct of life.

Albert Einstein

[H]e that will not apply new remedies must expect new evils: for time is the greatest innovator; and if time of course alter things to the worse, and wisdom and counsel shall not alter them to the better, what shall be the end?

Francis Bacon "Of Innovations" (1625)

The educational process has no end beyond itself; it is its own end; and ... the educational process is one of continual reorganizing, reconstructuring, transforming ... Since in reality there is nothing to which growth is relative save more growth, there is nothing to which education is subordinate save more education.

John Dewey (1920)

Many people had reservations when ideas that had been developed in a criminal and juvenile justice context were being introduced to schools. These reservations are healthy. Schools have a very different institutional mandate to the courts and other mechanisms of criminal and juvenile justice. The implementation and development of restorative justice in schools needs to be both responsive to the needs of individuals within the school community and responsive to the needs of the institution itself. Adapting restorative justice to the needs of schools has been one of the most significant challenges for the practice of restorative justice over the last ten years. While much has been learnt, there is still much more to learn. This chapter summarises some of the adaptations that have been made to restorative justice practices and proposes a restorative framework for further development of restorative justice in schools that supports sustainable outcomes. Sustainable development relates to implementation issues, and particularly to what is intended when restorative practices are introduced into schools. For restorative practices to be supported and developed with integrity within the school community, there must be at least four aspects to the development process. These four aspects involve intentions to:

- develop restorative practices (integrating values, skills and processes) across all levels of behavioural concern (eg, universal, targeted, intensive);

- measure the effectiveness of these practices across all levels of behavioural outcomes (eg, universal, targeted, intensive);

- provide professional and institutional development opportunities where concerns are raised; and

- integrate restorative values, skills and processes into the vision and policy of the school.

Adapting restorative justice to schools

One of the first lessons from the early trials of restorative conferencing in schools was that the practice of restorative justice in schools was not simply a matter of holding a few conferences for serious incidents – wider institutional reform was necessary (see Cameron & Thorsborne, 2001; Morrison, 2001; Ritchie & O'Connell, 2001). These institutional reforms included developing a continuum of responses that was based on the values, skills and processes of restorative justice, as outlined in Chapter 5, as well as a number of other reforms.

It was in the context of schools that the language of restorative justice adapted and changed. For many, the term "restorative justice", and its association with the institution of justice, was no longer appropriate and phrases such as "restorative practices", "restorative measures", "restorative discipline", "restorative milieu", "restorative approaches" and "restorative action", emerged. Also, there were concerns over the criminalisation of children through the use of the terms "victim" and "offender", and subsequently there was a preference for phrases such as "students who have harmed others" and/or "students who have been harmed by others". In general, the preference is to separate the person from the behaviour, so phrases such as "students who bully" (rather than bullies per se) and "students who have been victims of bullying behaviour" (rather than victims per se) are also preferred. The aim with these preferred terms is to avoid the temptation to pathologise student behaviour, thus enabling behaviour to be thought about in terms of a wider sphere of influence (as reviewed in Chapter 1). With these adaptations, restorative justice itself has been responsive to the institutional culture of schools. These institutional adaptations have been useful but schools also recognise there is a lot more to school reform than these initial adaptations.

Next generation of institutional development

The rising concern within schools and school districts now relates to how to implement, develop, and sustain the practice of restorative justice in schools (see also Blood and Thorsborne, 2005; Morrison, Blood and Thorsborne, 2005). The focus needs to be shifted from a range of responsive practices that restore relationships, to a responsive framework that regulates – that is that manages – the implementation, development and sustainability of restorative practices in schools. Thus, in this chapter, the single-faced pyramid that was initially presented in Chapter 5 is further developed into a four-sided pyramid that provides a model for a fully responsive and restorative framework. As was stated earlier, restoring safe and healthy school communities goes hand-in-hand with how safe and healthy schools are regulated – socially, emotionally and economically.

The regulatory framework to be presented capitalises again on Braithwaite's notion of separating the behaviour from the person; for both the behavioural and the social aspects (that is, the web of relationships) of individuals' lives, in different ways, need to be considered. It seems that many policies and practices that seek to regulate safe school communities focus on behaviour, over the person; that is, they emphasise the rules of behaviour, while failing to address the needs of the individual and the web of relationships (and hence influence) that sustains that person's behaviour and wellbeing. It is important to understand behaviour in the context of the relationships that regulate that behaviour.

The framework to be outlined focuses not only on behaviour, but also on the relationships that sustain behaviour and empower growth. Further, responsive and restorative policy and development need to be embedded in the cultural life of the school, as policy is less effective when it is simply handed down from a higher authority (Braithwaite, Braithwaite, Gibson & Makkai, 1994). In summary, the policies and practices that regulate safe school communities need to be responsive to the needs of individuals, as well as to the needs of institutions. Finding this balance is the hard work that schools must take on, with the empowerment of both the institution and individuals being essential to long-term value for both. We cannot expect change at the level of the individual, without expecting change at the level of the institution. To drive this institutional development, the hard work of visionary leadership is needed, because if the intention is clear and well planned, the social and emotional climate of schools can change. As Hatch recognises:

> Rather than being seen as exceptions to the rule that schools cannot change, the development of a small number of innovative practices and schools may instead reflect the rule that schools can only change through the monumental effort, unusual resourcefulness, and strong leadership of key individuals or groups. (2000, p 581)

The responsive and restorative framework to be presented goes a step in this direction. While initiatives typically begin with a small committed group of people, momentum grows through the empowerment of others, as understanding and influence develops.

The model presented aims to keep empowerment and development at the heart of everything schools accomplish. The hope is that schools can maintain inclusive environments and build social capital through bridging and bonding. Cultivating responsible leadership and participation is the primary goal, as schools activate and sustain the development process of a committed and caring community of learners. Creating this culture requires that school communities invest in:

- practices that restore individuals to communities when challenges arise;
- evidence of what works, what doesn't, and what could;
- partnerships that enhance the school's mission;
- visionary and responsive policy development.

To sustain school-wide behavioural change, it is important to invest in an ongoing system of growth and development – in other words, a learning community – at both the individual and the institutional levels. How might this be realised? Perhaps through a dynamic system of responsive and restorative regulation that capitalises on the investments of the learning community. This system would bring together four interconnected elements:

1. *Institutional vision* that empowers responsive policy development and integration.

2. *Restorative practices* that empower individual integrity and development.

3. *Behavioural evidence* that empowers responsive decision-making and planning.

4. *Professional bridging* that empowers institutional integrity and development.

Figure 7.1. Responsive & Restorative Safe School Pyramid

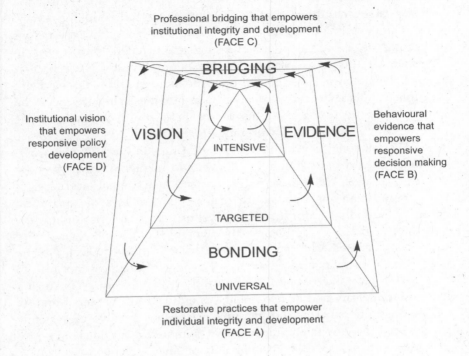

Professional bridging that empowers
institutional integrity and development
(FACE C)

Institutional vision
that empowers
responsive policy
development
(FACE D)

Behavioural
evidence that
empowers
responsive
decision making
(FACE B)

Restorative practices that empower
individual integrity and development
(FACE A)

A responsive and restorative framework

This responsive and restorative framework is developed through the use of a regulatory pyramid, with four faces (or sides). Two faces of the regulatory pyramid focus on relationships, both individual and institutional (the relational pair, Faces A and C), while the other two focus on behaviour, in terms of outcomes sought and outcomes achieved (the behavioural pair, Faces B and D). This regulatory framework outlines a process through which schools can be *responsive to behaviour* and *restorative to relationships*. Hence, behavioural policies are not forgotten but imbedded in a broader framework that recognises the importance of relationships to individuals. For each pair – the two behavioural and two relational – the two faces stand opposite each other, supporting the opposite sides of the pyramid (opposed to standing adjacent to each other). Thus, as one moves around the pyramid, the behavioural and relational faces alternate, tapping into both institutional and individual needs and concerns.

The behavioural pair focuses on behaviour in two different ways: behavioural vision and behavioural data. Behavioural vision clearly and formally establishes the institutional philosophy, clearly outlining every-thing from the mission statement and values, to behavioural expectations and standards, as well as policy in response to behavioural concerns. In other works, this face specifies the behavioural vision the school is seeking. Behavioural data, on the opposite side, provides the evidence base for the policy. In other words, the data provides a "reality check" on how schools are doing in terms of the behavioural policy, and the restorative practices the policy promotes and fosters.

The relational pair focuses on relationships in two different ways: relational practices at the individual level and relational practices at the institutional level. Having the individual and institutional level faces of the pyramid standing opposite to one another, reflects the reciprocal nature of individual and institutional level processes, in terms of how the dynamics of one level influences the dynamics of the other, and vice versa (as discussed in Chapter 2, and earlier in this chapter). On the individual side, the pyramid establishes a range of practices that seek to re-affirm, repair and re-build relationships with the aim of nurturing individual integrity and development, (as outlined in Chapters 5 and 6). On the institutional side, the pyramid establishes a range of systemic professional development practices that support institutional integrity and development, as well as sustainability of development.

In comparative terms, the behavioural pair involves more reflec-tion and planning, while the relational pair involves more outreach and development. Hence, given that the pairs stand opposite each other, the framework is constantly moving within a broad action learning frame-work that acknowledges the importance of reflection, planning and action. At the same time there is action learning happening within each face, as follows, starting with face (A), and then moving clockwise.

- Face A: *Relational practices* – One way of thinking about the relational practices at the individual level is to think about these processes as giving a voice to those affected by harm and wrongdoing in the school community. As outlined in Chapters 5 and 6, restorative justice is about creating safe spaces and opportunities to listen and respond to stories of harm. Through this discursive practice that emphasises restoring rela-tionships, individuals are involved in their own action learning process.

- Face B: *Behavioural evidence* – Schools also need to take time to respond to the evidence of what is working, what is not, and what looks promising, or what could work given time or resources; thus, investing in evidence-based decision-making. Schools often collect data, for accountability purposes, but fail to use the data as a support mechanism to enhance responsive decision-making. The process of reflecting on the data affirms which behaviours are responding positively to current policies and practices, and those that are responding poorly, or even negatively. Looking at the data allows schools to clearly acknowledge what they are doing well, and where more development is needed. Thus, action learning is occurring through data-driven decision-making that is responsive to the needs of the school community.

- Face C: *Professional bridging* – Once decisions are made, opportunities must be created and developed to effect the change needed to better address the problems and concerns raised by the data. In a nutshell, this is about professional and institutional development so that practice within the school does not remain stagnant, but responds to the cultural and social realities of the school. This process requires bridging with others to enhance knowledge, skills and partnerships that foster professional and institutional development. It is about building the scaffolding to secure the institutional hope of effecting positive and sustained change. Thus, on this side of the pyramid action learning is occurring at an institutional level.

- Face D: *Institutional vision* – Finally, policy is established, or modified that formalises the learning from the institutional development process; and this process secures the hopes that enable the vision to be realised. These policies set the direction for the new practices that were outlined under Face A. Effective policies secure our hopes and vision for the future of our schools and children. This final process brings together the learning and formalises the direction.

Taken together, each face of the pyramid informs the adjacent face, driving an action learning framework that is ongoing and responsive to arising needs and concerns at both the individual and institutional level. Put another way, responsive regulation and restorative justice are about responding to behaviour and restoring relationships. The regulatory idea is to broaden this vision – the macro regulatory practice of responsive regulation within schools aims to strengthen the responsive infrastructure of the school; while the micro regulatory practice of restorative justice strengthens the relational base of the everyday life of school communities.

The remainder of this chapter will take a closer look at the three levels within each of the four faces of the pyramid. The focus will be on the drivers that sustain and develop the primary (universal); secondary (targeted) and tertiary (intensive) regulatory responses. The aim here is not to develop a prescriptive "how to" approach, but to be more descriptive about what type of activities can characterise these responses on each of the four sides of the pyramid.

Figure 7.2 A whole school model of restorative practices

INTENSIVE
(TERTIARY)
eg Restorative
conferencing

1-5% of population

REBUILDING

RELATIONSHIPS

TARGETED
(SECONDARY)
eg Problem-
solving circles,
peer mediation

REPAIRING

RELATIONSHIPS

UNIVERSAL
(PRIMARY)
eg RCP,
HIPP, RCCP

RE-AFFIRMING RELATIONSHIPS

THROUGH DEVELOPING

SOCIAL AND EMOTIONAL SKILLS

Whole
School

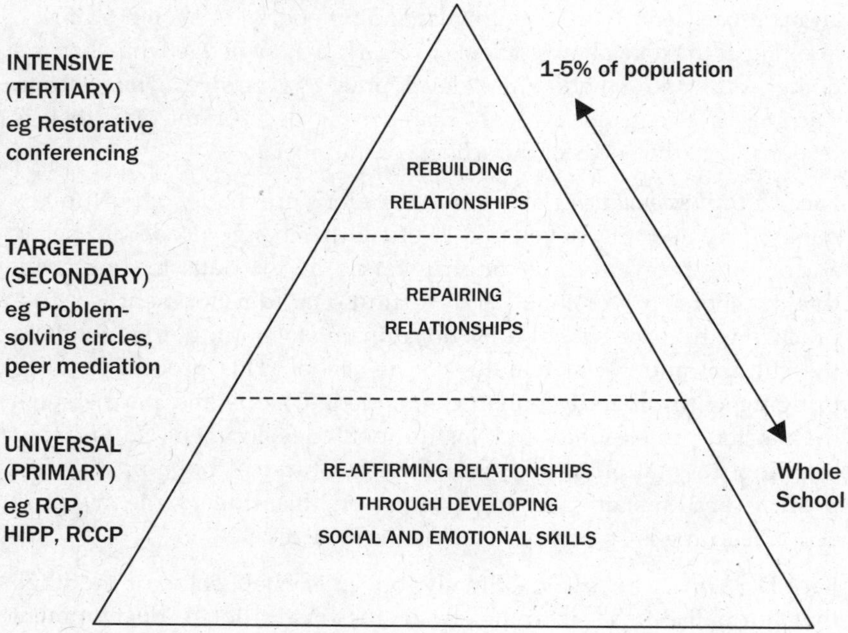

Relational practices that empower individual integrity and development

The starting point for implementation is the side of the pyramid that focuses on the practices underpinning restorative justice in schools, as developed in earlier chapters. These practices and programs aim to foster responsible and emotionally intelligent *behaviour* that engage all members of the school community. To this end, it is important that the whole school community understand and relate to the principles of restorative justice at a personal level, such that they can map the language and the practice of restorative justice into their everyday lives in the classroom, the administration offices, the cafeteria, the corridors and the schoolyard. It is also important to provide opportunities for parents and others important to the school community, to learn about and participate in restorative practices. While these practices alone are insufficient for the sustained development of restorative justice in school, they are often the point of entry for further school development.

Limiting the focus to the development of these practices for the moment, the recommendation is for schools to adopt a health care app-roach to school safety through implementing three levels of intervention, as outlined in Chapter 5:

- primary or universal practices;
- secondary or targeted practices;
- tertiary or intensive practices.

These practices come together within the pyramid above, which was first introduced in Chapter 5.

Behavioural evidence that empowers responsive decision-making

For the present purposes, a single school will be the focus of attention; however, it should be noted that professional development process across but school districts where comparative school data is stored can also be a powerful development tool (for example, see School Stat, 2006). Within schools, there are many different types of data that are important to student outcomes. The focus here will be on behavioural outcomes that relate to the safety and climate of the school. Data collection extends beyond an accountability mechanism when it is used support responsive decision-making. Often, in the name of accountability, the idea of data evokes fear and, in response, many school communities choose to ignore data as much as possible. Yet behavioural data can provide clear indicators of what the community is doing well, where it is improving, and what needs more attention and development. Data-driven decision-making also allows school communities to celebrate achievements and provides a rationale for future development.

The second face of the pyramid specifies the levels at which *behavioural* data need to be collected, so that the school community can determine which practices are effective in reducing harmful behaviour. The practice of restorative justice is not a panacea and will not address all the ills and concerns raised by harmful behaviour in schools. We need to become much more sophisticated at knowing what works when, and for whom. For example, just as the recidivism rate is variable across offence type (eg, violent, property etc) in the context of juvenile and criminal justice (see Chapter 6), variance should also be expected, across a range of factors, within the context of schools. Besides large systematic trials within school districts, individual schools should build their own database, as the same process can produce dramatically different results from place to place.

For example (as reviewed in Chapter 6), the randomised control trials in Canberra, Australia found that restorative conferencing was most effective for reducing repeat offending with violent crime, yet in England it was found to be most effective for property crime and not violent crime. Further, gender and race differences are emerging as well.

This evidence-based practice enables school communities to respond to areas that need attention through providing ongoing monitoring and evaluation across all levels of the pyramid. For example, schools typically collect data on suspensions, office referrals and classroom detentions that can be used to inform decision-making. Rather than collecting data purely for auditing or record-keeping purposes data can be collected so as to inform and support responsive decision-making in the further development of programs and practices. Through carefully looking at data trends, data has the potential to reveal patterns across individuals, groups (based on race, gender, and so on), time (hour, day, month), place (classroom, gym, playground, and so on), and many other variables of interest. Where the pattern is less than optimal, further resources and development can be put in place. This information can be used to focus professional development in specific areas, rather than responding to the latest trend. For instance, better training and resources might be needed to address the behaviours that are exposed at the second level of the pyramid before they escalate to the third level. It could also be the case that the practice works better for girls than for boys, and the reasons for this could be explored through focus groups and professional development.

In the same way that there is a continuum of practices, there is also a continuum of the types of data that can be collected.

Primary data

Primary data provides information about the population as a whole. Schools will typically already collect an array of basic demographic data which is important for understanding the heterogeneity of the school population. At the universal level, attendance data is a good indicator of school health and safety. It is also important to carry out regular school climate surveys to help bring the hidden curriculum of school life to the surface. There are everyday incidents of harm in schools that go untold and it is important for schools to become aware of these incidents. Confidentiality is essential for gathering data on school climate. Surveys should be anonymous, and canvas as many voices in the school community as possible; at the same time, they should offer an opportunity for people to give their name and contact details, and/or the name of a person who they can talk to, if they have a concern. But again, confidentiality must be ensured. While individual concerns are important to address when they arise, the data should also be disaggregated so patterns can be established across a range of demographic variables. While schools can employ professionals to carry out this process, it is also possible to set up a simple questionnaire, using established measures, and then enter the data into a spreadsheet, while always adhering to the ethical guidelines established by school districts.

Secondary data

Secondary data focuses on behaviour that has become more of a concern. Typically these incidents are referred to a more senior person in the school, with information being recorded on referral forms. These forms typically include a range of categories of information: student name; student demographic information (sex and race); student grade and class; name of reporting teacher; reason for referral; date, time and place of incident; name of other individual(s) who have been involved; measures taken before referral; and measures taken as a result of referral. Again, much of this data can be coded and entered on a spreadsheet. Thus, schools can look for trends over time (for example, month by month) by location, age, offence type, student and teacher. For example, a school might find that a significant proportion of the referrals are coming from the playground or the gym or particular classrooms. They might also find that particular times of the year are more problematic than others, or that particular times of the day are problematic. When these trends are highlighted, schools can then respond as appropriate.

Tertiary data

Tertiary data refers to behavioural information about the most serious incidents in schools. Typically, behaviour is becoming much more of a concern when students are suspended from school; thus, suspension data are an indicator of how well schools are able to curb the escalation of harmful behaviour. When this is matched with basic demographic data, we know who is getting suspended and who is not. The data provides the schools with the indicators of what they are achieving. If the results are not satisfactory, the school can respond through further analysis, discussion and professional development. Often the same people rise to the top of the pyramid again and again, often because the original problem was not addressed at its root cause. When it comes to these behaviour patterns, it is often helpful to collect individual behaviour profiles. Do the incidents typically happen during a certain time or in a certain place, or when certain people are present? While it is important to collect aggregate data across the school population, at the tertiary level, it is also helpful to collect aggregate data for an individual.

Professional bridging that empowers institutional integrity and development

Schools draw a large number of people together on a daily basis for the purpose of learning; yet, schools can be very isolating and anxiety-provoking places for parents, teachers, and students, especially when things are not going well. Getting the "together" part right is challenging. Robert Putnam, in his book *Better Together* (2003), argues that we need both bonding social capital and bridging social capital. Bonding social capital reflects our similarities (or homogeneity), while bridging social capital reflects our differences (or heterogeneity). While both are important, Putnam (2003) argues that bridging is harder than bonding. Schools must create and maintain many bridges. Schools are made up of many communities – communities of teachers, administrators, students, parents, and so on – and efforts must be made to bridge these communities. Building effective bridges through thoughtful communication processes is essential to the healthy functioning and development of schools.

Often when the bridges are not properly in place or not properly maintained, an alienating and antagonistic process of "us" and "them" develops, and communication and understanding break down. Even when two groups want the same outcome, they may act like they want different outcomes, as they perceive themselves to be in different "camps". For example, one study of parents' and teachers' attitudes towards bullying showed that while both teachers and parents preferred dialogue over punishment, each thought the other preferred punishment over dialogue (Morrison, 2001). Thus, one of the priorities of the effective implementation of restorative justice is to create the bridges that will open communication channels between the range of communities within schools. This is particularly important when change and reform are developing within the community.

Resistance to change, and the tensions arising from change, are commonplace in communities, and the reactions to the changes associated with the implementation of restorative justice are no different. Tensions arose in the context of criminal and juvenile justice (see Strang, 2001) and we should expect tensions in the context of schools too. Effective bridging between the many community constituents involved in education systems is essential to sustained institutional reform that seeks to be restorative. As one moves up the levels of the pyramid, bridging with professionals outside the school community becomes more important.

Restorative practices at an individual level can reveal our common humanity, common needs and common predicament; that is, a sense of how we are homogeneous, or similar. Institutions must also acknowledge our heterogeneity; that is, how we are different, and how we have different needs individually and collectively, as members of different communities within the larger school community. Through the practice of bridging, schools enhance their capacity for different communities to work together. Participatory deliberation at a group level is essential to this process.

The bottom line is that schools need to build strong partnerships with many different constituents to be effective, and different partnerships will be needed as schools seek to re-affirm, repair and rebuild relationships that sustain the school community. This is particularly important when new concerns arise from the ongoing research and development that responsive regulation seeks to achieve. Further, not only will schools need to build bridges to their constituents, they will also need to build bridges to the researchers and practitioners that facilitate the development of new ideas and directions that emerge from thoughtful deliberation.

Research is needed to help provide the evidence to support the new ideas. Optimally, this research can be carried out at a school or district level, as this evidence helps to build the rationale for change. This evidence needs to include stories of when schools got it right and when they got it wrong (Howard Zehr refers to this as sharing our butterflies and our bullfrogs) and it also needs to include the hard aggregate behavioural data at each of the three levels of intervention. Stories touch the heart; numbers engage the mind. Both are needed. Facilitators and trainers are needed to implement and develop new directions within and between the different constituents. Schools and school districts implementing restorative practices should not expect an easy road; instead, they should expect significant, and sometimes surprising, challenges. The implementation of institutional reforms will be fraught with a range and depth of emotions. By putting bridges in place, as necessary aspects of policy and practice reform, the implementation process can be much less hazardous. Effective schools build confidence and gain commitment through building bridges with their constituents. Bridging and development will also require different focuses as one moves up the pyramid.

Universal bridging and development

Universal bridging and development recognises the need to create formal and informal spaces for people to affirm themselves, both as individuals and members of the various school constituencies. Each of these constituencies will need basic information about restorative justice at the outset and a rationale about the need for change. Data from school-wide safety questionnaires can help to establish the rationale and can help to drive the process, as well as help to set clear and definable goals. As implementation progresses, each of these groups will also require professional development and training in the basic values and processes of restorative justice. Remember that the universal level is about affirming relationships through building a climate of nurturing and caring; hence, this process is about creating a shared culture and a common language around restorative practices. Because this is a process of socialisation, if the voice of a particular constituency is missing the process as a whole will be affected. The aim is to maximise inclusion. Strengthening the voice within constituencies is as important as building the bridges between constituencies: teachers with administrators; students with teachers; parents with students; administrators with parents; and so on. This process is about creating channels of communication. When institutions are not open to hearing many different voices, they will continually repress the same people again and again. When these voices are repressed, alienation kicks in and the consequences become evident later on.

In the context of this regulatory pyramid, restorative and relational practices at the individual level empower the "I" story, while restorative and relational practices at the institutional level empower the "We" story (see Chapter 2). Taken together, one drives the other. By way of simple example, at the institutional level, it could be that teachers think, and the data reflects that they are not getting enough support at lunch to adequately address the range of behavioural problems they need to respond to. Teachers and administrators would need to explore why this was the case; for instance, what were the drivers? Using existing data as a baseline, new responses could be tested for effectiveness, and if successful, new policy established. Another simple example that often arises from school-wide questionnaires is that parents think that communication between the school and home needs to be improved. These concerns always need to be taken seriously and explored both within and between the different constituencies.

These bridges are all about re-affirming the voices of the different constituents of the school community. When voices are affirmed, much of the groundwork for gaining commitment and developing a shared vision is in place. Part of creating a shared vision is creating a common language and practice. People will come to share this vision in different ways. For some, the sharing of personal stories will capture their hearts, for others the sharing of information and looking at the data trends will capture their minds. Often it is a bit of both, with both the stories and the numbers being important. Building the base of the pyramid on solid ground is essential. This involves developing a shared vision with all members, and constituents, of the school community. Creating this vision involves:

- creating safe spaces where a culture of care, respect and deliberation is upheld;

- celebrating strengths and acknowledging weaknesses through sharing stories and numbers;

- developing a shared language and practice, through information and training;

- providing opportunities to participate in policy development at all levels of intervention, and in all spaces in the school, from classroom to boardroom.

This requires time for shared reflection and will have to be ongoing as students, parents and teachers constantly move into and out of the school community.

Secondary bridges

Secondary bridges will be enhanced through having strong primary bridges at the base of the pyramid, as they act as a foundation for the specialised training at the secondary level. Representatives from the different constituencies – teachers, parents, students, administrators, and so on – will emerge, who can be trained in processes such as peer mediation and running restorative circles. Generally, especially when funding is a scarce resource, it is better to work with representatives who volunteer for secondary training and development. Based on their success, these people will become the facilitators for bringing others on board. While the ideal is for all teachers to have basic training in resolving conflict at all levels of the pyramid, often schools will not have the resources available for this and will need to pace the training with development opportunities. Teachers will also be more able to integrate the learning when they are ready and willing to learn. Schools can manage this in a variety of ways: some will train a cross-section of the school community in basic skills and only one or two at the higher levels; some schools will employ one staff member to work as the restorative justice coordinator, who will work as a facilitator and trainer; and some districts will share facilitators and/or partner with an outside agency. Depending on the issue being addressed, schools may also want to bridge with professional agencies that specialise in areas of concern such as drug and alcohol, sexuality, and so on. The ongoing questions that need to be raised are: Do teachers and other members of the school community have the skills to respond to behavioural problems restoratively? Is more professional development in this area required? Do these behavioural concerns have common themes? Are they associated with any particular sub-population of the school community? Does the school need to participate in some outreach activities with these populations?

Tertiary bridges

Tertiary bridges involve even more specialised training and development. It takes time to hone the skills needed at this level. A typical intervention at this level is a restorative justice conference, and running an effective conference takes time, training and support. Conferences are emotionally powerful processes that should never be taken lightly. Many school districts have teams that work with a cluster of schools. The make-up of these teams will vary from school to school and district to district. In some schools these teams will be made up solely of teachers and administrators within the school, some schools will partner with other schools, some districts will train regional personnel, while others may use a range of community groups. In some areas, bridges will need to be developed with the courts, police and social welfare agencies, as the behavioural concerns grow and affect others.

Some of the most challenging bridges to build will be between the schools and other government institutions, such as courts. With the growing concern about school and community safety, the intersection of duties between courts and schools has also grown: schools are increasingly involved in processes that divert young people from court and courts are increasingly involved in processes that place students back into schools and communities. We can no longer afford to say that we create safer schools through shifting the responsibility for individuals from schools to courts, when behaviour gets this bad. Further, more and more juveniles are coming out of detention facilities and residential placements and back into schools. There needs to be integrated policy that ensures this process reintegrates youth back into schools and communities in healthy ways.

Institutional vision that empowers responsive policy development and integration

Policy is often an abstract concept in the everyday reality for most of the school community, whereas, optimally, it should be integrated at all levels. Policy must drive the vision of the school so that every member of the school community is empowered to work towards the behavioural outcome sought by that vision. Within the responsive regulatory framework outlined, schools should have clear policy at the universal, secondary and tertiary levels. Members of the school community, including the student body and the parent association, should be involved in policy development and review.

Universal policy

Developing a strong policy base at the universal level is essential to the development of a sustainable whole school response to school safety. Policy must be proactive as well as reactive. Too much policy focuses on when things go wrong, instead of building a firm foundation for getting it right. Establishing clear and consistent behavioural expectations is an important policy initiative. In the context of responsive regulation, this means more than booklets outlining the schools behavioural code of conduct. The code of conduct must also be an active document that is discussed regularly, particularly at the beginning of each year. Students within each classroom should be involved in developing a number of classroom agreements that will guide behaviour for the year. Developing these classroom agreements can be facilitated in the context of circle time (see Roffey, 2006; Weare, 2004). Other proactive policy includes outlining the institutional initiatives that will be used in the development of the social and emotional curriculum to develop sound relational skills. These initiatives need to be developmentally appropriate and work in concert as students' progress from year to year. Many programs, such as the Resolving Conflicts Creatively Program (reviewed in Chapter 6), have developed age-appropriate curriculum. Such initiatives should strengthen and develop the *values* of restorative justice: empowerment, honesty, respect, engagement, voluntarism, healing, restoration, personal accountability, inclusiveness, collaboration, and problem-solving. Any initiatives should also strengthen the *practice* of restorative justice – including skills such as active listening, communication and problem solving.

Secondary policy

While a strong foundation at the universal (or primary) level is essential, these proactive policies and practices need to be backed up by a range of reactive policy initiatives at the secondary and tertiary levels. The most challenging aspect of moving from the universal to the secondary level is developing policy that is congruent with the values and practices developed at the primary level. Effectively managing this slippery slope becomes more achievable if viewed in the context of culture change with a long-term vision. For example, practicing the value of "inclusiveness" at the secondary level is a challenge for schools, for typical reactive policies for managing classroom behaviour include "time out" or a referral to a high authority, such as the deputy principal, or being given detention. These practices by their very nature are exclusionary rather than inclusionary. It is important for schools to recognise this and address this issue as much as possible. In particular, students who have been excluded from the classroom need to be re-integrated back into the classroom.

There are many ways to manage the re-integration process. For example, when Massey High School in New Zealand began developing a range of restorative practices in their school, they developed the Restorative Thinking Program (RTP), based on a program they already had in place. Students are referred to the RTP classroom when their behaviour is affecting the learning opportunities of others. The Massey RTP referral policy is explained as follows:

> Teachers apply a questioning process prior to the referral to prompt the student to self-monitor and self-correct so that referral may no longer be necessary. Further disruption beyond this point results in the student being sent out of class to RTP where they work with specialized staff to problem solve the issues that caused them to be sent out.
>
> RTP staff use questions to prompt the student to understand the event from a wider perspective. Students tell their version of the events and are supported to explore the harm and impact on others. They are encouraged to identify and prioritise their goals. This enables the student to find another way that will work for themselves and others in the classroom, and prepares them for classroom re-entry.
>
> The student completes a written plan and returns to class to discuss it with the teacher. The dialogue that accompanies the plan, the "Restorative Chat", is an opportunity to develop understanding between the teacher and student, repair the relationship and facilitate successful reintegration into the classroom. (Moxon, 2005)

This process is documented on a referral sheet that begins with explicitly stating that behaviour agreement that was discussed during the development of school-wide classroom behavioural expectations: "The teacher has the right to teach and every student has the right to learn". Massey High School has developed a code of conduct based on five statements which are discussed and posted in every classroom. This code of conduct is referred to as "The Massey Way". Besides the RTP, Massey also manages behavioural issues within classrooms using classroom conferencing, which by their nature are more firmly grounded in the values of inclusiveness and empowerment (see "Problem solving circles" in Chapter 6). Thus, in working towards a sustainable whole school approach, Massey is augmenting current practice to better fit the restorative values while also introducing new practices and carefully monitoring progress along the way.

In line with this example, schools should begin the process of implementing restorative justice by first reviewing current policy and practice in the context of the values and practice of restorative justice. Adapting and developing current school practices to link with a broad school vision based on restorative justice, makes the transition to new practices and policy much easier.

Tertiary policy

As with secondary policy, responsive and restorative tertiary policy can be a slippery slope for school to manage, particularly when state or federal policy mandates suspension and expulsion for specific behaviour (for example, possession of weapons and drugs on school property). Most schools and districts have explicit exclusionary policies for managing serious incidents in schools. The question for schools is how to manage these incidents as restoratively as possible, such that concerns of all involved can be best addressed, with the aim of repairing the harm done, particularly for victims.

Tertiary policy is typically "offender" focused; restorative justice shifts the emphasis to include the victim and the wider community. For serious incidents, schools can follow up a suspension with a restorative justice conference that brings together all those affected by the incident, together with their respective communities of care. The suspension allows for a cooling-down period and the time necessary to prepare an effective conference. Schools are face-to-face communities and managing the contact between "victims" and "offenders" needs to be managed thoughtfully. The agreements that are decided upon during the conference are recorded and followed up as part of the schools tracking system, providing part of the evidence base for how responsive and restorative schools are managing behavioural concerns. As schools become more restorative, suspension rates should fall (as reviewed in Chapter 6) but this is often a reflection of what is happening at the primary and secondary level, as well as the tertiary level.

The three policy levels need to fit together making holistic sense as one moves up and down the pyramid. The policy also needs to be as visible as possible, for example, by posting both the code of conduct and the policy pyramid throughout the school.

Policy should not be changed for the sake of change. Rather, there needs to be an evidence base for change and further deliberation with the implementation of any new policy. Evidence-based decision-making allows all constituents to participate as individuals and collectives. Thus policy development works hand-in-hand with the development of all sides of the pyramid, and at all levels. In a recursive manner policy, practice, evidence, and professional development work together to inform new policy, practice and evidence, from which new professional development opportunities will emerge.

Restorative justice and empowerment

When the changes associated with reforms and new practices are not realistic and thoughtful, new innovations will rise and fall; this is particularly true with restorative justice, because it is about empowerment. Russell offers a vivid case history of the rise and fall of restorative justice in Boulder, Colorado, concluding:

> Restorative justice fell on the Hill [in Boulder] because restorative justice empowered members of the community to ask for effective enforcement of Boulder's laws in order to repair harm to the neighborhood and prevent more harm from happening. Restorative justice empowered us to make more demands on our local government. Meeting our demands … was something the city of Boulder was not prepared to do. (2003, p 130)

In Minnesota, where some of the longest-standing restorative justice reforms have developed in the United States, empowerment "stories from the street" have been well documented. Below are three stories of empowerment.

> In an upper middle class suburb of St Paul, an adolescent girl was charged with marijuana possession. Initially, the mother could not believe her daughter could be involved with drugs. In the family group conferencing process, which this city uses for all diversion cases, the mother was confronted with the reality of her daughter's use of drugs. The mother became concerned about the role of the broader community context in her daughter's behavior. She suggested to the police department that there was a need for a community wide dialog on shared values and community standards to communicate clear boundaries to the young people of the community. The police department worked with this mother to organize a process called Focus on Community United by Shared Values, whose aims are to establish a committed relationship between the youth and adults of the city, to focus on developing the character and capabilities of all people, young and old alike, and to be responsible members of the community.

> Twelve middle school students were involved in vandalizing an empty home in the community. During the peacemaking circle process the students and their parents identified the lack of a place for students to hang out together as a contributing factor. Members of the community justice council worked with Community Education to develop additional teen activities in their summer program and are exploring the feasibility of a teen center in the community.

> A community member felt empowered after participation in a restorative justice conference to speak to a man smoking marijuana at her bus stop. She told him that she has to catch the bus there and it is not okay

for him to smoke marijuana in the bus stop. The man left. She stated that she would never have done that prior to her experience in the community conferencing process. (Minnesota Department of Education, 2005)

Thus, schools and administrations should expect many layers of tensions with these types of changes. Tensions will arise with the introduction of the new ideas for building safe school communities. The values and processes grounding the practice of restorative justice will challenge the mind-set of members of the school community, some more so than others. Giving members of the school community time to take these ideas in, work with them and experience them, is essential. As the implementation of the practice of restorative justice develops, and affects more people (particularly when it affects them deeply) further tensions will arise. And when members of the school community become empowered, expect further tensions within the institution, and also between institutions. Effective bridging is essential throughout the entire implementation process, which should be a long-term vision. Schools need to be involved in these processes of reform for the long haul. To endure this long journey, it is important to have short-term goals, where the expectations are clearly established with those who will be involved and affected. Having said this, there will be many simultaneous journeys as individuals come to understand restorative practices and reform their own practice. Some will quickly rejoice while others will grumble. All of these voices need to be heard, through effective leadership, bridging, communication and development. Responsive regulation and restorative justice are about empowerment and change, at an individual level and an institutional level. It is about micro-institutional change feeding macro-institution change at all levels of the pyramid.

Participation and change

Just as individuals are all different, schools are all different. What is right for one individual or school may not be right for another. This discussion has attempted to avoid prescription in discussing the processes of implementation, sustainability and development. School communities must be self-reflective and engage with their own constituents. School life will always be organic in nature, changing with the realities of the time. There needs to be an ongoing process of research and development at the school, region and district levels. There is no one perfect template across place nor time. Indeed, we have probably been using the same template within our schools for far too long, with society leaving our schools behind. One small but telling example of this is that most school districts in North America still use the Farmer's Almanac as the basis for their school calendar, while not many children today are expected to help in the fields over the summer.

It is a matter of carrying out an ongoing needs assessment. There is no one perfect place to start with the implementation and practice of restorative processes. In some sense it must start all at once, through careful consideration of all the sides and levels of the pyramid. Generally, it is effective for schools to map current policy, practice, data and development opportunities onto this regulatory pyramid. This process will reveal gaps in the system, and while some gaps will be revealed quickly others will emerge through deliberative dialogue within and between constituents. When gaps are revealed, they will help to indicate the direction that strategic development needs to take. Through this process schools can develop a comprehensive needs analysis.

The basic questions that school communities need to ask themselves as part of their needs assessment are:

- What practices do we use to support behaviour at the primary, secondary and tertiary levels? Do these practices fit with our underlying philosophy and values? Are these practices responsive to the needs of the community? Do they seek to engage and empower or exclude?

- What data do we collect that will reveal the success, failures and potential of our practices for the individuals and groups that make up our community?

- What systems do we use to bridge learning and development for the different constituents within the school communities?

- What policies do we hold that clearly specify the values, vision and behavioural expectations for our school?

Common characteristics of successful reform

While recognising differences, there are some common characteristics to successful school reform that integrates academic, social and emotional learning. Specific to programs that seek to build social and emotional learning, Gager and Elias (1997) came up with this list of factors that lead to successful implementation (see Elias, Zins, Graczyk & Weissberg, 2003, p 311): (a) presence of a program coordinator or committee to oversee implementation and resolution of day-to-day problems; (b) involvement of individuals with high shared morale, good communication, and a sense of ownership; (c) ongoing processes of formal and informal training, including involvement of acknowledged experts; (d) inclusion of all school populations; (e) visibility in the school and the community; (f) components that explicitly foster mutual respect and support among students; (g) varied and engaging instructional approaches; (h) linkage to stated goals of schools or districts; (i) consistent support from school principals; and (j) balanced support from both new and seasoned admini-strators. They also note that many attempts to "scale up" school reform initiatives have lead to disappointing outcomes. Elias, Zins, Graczyk and Weissberg's (2003, p 303) conclusions centre on three points: (a) the need to prepare professions with the array of skills needed to lead efforts at scaling up school reform; (b) the importance of an action-research perspective; and (c) the need to better document the stories of educa-tional innovation and scaling-up efforts so that contextual details can enrich an understanding of what is required for success. Each of these points are captured in the regulatory pyramid developed above, the hope is that they are not lost as school communities develop and engage in their own journey of restorative justice and responsive regulation.

School reform and productive leadership

Leadership has been identified as the single most critical aspect of school reform as it influences every aspect of what it takes to enhance student achievement in schools (Marzano, 2003). Effective leadership harnesses the energy needed to develop a responsive and restorative pedagogy, in that leadership, like restorative justice, is about empowerment of the school community. Developing this new pedagogy requires a vigilantly led transformational process as Lee explains:

> [A] transformational process will change mind-sets, target values and build a culture which can truly support new strategies and organisa-tional aspirations. However it can only be driven by passionate and per-sistent leadership at the top. Therefore, transformational change begins with transforming the mind-sets of managers. (Lee, 2004, p 39)

While having executive staff on board is essential, leadership can not be confined to this level. A reciprocal relationship between leadership and empowerment must be developed; in other words, leadership drives community empowerment, and community empowerment drives leader-ship. To be effective, both must permeate all levels and domains of the school community. This resonates with Lambert who argues:

> [L]eadership needs to be embedded in the school community as a whole [because] leadership is about learning together, and constructing mean-ing and knowledge collectively and collaboratively. (2003, p 3)

Through leadership and empowerment all members of the school community learn to "walk the talk" and "build bridges".

Effective leadership must shape the development of five key elements of productive and professional school communities: shared norms and values, focus on student learning, reflective dialogue, deprivatisation of practice, and collaboration (Louis, Kruse and Marks, 1996). These elements align with the characteristics of productive leadership outlined by Hayes, Mills, Lingard and Christie (2001), who concur with the conclusions of Louis, Kruse and Marks (1996, p 193) that "the most effective administrative leaders delegated authority, developed collaborative decision-making processes, and stepped back from being the central problem solver".

Further, in line with restorative justice, the process of leadership must go beyond the procedural aspect of engagement to the emotional aspect of engagement. Not only do leaders need to "walk the talk", they need to create the safe spaces where others can be engaged socially and emotionally. Lingard, Mills, and Hayes (2000) have identified this as building the emotional economy of the school: "Leadership in schools needs to give effect to a new emotional economy that supports teachers and the school's learning community" (p 105). Balancing the development of the emotional economy (or capital), must be balanced with the development of human and social capital. Each are important, yet getting the balance right is the key to developing a learning process that produces just and equitable outcomes for all students..

Lingard and colleagues (2000) make a strong case for educational systems to learn to:

- be more reflective on the impact of their policies and funding arrangements;

- enhance accountability from top-down to two-way;

- support capacity building;

- support innovative practice;

- support systematic professional development that enhances outcomes for both teachers and students, and does not marginalise productive pedagogy for the sake of standardisation.

As with the restorative and responsive framework outlined, productive pedagogy pays simultaneous attention to already existing aspects of classroom practice and focuses teachers on the academic, social and emotional aspects of learning and development. The regulatory framework outlined not only develops and sustains safe school communities; it provided a platform for the development of productive pedagogies in all aspects of learning.

The synergy of congruence and inclusion

Fully realised, restorative justice is not about adding another program, or set of practices, to the grab bag of school life; it is about institutionalising a processes of micro-institutional change that drives macro-institutional change, responding to the ongoing and emergent needs and concerns of individuals and communities. For this change to be effective, it must broach both the everyday practice of managing student outcomes, as well as the institutional culture that sustains the development of those practices. It is on this second point that the practice of restorative justice in schools can become more fully realised. The hope is that through the marriage of restorative justice and responsive regulation within a regulatory pyramid, the practice of restorative justice will serve the needs of individuals and institutions more fully, and in doing so will become a regular practice within schools that enhances opportunities for learning and growth.

The broad aim in developing this responsive and restorative pyramid of restorative justice and responsive regulation to develop the emancipatory politics of hope through the reciprocal relationship between institutional and individual processes. Braithwaite discusses this in terms of the reciprocal relationship between hope and emancipation, arguing that:

> Handouts to the poor without nurturing optimism to empower them-selves to solve their own problems are not the solution. Neither is psychologism that builds hope without concrete support and the flow of resources needed for structural change. Cognitive change is how people imagine a better world, micro-institutional change [illustrated through a range of restorative practices], and macro-structural change must be strategically integrated for emancipatory politics to be credible. (2004, p 79)

As Hargreaves and Fullan (1998) suggest, reform is a process of re-structuring as well as "re-culturing", with re-culturing often leading the way to sustained re-structuring. Restorative justice aims to transform the culture of the school through empowering the relationship structure.

The framework developed above outlines a recursive process of ongoing monitoring and development that must constantly be in place in schools, and which allows schools to respond to concerns as they arise. For new problems will always arise, and new actors and new behaviours will always appear. There will always be deviance from the status quo within schools – some of this deviance will breed new life into the school community, while some of this deviance will eat away at the foundation of the community. Schools today reflect the divisions within our communities in many ways. This is increasingly evident in the flight to private schools for those who can afford it, leaving the public school to those who cannot afford this opportunity.

We have a lot of work to do; providing schools with the capacity to better address the realities of society today will not be a straight-forward journey. The journey will require resolve and resources. Schools, as our primary developmental institution, have the capacity to divide us and unite us. Schools foster harmony and security. In a local context, they promote human and social capital, as well as safety and security, for individuals and their communities. In a global context, schools are the institutional heart and mind for the development of homeland security and civil society. Thus, they are an important instrument of the promotion of local and global democracy. As Putnam concludes:

> Reweaving social webs will depend in part on the efforts of dedicated local leaders who choose to pursue their goals ... through the sometimes slow, frequently fractious, and profoundly transformative route of social-capital building. But reweaving will also depend on our ability to create new spaces for recognition, reconnection, conversation, and debate. Creating these spaces will require innovative uses of technology, creative urban planning, and political will. (2003, p 294)

The many threads that make up the web of social life will always be changing. It is the responsibility of social institutions to maintain the integrity of these webs, in different ways promoting harmony and security. As our primary developmental institutions, schools have the hard work of weaving together a number of threads of social life, in the primary years of a young person's life.

Schools are directed to have policies on everything from bullying to drugs. Sometimes this can result in knee-jerk reactions or the overall climate can become too formalised. Restorative justice and responsive regulation offers an approach to address the needs of the individual students, school personnel and the school community as a whole and to build a culture of emotional resilience and responsible citizenship. The hope is that the regulatory framework outlined in the chapter can guide the process.

Chapter 8

Reflections and revelations on being responsive and restorative

The world we have made as a result of the level of thinking we have done thus far creates problems we cannot solve at the same level at which we created them.

Albert Einstein (cited in MacHale, 2002)

If prisons and punitive mechanisms are transformed, it won't be because a plan of reform has found its way into the heads of the social workers; it will be when those who have to deal with that penal reality, all those people, have come into collision with each other and with themselves, run into dead-ends, problems and impossibilities, been through conflicts and confrontations; when critique has been played out in the real, not when reformers have realised their ideals.

Foucault (1981, p 13)

Bullying and Pandora's box

Bullying, because of its insidious nature, is often easier to ignore than confront. At least since the time of Charles Dickens, bullying has been rationalised as character building and a lesson in the ways of the world. Through these rationalisations, the emotional impact of the problem has been minimised. Today, there is mounting evidence of the emotional harm that bullying behaviour can cause. We also have evidence that there is an effective intervention that aims to repair the harm done, in particular, the emotional harm. That intervention is restorative justice, and when it is coupled with responsive regulation, we have a potentially powerful method for dealing with harmful behaviour in schools and for building safe school communities. Safe school communities provide the social foundation for growth and development, through the web of relationships they build for students. This web of relationships also secures hope for students.

Yet to confront bullying and other harmful behaviour in schools is akin to opening Pandora's box. Today, the tendency is to exclude rather than include. Society, local communities, and their authorities can (and do) legitimise exclusion and bullying – and thus condone the systematic abuse of power. Those that legitimise it often do not see the problem, so the status quo remains. There are many layers, and sides, to addressing these issues, as indicated in the regulatory framework in Chapter 7. There are also many questions arising from these issues. There are a host of questions that arise from a deeper exploration of the individual and collective aspects of power abuse and exclusion. For example: in what way do individual and collectives feel safer through these practices? How do they affect the security, hopes and dreams of the next generation? What is the interplay between emotional security and homeland security? This is important territory to map and while the journey is not without its hazards, pitfalls, and blind turns, it is important to make a start. Pandora's box needs to be opened. We, individually and collectively, must confront the problem. This often means confronting ourselves. While, proverbially, Pandora's box does contain the destructive forces of human nature, confronting these destructive forces reveals hope. Developing hopeful futures involves confronting our own demons, our own shame, as individuals and as a society.

Bullying relationships thwart a student's potential. Students cannot gain their sense of autonomy when they are caught in these relationship patterns. In schools, bullying can be legitimised in many ways: through the principal's relationship with the teachers and students, through teachers' relationships with each other and with the students, and with students' relationships with each other. Bullying is about power, domination and control. It puts value on some students and teachers, and not on others, often through valuing particular outcomes, such as grades. Once the value of one person over another has been legitimised (often through inaction rather than action), the scene is set for further dominance and control. The pattern then becomes self-perpetuating. Bullying is a difficult and complex issue. The only way forward is through working together to build strong relationships that value all members of the school community. As part of this process, individuals may need to acknowledge that they could be a part of the problem, however worthy their intentions. We must create the safe spaces where we can support each other in finding better ways to work through our differences, as well as the harms of our actions and inactions, as individuals and institutions. Schools have a duty of care to this end, as well as the responsibility of developing hopeful futures for the next generation.

Schools and their duty of care

As Slee and Ford (1999; see also Bailey, 2006) point out, bullying is not only a serious issue, much of it is criminal. Schools must take the problem seriously; if they fail to do this, they may expose themselves to litigation through their failure to fully discharge their duty of care. A school can be found culpable when: (a) a duty of care is established; (b) that duty of care has been breached; and (c) that breach has caused injury to the party involved. A British editorial warned: "Schools will face legal bills of tens of thousands of pounds if they fail to protect pupils and staff from bullying ... The bill to the taxpayer could run into millions of pounds" (O'Leary, 2000). In fact, this is already starting to happen. For example, in early 2005, a case was heard in Aberdeen Scotland, in which a 16-year-old sought £20,000 in compensation from the city council, after years of being victimised through bullying. While many of these cases are settled out of court, this is not always the case. One Canadian student won his case against a school district which argued that the school "shouldn't be held legally responsible for the behavior of its students". The student felt it was a "victory for all students who face bullying in school. He says his fight has been an emotional roller-coaster, but says it was worth it because no one ever apologized" (CBC, 2005).

But before we burden the courts, the health care system, the education system and the tax system with the effects of dealing with the aftermath of bullying behaviour, we owe it to ourselves to invest in a range of programs and practices that help heal the scars of harmful behaviour and enable individuals to take responsibility for their actions. This is a more efficient way to spend our tax dollar and our private dollar. Litigation does not heal the emotional scars, nor does it necessarily encourage responsible behaviour. Indeed, at an emotional level, the result can arouse more harm than good, resulting in further reactionary policies driven by shame and fear. The safety and emotional wellbeing of our students needs to be at the heart of our policy-making. The health of all nations and the health of their homeland security, begins with the health of the next generation.

Dealing with actions that breach safety

One way of keeping schools safe, and minimising the prospect of litigation from individuals who are bullied, is to cast out the perpetrators. While this may be effective in the short-term, it is seldom effective in the long-term. When we cast offenders from the schoolyard to the community, we only widen the sphere of alienation. Those who offend in classrooms and schoolyards will potentially offend in the community.

Safe schools work hand-in-hand with safe communities. Suspensions typically put our most vulnerable students at further risk, oftentimes the behaviour that caused the suspension is the result of poor social and emotional support. These students are already enmeshed in unresolved conflict and alienation in the family or at school. Yet schools are willing to cast them out again. When we do take these students back, suspended students are more likely to re-offend and disrupt class, because the root cause has not been addressed. Thus, the cycle is perpetuated, laying the foundation that establishes the school house to jail house track (Advancement Project, 2005).

Suspensions have been found to be effective only when the student has received support or participated in a program that aids the transition to and from the suspension (Wilcox, Brigham & Nicolai, 1998). Suspensions need to be addressed on a case-by-case basis to address the motivations of the students involved and to give the parties involved an opportunity to repair the harm done. These students have a story to tell us, as do the students who were bullied. Through listening to their respective stories in an environment that sanctions the value of social relationships, these students are more likely to take on measures of responsibility and self-control (Pranis, 2000). Collett (1999, p 41) concludes that: "What emerges from the research literature [on suspensions] is the importance of valuing all perspectives of a suspension situation because it is not just individual deficits but relationship dynamics and social environments that shape behaviour". Restorative practices, through affirming the value of relationships, has the capacity to shift behavioural dynamics. It is a process that offers each person care and support, while valuing accountability and responsibility. While some schools will be legally bound to suspend some students in some situations, a re-integration conference to assist a student's re-entry into the school community can be used to build deeper understanding of the incident and to repair the harm.

Better yet, schools need to invest in a range of responsive interventions that truly address the causes of harmful behaviour in schools, before they escalate into serious events. These interventions need to address the relational dynamics within schools, and along with these the power dynamics. This involves a process of socialisation and this takes time. There are no quick-fix solutions. As Slee and Ford note:

> Unfortunately ... the push for "quick-fix" solutions to school bullying has had some negative outcomes including undue pathologising of the individual. Construing bullying as aberrant behaviour with its origins in personality flaws or dark family history has focussed attention on remedying deficiencies in the individual ... Schools must confront how [broader] issues impinge on school life, feeding and amplifying bullying

problems. Instead of simply reflecting dominant cultural themes played out in behaviour such as bullying, schools must be agents for change. (1999, p 30)

This is a tough agenda. Schools are already feeling overburdened and under-resourced. Subsequently, the "quick fix" becomes one of isolating "the problem", focusing on an individual's aberrant behaviour rather than the enmeshed power dynamics within the school community. By way of simple example, too often students who bully get anger management classes, and students who are bullied get assertiveness training. The situational power dynamics, which lay at the heart of the matter, are not addressed; and with this the role of bystanders and authorities in perpetuating these power dynamics, also remain unaddressed. These issues are further sidelined through programs that are more informational than relational, in that they focus on describing the problem and what to do about it, often in an abstract, recipe-book manner. And more often than not, emotions are sidelined in fear of the situation becoming out of control. Emotions send us important messages, and more often than not, we ignore the message. We must learn to listen to the message. This is crucial for safe and healthy social and emotional learning and development.

In summary, the informational aspects of anti-bullying campaigns must also embrace the relational aspects of bullying behaviour. Indeed interventions based on information alone may fuel the power dynamics, rather than address them. Efforts to address bullying and victimisation at an individual level, also need to acknowledge the social and collective reality of individual behaviour. We must move beyond pathologising behaviour and labelling individual attributes and we must learn to take collective responsibility. Many programs have already made these shifts in addressing bullying behaviour in schools. However, there is another shift to make and this is the shift that is the most confronting: it is the shift that embraces both reason and emotion. It is the shift that requires us to open Pandora's Box.

Bullying, alienation and restorative justice

Why is it that if bullying behaviour has always been with us, only now have bullying, violence, and alienation become pressing issues? Why is there increasing social pressure to adopt restorative justice beyond the criminal justice system, as evidenced in New Zealand (*New Zealand Herald*, 2006)? Interestingly, bullying and restorative justice have a serendipitous fit: bullying is defined as the systematic abuse of power and restorative justice aims to restore the power imbalances that affect our relationships. Further, there is an interesting synchronicity to the emergence of these two growing fields of study: both have a recent history, having emerged strongly in the 1990s. This coincides with Braithwaite's analysis of the decline of democracy, where: "The lived experience of modern democracy is alienation. The feeling that elites run things, that we do not have a say in any meaningful sense" (2002, p 1). By way of illustration, the Index of Leading Cultural Indicators (Bennett, 1999) stated that over the past three decades there has been "substantial social regression", with a reported 560 per cent increase in violent crime, and the fastest growing segment of the criminal population was children. The teenage suicide rate is another worrying indicator, with the rate being more than three times what it was in 1960. Violence towards the self or others is a strong indicator of alienation. Sadly, it is evident in our schools. Indeed, violence in schools was another international concern that emerged in the 1990s, and in response the first international conference on violence in schools was held by the United Nations Educational, Scientific and Cultural Organisation (UNESCO) in Paris, in 2001. Further, UNESCO declared the period of 2001–2010 to be the International Decade for a Culture of Peace and Non-violence for the Children of the World.

Yet, with our rising concerns about violence in our schools and society, we have become less tolerant and more punitive and excluding. The zero-tolerance policies introduced to address petty crime on the streets of New York now pervade our schools. And while not all schools hold explicit zero-tolerance policies, the language and the mind-set of zero tolerance is clearly with us.

Practising restorative justice in schools

Restorative practices, through valuing relationships, challenge everyone involved. This is an important challenge. To sustain any shift in the way schools operate, each party must question, in the most fundamental way, their own beliefs and practices. The central and dominant theme to be addressed is the use of punishment and control in achieving behavioural compliance. These practices value domination. Restorative justice does not value domination, but rather, it values relationships of non-domination. Respect for authorities, as engendered through restorative justice, does not necessarily equate to domination.

Herein lies the problem that restorative justice must confront, because it does value relationships. Because of the embedded basis of relationships in schools and in society, real change will not be sustainable until a critical mass of individuals makes the shift towards restorative processes. One individual alone cannot sustain the practice of restorative justice. Only through changing our language and discourse around compliance and deviance can we expect a sustainable shift in practice. The route to compliance has many paths, but the compliance that we should strive for is one that values positive relationships, a sense of community, and mutual respect and understanding. Blind compliance, without the relationship network, should not be the result we strive for. We want engaged and passionate students, not students that blindly follow. Cameron and Thorsborne see it like this:

> School behaviour management plans have focused largely on what should happen (penalties and tariffs) to offenders when (school) rules are broken, with only limited understanding of the impact on those in the school community of the offending behaviour. Restorative justice in the school setting views misconduct not as school-rule-breaking, and therefore a violation of the institution, but as a violation against people and relationships in the school and wider school community. (2001, p 183)

The emphasis needs to be on behavioural education, over control, in working towards achieving compliance. The aim should be to take a student, and other members of the school community, through a process by which they can understand the consequences of their behaviour for themselves and others, so as to develop relational thinking and bring understanding to a collective level. Punishment instils a narrow and selfish way of thinking because the focus is on oneself rather than others; likewise, delinquency can be understood as broken links with others. When we put the focus on others, on relationships and on connections with school communities, shame becomes a powerful social regulator. Rather than a focus on guilt and punishment, the focus becomes one of shame and reintegration. We can only manage our shame over wrong-doings in healthy ways, when we are part of a healthy community, one that respects us, cares for us, and allows us to work through our differences. Schools must be emotionally intelligent to emotionally engage students. This is the heart of safe and healthy school communities.

Stronger communities: Bridging and bonding

Can the development of strong citizens in schools lead to the development of strong communities? What characterises a strong and productive community? Schorr (1997) has examined a number of community-building programs in America, addressing the question: why do many promising community-building initiatives fail to reach their full potential? Through closely examining those that have succeeded, she highlights a number of elements that exemplify outstanding programs. The building of "common purpose" is an overriding theme and schools, she argues, are the institution to build and strengthen the relationships between families and neighbourhoods. This is important because safe schools go hand-in-hand with safe communities. Schorr's (1997) research highlights four key elements that characterise effective community initiatives:

1. Action or activity that draws on the overlapping domains of community life, and which enables economic, service, educational, physical and community development.

2. The community itself is the foundation from which resources are drawn and strengthened; in other words, the community becomes the source of individual, social and physical capital – each having an important role.

3. From this foundation, external resources are brought in to further strengthen the foundation. Typically these resources will include public and private funds, professional expertise, and partnerships that bring clout and influence.

4. They are grounded in a theoretical framework of social change that provides an optimistic basis for the efficacy of the program.

These elements characterise the whole school approach to behaviour management that was taken up by Mayfield Primary school in Tasmania, when they decided to get serious about dealing with harmful behaviour. "Making Peace at Mayfield" (1996) is the story of their journey. Schools need to share the stories of their journeys. Each journey is unique and important. Sharing these stories will help others begin their journey. Storytelling is important: it is restorative, empowering, and builds hope. Mayfield's story offers hope. The community worked long and hard to make Mayfield the place it is now:

> [A] place to belong, to feel safe, to enjoy and learn respect, to learn, to grow ... It didn't just happen. In turning the school around, a team effort had to come to terms with what its community was and what they could do to build a positive ethos, climate and learning environment. They addressed a wide range of issues affecting curriculum, teaching and learning styles, physical layout and environment, the way they encouraged and celebrated individual and group success, and, most of all, how they could enable students to manage their behaviour in a positive, non-violent way. (1996, pp ii-iii)

The forces for change at Mayfield included: (a) leadership towards a shared vision; (b) leadership through an organisational culture characterised by rights and responsibilities; (c) focus on professional and curriculum development; and (d) opportunities for parent education and participation. As highlighted here, the forces for change were that of empowerment for all members of the school community. Furthermore, the change process focused on harnessing the resources of the local community.

The role of the broader education system is not to impose new rules and standards, but to support, legitimate and strengthen the efforts of local school communities. A change in culture, even a culture of bully-ing, must come from within. It cannot be imposed as this is often met with resistance. A thoughtful process of socialisation is what is necessary.

The program at Mayfield, like that at many other schools, captures key components of an effective community-building program. Schorr (1997) argues that these programs:

- are comprehensive, flexible and persevering;

- see people in the context of their families;

- deal with families as part of neighbourhoods and communities;

- have a long-term preventative orientation and a clear mission;

- and continue to evolve over time.

These programs are also well managed by competent and committed individuals with clearly identifiable skills; they train and support staff to provide high quality and responsive services; and they operate in settings that encourage practitioners to build strong relationships based on mutual trust and respect. Each of these elements is captured in the frame-work provided in this book. The challenge for schools is putting the framework into practice.

The work done by school communities who introduce restorative practices has not been easy. The work done everyday in schools around the world is not easy. There are daily frustrations. For every school faces the "relentless intrusion of social problems into the classroom" (Schorr, 1997, p 283). Teachers increasingly feel that they are being asked to address problems that society has created. These problems manifest themselves in classroom behaviours. Schools should not have to face these problems alone. Schools too, must build partnerships and they need the support of government, bureaucracies and their local commu-nities. Schorr (1997) finds that schools who are faring well have:

1. Improvised and linked themselves with whatever services/resources are available.

2. Put their buildings at the disposal of the neighbourhood.

3.   Become partners in efforts to reform services and build communities.

4.   Supported families as valued partners in promoting children's learning.

The theme that emerges from this analysis is that the building of relationships – through both bridging and bonding – is the key component underlying effective programs. This, too, is the message of restorative justice and responsive regulation.

Policies of hope

It is important to get the policies right. Policies must capture the vision of safe school communities and they cannot be driven by fear of litigation. The possibility of litigation must be considered but it should not drive the process. According to Hutchinson, defensive policies are wrapped up in paradigms of control:

> [W]hich limits the potential for addressing the culture, curriculum, organisation and pedagogies of schooling which contribute to indiscipline. Education authorities' concern tends to revolve around questions of after-the-fact responses to disruption and is beholden to political dynamics of competing cultures within the education organisation and to electoral politics which shape governments and, in turn bureaucratic agendas. (1996, p 167)

Clearly, we need to get past this.

Hutchinson, in his book *Educating Beyond Violent Futures* (1996), challenges us to change our approach to education and learning. He tells us why we need to expand our ways of knowing and vocabularies of hope. He argues that we must question our contemporary rationalisations. Statements such as "Don't worry. It's just a phase" or "Boys will be boys", often characterise the rhetoric around school bullying and help to legitimise the status quo. Hence, endeavouring to implement a change in attitude is difficult and often met with resistance. It becomes too easy to cut down those who are interested in change. Those involved are often accused of trying to change what is; what will always be. This is certainly the case with school bullying.

Schools should not be characterised as places that legitimise resistance to change. Schools should be places for change. They need to challenge the past, the present, the future. Hutchinson concludes:

> Perhaps the most important lesson to be drawn here is, despite the many setbacks and disappointments that we may experience in our schools and societies, not to give up, not to become overly cynical but to keep trying. Fatalism and cynicism may be commonsensical but they dissipate

our social imagination and that of our children. Whether for our schools or societies, they fragment hopes of any real social transcendence ... [They] obscure the potential value of schools and teachers to actively listen to children's voices on the future, to contribute to student empowerment by planting seeds of hope and to facilitate the acquisition of non-violent action competencies. (1996, p 270)

The practice of restorative justice offers hope. This was the experience of the Truth and Reconciliation Commission (1999), which offered hope to South Africans.. The cover of *No Future Without Forgiveness* by Desmond Tutu provides a compelling synopsis of the book:

[D]eeply rooted in the conviction that our relationship to others is central to our existence as human beings. By describing its unique, harrowing and thought-provoking process, Archbishop Tutu shows that reconciliation after conflict is not easy but is the only way forward – whether at the political or personal level – and he offers inspirational advice on how we might make this principle work in a better, more humane future. (1999)

In his book Tutu tells us of "ubuntu" – the essence of being human. That we "live in a delicate network of interdependence ... That a person is a person through other people ... It says 'I am human because I belong.' I participate, I share" (1999, p 35). A sense of belonging, participation and sharing for each student, is what our schools need.

When people who have been bullied and those who have bullied come together, the common reason that they share in confronting each other, and confronting their demons, is that the process offers them hope. Through each telling their personal stories of the harm caused, reconciliation and forgiveness can follow. The process gives them hope for a better tomorrow, where they may feel safer and more secure within their community. Restoration of the individual becomes restoration for the community as a whole.

Hutchinson's (1996) vision for a better tomorrow is spelt out in UNESCO's declaration and program of action on a Culture of Peace. Each Article within that declaration makes an important point. Article 4 is particularly noteworthy here. It states that education at all levels is one of the principal means to build a culture of peace. We must ensure that children from an early age benefit from an education on the values, attitudes, modes of behaviour and ways of life, to enable them to resolve any dispute peacefully and in the spirit of respect for human dignity and of tolerance and non-discrimination. Schools have an important agenda to take up here. This past century has been characterised by a lack of hope. Let's make this next century one that instils hope. Let's develop practices based on the institutionalisation of hope. Instead of teaching our children to expect the worst, let's teach our children to expect the best.

Safe spaces, epiphanies and revelations

Many students are able to successfully negotiate their way through the current institutional systems; however, a good number are less successful. Harmful behaviour comes in many forms. Success comes in many forms, as well. We must be fully cognate of the range of harmful behaviours in schools. While bullying and violence are important to address, there are many more examples of harmful behaviours in schools. By way of example, the rate of cheating on exams in high school and colleges has risen steadily over the last half a century (Pearson Education, 2001). *The Cheating Culture* (Callahan, 2004) provides many examples of "doing wrong to get ahead". So students may be getting the right grades, but for the wrong reasons. This cultural trend harks back to the issues of compliance and regulation; specifically, that when we focus too much on the behavioural outcomes, over the relational outcomes, we may get the right outcomes for the wrong reason. Without doubt, there are many problems to address as schools wrestle to improve character education and citizenship within an alienated society.

One of the problems is that we have segmented society to unprecedented levels. We have also become increasingly time poor. As this happens we need to compartmentalise to keep things manageable. Different domains take on the responsibility for different tasks. For example, schools' core business is largely seen as one of numeracy and literacy development, while parents are responsible for their children's moral development. There is, of course, some cross-fertilisation in that both schools and parents share in many aspects of child development. But overall, we like to compartmentalise our respective responsibilities. Overall, this is a very mechanistic view and one that is endemic in modern society. In the end it is not sustainable.

Likewise, our rituals have become much more private, rather than public. Truly holistic and deeply meaningful experiences have become rare. School life has become mundane, as students jump through the academic hoops towards graduation. One of the consequences is that children are being denied their childhood and their rites of passage into adult life (Hinkle & Henry, 2000). When grounded in mundane experiences, Staples argues that:

> [Children] see a world without hope and are taught not to feel passionate about anything … [Violence is] both a reaction to hopelessness and powerlessness and, paradoxically, an attempt to assert one's will that often becomes addictive. (2000, pp 32–3)

Welsh (2000, p 30) characterises "violence [as] a failed epiphany, that is, a heightened moment of awareness emerging out of the everyday flow of experience that seeks to overcome alienation. Violence fails because it cannot create a world of sustained meaning". While violence can be characterised as a failed epiphany, restorative justice can be characterised as a sustained epiphany. When the powerful emotional forces of a face-to-face restorative justice conference touch those involved, the moment is often explained in terms of an epiphany. This epiphany involves a realisation of collective vulnerability and purpose that touches, and gives meaning to, each individual involved. It allows each individual to move forward in their life, through a sustained meaning experience within a collective process. This can only be realised through the creation of safe spaces where individuals can connect at an emotional level.

We must recreate the safe spaces where epiphanies and revelations can be experienced, particularly by young people. Our safe spaces have receded as parents and communities fear for the safety of their children. With this, the many community eyes that once supported children and held them accountable and thus kept communities safe, have now become downcast in the name of privacy. These spaces must not only be created to address harmful behaviour; they must be created to celebrate our joys and rites of passage.

Based on the work of Durkheim and Goffman, Collins (2004; see also Sherman et al, 2005) has conceptualised restorative justice conferences as an example of what he defines as "interaction rituals", which embody four distinct features:

1. people are physically together so that they are influenced by each others' bodily presence;

2. the boundaries of interaction membership are clearly defined so that everyone known who is participating and who is not;

3. participants focus on a common purpose and know that all are focusing on it; and

4. participants share a common emotional experience. The interaction between these elements produces a shared experience at both an emotional and cognitive level through the focus on mutual entrainment of emotion and attention (Collins, 2004, p 48).

Durkheim characterised this shared emotional experience as one of collective effervescence, wherein it is the intensity of the interaction ritual, rather than the content, that drives the feeling of group solidarity and the outcomes achieved. These outcomes include feelings of confidence, elation, initiative and a recommitment to the group's standards of morality, each being relevant to a successful restorative justice conference.

While Collins (2004) refers specifically to restorative justice conferences, the face-to-face communities of schools and classroom offer abundant opportunities for successful, and failed, interaction rituals. Interaction rituals fail when there is:

> [A] low level of collective effervescence ... no shared entrainment ... [and] on the output side: little or no feeling of group solidarity; no sense of one's identity as affirmed or changed ... no heightened emotional energy – either a flat feeling unaffected by the ritual, or worse yet, a sense of a drag ... These imply a continuum of just how badly rituals fail (Collins, 2004, p 51).

In this context, through policies of exclusion, schools may fail to engage students in effective behaviour change by failing to optimise the conditions necessary for a successful interaction ritual.

Children are gaining meaning about social life in ways very different from even 20 years ago. These days children have access to a wide range of electronic media. They can be entertained for hours, alone, in front of a range of multimedia devices. As a consequence, the pattern of interactions with peers and adults has changed. Children today are socialised within different relationship patterns than their parents. This, of course, has its consequences for many different domains of life. We must work through the consequences of these shifts in how we manage our relationships when developing the policies and practices that mould our institutions.

Policies and practices need to embrace the person behind the behaviour, socially and emotionally. To embrace the person, we must weave a web of relationships around that person. This web must be strong on both accountability and support; indeed, must marry accountability and support. When relationships are important to us we hold people accountable for their behaviour and we also support them. Too often, accountability and support mechanisms do not work together. When accountability and support break down in the everyday lives of communities, relationships with others are eroded. These relationships can then be affected by shame if we fail to recognise and respond to harmful behaviour.

Willingness to disturb the universe

Schools are central to the development of responsible citizenship. Schools need to provide opportunities for students to engage in meaningful ways through creating safe places for relationships to be affirmed, repaired and rebuilt. Governments, bureaucracies, and communities must support them in this task. Schools must legitimise and promote: respect for the individual; consideration of difference; and participation within the community. To do this, we must be willing and able to engage with each other socially and emotionally. This requires the creation of safe spaces. If the development of students' capacity to live a life of productive citizenship continues to take second place to numeracy and literacy, we face heavy consequences. These will be reflected back on each of us through the growing burdens within the social justice and health care systems.

Restorative justice grew from a dissatisfaction within the courts, in particular within the juvenile and criminal justice system. Yet courts have a very different mandate than schools. Schools are a developmental institution. Because of this, within schools we can broaden our vision for restorative justice to a mechanism that works towards achieving social justice. This vision is about achieving just outcomes for all students on all levels, including safety, health, and academic outcomes.

In his seminal paper, Nils Christie (1977) characterised conflict as property, describing court systems as stealing conflict from those most affected, through stealing the voice of those most affected. The practice of restorative justice gives voice to those most affected by harmful behaviour. Within schools, there are many conflicts stolen and voices not heard, through regulatory systems and practices that focus on behaviours rather than individuals. With this, the education system steals more than conflict, it steals the hopes, dreams and potential of our children. And with that, we do ourselves, as individuals and as a society, a great disservice.

Our children are our mirror, our reflection. We know how well we are doing as a democracy when we look at the health and safety of our children. When our children are hurting themselves and each other, they are sending us a powerful message – one that we need to heed. Restorative justice and responsive regulation lay the foundation so that we can build a just world for our children and ourselves. Let us build the scaffolding of hope for the next generation together. The children deserve it and we deserve it, too. Together, let's raise the bar in promoting justice in our schools. Justice – not just for some members of the school community – but for all members of the school community. In doing so, we will be working towards not only just schools, but towards a more just society. To begin this journey, in the words of TS Elliott, we must be willing to disturb the universe, to open Pandora's Box. Together, let's raise our voices and empower others to raise theirs. The universe needs to be disturbed with due care and respect for all. Let us share our stories of harm and our stories of hope. Together let us begin to heal the harm and restore safe school communities.

Please Remember
Please take a minute to remember
What teasing, name calling, and ridiculing can do
The harm that it can cause
The people that it can hurt
The turmoil that it adds to
As I try to figure out where I fit in
I am someone's son
I am someone's daughter
I am someone's pride and joy
I am the center of someone's universe
Please don't classify me
For the clothes that I wear
Or for the music that I listen to
Because I may be short or tall
Because I am fat or thin
Don't classify me
For the color of my skin

Please don't categorize me
Because I excel academically or athletically
Because I may be an honor student
Because I may play sports
Or because I'm none of the above
Don't call me a nerd, geek, preppy, or a jock
I just do some things better than you
And other things not as well
Am I different from you, or
Are you different from me
Aren't we just individuals
Each trying to make our own way in life
Please take a minute to remember
I am someone's son
I am someone's daughter
I am someone's pride and joy
I am the center of someone's universe

PS Walker (Student at Columbine)

Appendix 1

Principles of restorative justice:
As applied in a school setting
Restorative Justice Consortium, 2005

Values

Restorative practices are underpinned by a set of values, these include: Empowerment, Honesty, Respect, Engagement, Voluntarism, Healing, Restoration, Personal Accountability, Inclusiveness, Collaboration, and Problem-solving.

Processes

1. Primary aim to be the repair of harm.

2. Agreement about essential facts of the incident and an acceptance of some involvement by the person who caused the harm.

3. Participation to be voluntary for all participants and based on informed choice. This also applies to what is included in any outcome agreement, and any consequence for non-participation/ compliance to be made clear.

4. Adequate time to be given to participants to decide whether to take part and to consult with others, if they wish.

5. Acknowledgement of the harm or loss experienced by the person harmed, respect for the feelings of participants, and an opportunity for the resulting needs to be considered and where possible met.

6. The person/s who have been harmed or suffered loss to be (if they wish) the primary beneficiary of any reparation agreed with the person who has caused the harm.

7. Where harm is repaired or amends made, this to be acknowledged and valued.

8. The person/s who has harmed and the person/s harmed are the primary participants of any restorative process.

9. Restorative practitioners to be seen as neutral by participants, and to act impartially.

Equalities/Diversity/Non-discrimination

10. Participants not to be discriminated against for any reason.

11. Diversity to be respected.

12. Respectful behaviour to be maintained in restorative processes, whilst enabling emotions and needs to be expressed.

13. The rule of law to be up-held.

14. Respect for the dignity of all participants at all times.

Information, Choice and Safety

15. Access to information and referral to other organisations who might offer assistance to participants, before, during, after or if they decline participation in a restorative process.

16. Opportunity to participate in a restorative process, except where there is a significant risk of further harm, there is disagreement about the critical facts, or parties do not wish to participate.

17. Ensuring choice is available to the participants regarding restorative processes, including direct and indirect forms of communication and the nature of any reparation.

18. Safety of participants before, during and after participation in a restorative process.

19. Additional protection and support for the particularly vulnerable to enable full participation.

20. Restorative practitioners to keep confidential the content of restorative communications and personal information, subject to the informed consent of participants, the requirements of the law, and their agencies' policies.

21. Restorative agreements to be fair, appropriate to the harm done and achievable.

Agreements/Outcomes

22. Outcomes of a restorative process to be monitored and timely action taken should a problem occur. Any developments should be communicated to participants, unless they have asked not to be contacted.

23. Evaluation of processes and outcomes to be carried out wherever possible.

24. Learning from restorative processes to lead to a reduction in harm and the fear of crime; whilst encouraging cultural and behavioural change amongst individuals and communities. This in turn can lead

to improved social harmony and safer communities. Therefore, where appropriate, practitioners and services are encouraged to find ways to safely promote this learning to others.

Organisation/policies

25. Those agencies/individuals carrying out restorative practices to have a commitment to practise based on the needs of the participants.

26. Organisations to be encouraged to use restorative principles in other areas of conflict, such as internal grievance, disciplinary systems, and external procedures, eg, client complaints, wherever possible.

27. Organisations and practitioners to have a commitment to high quality restorative practice through appropriate training, services and support for practitioners, and complying with the best practice guidance available at the time.

28. To provide best outcomes for participants, organisations carrying out restorative processes to ensure co-ordinated multi-agency working is established.

How restorative is your school?

Based on Van Ness's assessment model schools can evaluate how restorative the case and/or program is or could be under the circum-stances (Van Ness and Strong, 2002).

Four related elements of restorative process are used: encounter (meeting), amends, (re)-integration; and inclusion (involvement). For each element a continuum of possible responses are listed that range from not restorative to most restorative.

1. Encounter (meeting): separation; no encounter; agreement; meeting and agreement; communication; communication and meeting; communication and agreement; meeting, communication and agreement.

2. Amends: no amends; change; reparation; apology; reparation and change; apology and change; reparation and apology; reparation, apology and change.

3. (Re)-Integration: exclusion; stigmatisation of both parties; indifference to both; indifference to one or other of the parties; assistance; respect; respect and assistance.

4. Inclusion (involvement): coercion; prevention; indifference; permission; invitation; invitation and interests; invitation, interests and alternatives.

Taken together, a fully restorative process would involve: (1) meeting, communication and agreement; (2) reparation, apology and change; (3) respect and assistance; (4) invitation, interests and alternatives. At the other end of the continuum, the antithesis of a restorative process would involve: (1) separation; (2) no amends; (3) exclusion; and (4) coercion.

For more detail, please see:
<www.restorativejustice.org.uk/Resources/pdf/Principles_Schools_2005_2nd_ed.pdf>.

Appendix 2

Responsible Citizenship Program:
Building respect, consideration
and participation in schools

A world at peace is not, and can not be, a world without disagreement and conflict. Resolving in a peaceful way, conflict that occurs between nations, between interest groups and between individuals, is a key part of living in the "Peaceable Kingdom". It is also possibly the most important part of peace education aimed at elementary age children.

Tabachnick (1990, p 169)

The Responsible Citizenship Program incorporates a range of related processes that aim to develop, support and restore healthy relationships – including community building, social and emotional learning, conflict resolution and shame-management – under one conceptual umbrella. Each of these components is introduced successively, beginning with a community-building process that rests on three principles of restorative justice – respect, consideration and participation. At an emotional level, the program is grounded in the idea that restorative justice is about building positive affect, such as interest and excitement, and providing mechanisms to discharge negative affect, specifically the shame associated with damaged social relations. Modelling the core features of restorative processes (see Chapter 4), the program is grounded in the hallmarks of practices that work toward repairing the harm done: story telling; emotional engagement; and responsibility.

Throughout the program students are given opportunities to voice and express their views, through storytelling and emotional engagement; so initial emphasis is placed on creating a safe place where concerns and stories of harm at school can be voiced and integrated into the program. At the same time, the program aims to be fun and engaging for students. The program tries to strike a balance between building the positive emotions of social life, while recognising the importance of working through the negative emotions in productive ways. To this end, as relationships within the community strengthen, students are given an opportunity to learn productive conflict resolution skills, through a focus on the feelings associated with conflict and how to resolve those feelings.

Through this focus the social and emotional intelligence aspect of the program is integrated into the conflict resolution component, with the agenda being that of developing students' shame management skills. Another important aspect of the program is the peer-to-peer learning focus, which aids in shifting the culture of support and accountability within the school.

The program is grounded in a number of principles of restorative justice. One set of principles grounds the community-building process; a second set grounds the conflict-resolution process. Braithwaite's (1987) conceptualisation of restorative justice offers the first set of principles: he argues that restorative justice is a *participatory* process that addresses wrongdoing while offering *respect* to the parties involved, through *consideration* of the story each person tells of how they were affected by the harmful incident. Playing on the program acronym (RCP), respect (R), consideration (C), and participation (P) become the core program agreements. They are developed through the learning opportunities that the program provides. While these core principles remain relevant throughout the program, a second set of principles is used to develop students' strategies on how to resolve conflicts productively (a further play on RCP). The five principles, as outline below (see also Chapter 4), underpin the strategies that ground the conflict resolution process developed for this program.

1. All members of the school community, offenders and victims alike, are valued members of the school community whose supportive ties with others should be strengthened through participation in communities of care (see also Bazemore & Umbreit, 1994).

2. Regulation of harmful behaviour concerns actions and should not involve the denigration of the whole person; expect the best from the person without condoning the behaviour (see also Moore & O'Connell, 1994).

3. Each individual must take responsibility for their behaviour to move forward (see also Heimer, 1998).

4. The emotional, social and physical harm done must be acknowledged (Scheff & Retzinger, 1995).

5. Reparation for the harm done is essential (Retzinger & Scheff, 1996).

These principles are introduced within the program through the use of five keys that are important to unlocking conflict. They are called the REACT keys, to emphasise that resolving conflict requires active (but not antagonistic) participation. Building on each letter from the word REACT, the five principles are presented to the students as follows:

- Repair the harm done (Principle 5 – Restitution).

- Expect the best from others (Principle 2 – Separate the person from the behaviour).

- Acknowledge harm done (Principle 4 – Acknowledge emotional, social and physical harm).

- Care for others (Principle 1 – Building communities of care).

- Take responsibility for behaviour (Principle 3 – Personal resolution to move forward).

Given that restorative justice can be couched within the framework of participatory conflict resolution, this program is one in which participants have the opportunity to learn about effective strategies in Resolving Conflict Productively (RCP). Conflict is a natural part of social relationships yet can easily fall into an escalating cycle of antagonism, aggression and violence. We struggled with whether the "P" should stand for peacefully or productively. While peacefully reflects the non-violence ethos of the program, it also has a passive connotation; we want the active engagement aspect of restorative justice to ring true as well, reflecting the responsive and restorative elements of the program. By "productive" we mean not just ending the conflict (through disempowerment) but productive in the sense that it empowers participants, through the building of emotional, social and human capital. Hence, this program aims to build a more productive approach, in a holistic sense, to resolving conflict through providing a framework for students to reflect upon the wrongdoing and learn from their experience.

The curriculum for this program was developed for Year (Grade) 5 students, but is adaptable to other year levels. The students spent one or so hours with the facilitators twice a week over five weeks (10 hours in total). The ideas and concepts were introduced through the use of poster-making and role plays, working towards the development and production of a short video that told the story of a conflict within the school and how the students used the REACT keys to resolve the conflict.

Delimitations of the program

1. The lesson plan is appropriate for students in Year 4 through to Year 7 who have the ability to participate in an experiential education setting involving discussion, poster-making and role playing.

2. The curriculum is appropriate for use by teachers who have knowledge, experience and training in the principles of restorative justice.

3. The efficacy of this curriculum lies in the principles and ideas of restorative justice becoming adopted as part of the culture of the classroom and school.

4. While individuals and schools may use this program as it stands, the ideal (and the recommendation), is for students, teachers and parents to be supported and guided through the processes of developing a restorative justice culture within the school community.

5. The program outline is only meant to be a guide; the hope is that the program will be adapted to meet the needs and concerns of different school communities. The idea is that through school communities engaging in the principles of restorative justice, they will embark upon their own journey. Our hope is that these journeys will be evaluated, documented and shared.

6. Finally, this program draws on the experience of the three facilitators. It marks a significant learning curve on our part, as much as the students, if not more. This was our journey as much as the students' journey of growth and development.

Overview of program workshops

The program consists of 10 one-hour workshops with 12–15 participants:

	Activity
1 Introduction to the Responsible Citizenship Program (RCP)	Posters
2 Developing RCP agreements on respect, consideration, participation	Role play
3 Responsibility in our school community	Posters
4 Feelings – oops! and ouch!	Role play
5 REACT KEYS	Posters
6 VIDEO – school-based examples of oops!, ouch! and keys	Video
7 Planning an RCP video	Video
8 Rehearsing an RCP video	Video
9 Making an RCP video	Video
10 RCP wrap-up and Citizenship Charter	Poster

Core elements of program

1.   *Develop a common structured language that maps a restorative culture.*

The key concepts we wanted students to work with and practice were: respect, consideration and participation. Mapped onto this would be a language to acknowledge feelings when students are hurt (ouch!) and when students hurt another person (oops!). Students then learn about a structured approach to repair the harm done using the REACT keys.

2.   *Use mechanisms to bring the learning in the groups back into the classroom culture, so the learning is transferred and becomes part of the wider culture.*

To ground the concepts we had the students create some banners and posters that could be placed in the classroom as they were completed (becoming a learning focus for students to attend to and discuss). We wanted this process to be established from the onset of the program (establishing the relevance in the classroom early) and to remain in the classroom beyond the set time of the program (to sustain the learning outcomes of the program). To this end the students painted a number of posters, beginning with a *rainbow of respect*, a *considerate teddy*, and a *participation tree*.

3.   *Develop peer-to-peer experience and learning.*

Students needed to think about meaningful examples of respect, consideration and participation. To this end, to complement the posters, colourful pots were placed alongside each of the posters: pot of gold at the end of the rainbow; teddy's honey pot; and the pot from which the tree grows. At the end of each session, students would write on a colourful card (representing gold nuggets in the pot of gold, teddy's bow tie that fell into the honey pot, and seed pods from which the tree grows) the name of a student who showed respect, consideration and participation. At the beginning of the following session, one gold nugget, bow tie and seed pod would be drawn from each pot and the name of the student on the card would be read out. The group as a whole would then be asked: How did "Suzy" show respect last session? In what way was "Matthew" considerate last session? In what way did "Steven" encourage participation last week?

4.   *Use role plays to help ground the learning for the students.*

The concepts were also grounded in action through role playing stories of respect, consideration and participation developed by the students. The role plays also help the students to develop important skills for the production of their video. Role plays were also used to develop the students' understanding of oops! and ouch!.

5. *Place the learning within the program in a story relevant to the lives of students at school.*

    To this end the workshops build to the production of a video that gives the students an opportunity to tell a story about resolving a conflict situation (or harmful action) at school based on what they learnt in the program.

6. *Tangible outcomes for individuals and the group.*

    The video was one collective outcome that the students could share with others, and take pride in. We also wanted an individual outcome. This became a Citizenship Charter, or a small personal statement, that each student put in their personal portfolio.

7. *Involves a learning element that gives parents an opportunity to be involved.*

    The parents were invited to the wrap-up of the program, when the video was shown and we celebrated our accomplishments. This also became a learning opportunity for the parents and an opportunity for dialogue between students, parents and teachers. The parents were also invited to help their children develop their citizenship charter.

8. *Evaluate the learning process for the students on a regular basis.*

    At the end of each session, we asked each student how much respect, consideration and opportunity for participation was given to them. We also used two different surveys to evaluate the effectiveness of the learning process. One asked about the conceptual features of the program (for example, what does REACT mean?). The other examined, (through a pre- and post-test design) the levels of pride, respect, shame-management, school safety, and so on. The outcomes are reviewed in Chapter 6.

Some helpful hints for workshop facilitators

1. Facilitators need to be positive role models for the students and model explicitly the learning outcomes that each workshop aims to achieve.

2. Facilitators need to use humour appropriately and have fun themselves. When mistakes or hiccoughs happen, turn them into a learning opportunity for everyone.

3. Facilitators should participate equally especially in the working groups and discussion circles. The variety helps to keep the students engaged in the program.

4. Bring it to the group's attention when the members are not practising RCP, and encourage participants to self-regulate.

5. Before the program begins, parents need to be made aware that their child will be participating in the program and that parents will be invited to participate in the final workshop. They should also be encouraged to drop by at any time and participate in the program. Teachers and other members of the school community should also be given an opportunity to participate.

6. We aimed for a ratio of one facilitator per five students. The total group size was no more than 15. To achieve this we need to run two sets of 10 workshops.

Workshop 1: Introduction to the Responsible Citizenship Program

Aim

To introduce the program and the facilitators through simple and straightforward exercises. Specifically, to think about Responsible Citizenship at school in relation to three key components: respect, consideration and participation.

Activity

Make RCP Banners.

Materials

Three painting stations (each with a variety of colours of paint; paint brushes; pencils; water); roll of paper for making three banners; three pots to decorate.

Agenda

1. *Introduction and setting program expectations* (5 minutes)

    The introduction to the Responsible Citizenship Program is intended to be brief. It should set clear expectations of what the program involves. Each facilitator should introduce themselves and participate equally in this opening talk. The following points should be covered:

- The aim of the program is to develop responsible citizenship in the school.

- RCP is the students' program and their ideas will be used to develop the program along the way. It is important to listen to everyone's ideas and let everyone participate.

- What are we going to be doing? Making posters, doing some role plays and much more. Each of the activities will be used to develop students' ideas about responsible citizenship in school.

- The program will build to the production of a video. Everyone will be involved in the production. The video will tell a story about responsible citizenship at school. Tell the students that their parents will be invited to see the video and hear about what they have learnt in the program.

- The success of the video will depend on everyone working together.

- There is no assessment in the Responsible Citizenship Program. Achievement is a function of participation and contribution.

- Encourage students to think about using what they have learnt in the program on a day-to-day basis at home and at school.

2. *Participant introductions* – Name game (5 minutes)

    Once the tone of the program is set, give everyone the opportunity to introduce themselves using a fun name game that allows them to express themselves positively. The students, in some sense, can be encouraged to reinvent themselves, show people another side of themselves. The facilitators should be involved in this process, too and can set the right tone by going first and giving good examples.

3. *Students' expectations and agreements: respect, consideration and participation* (10 minutes)

    Get the students to generate a list of their expectations of each other in terms of making the program successful. All ideas are noted on a board or sheet of paper. The group as a whole brainstorms a number of possible agreements. Once this is done, tell the students that there is a simple way to remember how to be a good citizen at school. Three simple words are important and, if we took the **R**, the **C** and the **P** from the Responsible Citizenship Program, these three letters could help spell the way for us in a simple way. Encourage the students to figure out what each letter stands for: R is for respect; C is for consideration; P is for participation.

From the list that the students generated there are likely be examples of each. For example, listening to others is a sign of respect, considering other people's ideas is an example of consideration, allowing everyone to have a turn is an example of participation. Ask the students to define each of these words, say why it is important, and what it feels like.

- Respect – to see each person as worthy and valued within the group.

- Consideration – to be considerate of ideas/feeling/needs of each person.

Sometimes your own ideas/feeling/needs may not be the same as the others in the group but it is important to be considerate of a different point of view. Sometimes you may not even agree with someone but it is important to consider what they have to say and how they may be feeling. Storytelling and listening encourage consideration.

- Participation – to let everyone have a go and be involved. For the school to be a safe and healthy place for learning, it is everyone's responsibility, so everyone has to be involved.

Respect, consideration and participation will become the basic group's agreements. Get the students to agree to follow the guidelines they have set for themselves. This list should then be produced and hung at each subsequent workshop.

Agree on a way for everyone to stop and focus when the group is not upholding their agreements. Sometimes the use of a buzz phrase/word (a word that the group chooses that captures the nature of the agreements) is effective. For example, when someone notices that the agreements are not being upheld, they could say, "Where's the RCP?" Another idea is to raise hands in silence until everyone has their hand up. The silence offers an opportunity to go through the three restorative justice questions: what happened; who was affected; what needs to happen now?

4. *Activity – RCP banners* (25 min)

Divide the group into three smaller groups. Try to make the groups as diverse as possible and bring together students who often don't participate in activities together. Each group will make one poster on a different theme: respect, consideration and participation.

Each group should consider the following when making their poster:

- What does the word you were given mean? (for example, what does respect mean to you?)

- What would you see? (for example, what would you see if everyone was acting with respect for each other?)

- What would you hear? (for example, when respect is being offered?)

- What would you feel? (for example, when respect is being offered?)

- How would you know? (for example, when respect is being offered?)

The group tasks:

- *Respect*: Ask this group to make a banner of the rainbow of respect.

- *Consideration*: Ask this group to make a banner of the most considerate person in the world: someone who always listens, a teddy bear.

- *Participation*: Ask this group to make a tree because a tree has many different parts working together to help the tree grow: leaves gather sunlight; roots gather water; and the trunk helps the tree stand up straight.

We helped speed the process along by drawing the initial outlines of the rainbow, bear and tree.

5. *Parading the RCP banners* (5 minutes)

    Each group is given the opportunity to parade their banner and tell the other groups about it.

6. *Introduce nuggets/bows/seeds* (5 minutes)

    At the end of each session the group comes together for a closing exercise that affirms the group and provides an opportunity for each student to offer the name of one person (other than themselves) that showed respect, consideration and participation in the workshop activities of that day. Each student is given a gold nugget, bow tie and a green seed pod (cut from pieces of coloured cardboard). Each student writes the name of one student who they thought captured each of the three components of RCP. Students then place their answers in the appropriate pot: the gold nuggets go into the pot of gold (placed at the foot of the rainbow banner); the bow ties go into the teddy bear's honey pot (placed in front of the teddy bear banner); the seeds go into the tree's pot (placed at the foot of the tree).

7. *RCP Wrap-up – What I look forward to in RCP* (5 minutes)

    While sitting in a circle, each student is given the opportunity to express something they enjoyed in the day's workshop, something they didn't like or would do differently, and what they are looking forward to in the workshops ahead.

Facilitators' comments

- "Beginnings are difficult times and so there was a certain self-imposed pressure to make the first session a positive experience. Also trying to learn names and gain an appreciation of the individuals' characters were additional demands".

- "I believe that this first session was well focused. The balance that we achieved was between portraying RCP as fun and yet work. This meta-message needed to be clear".

- "It is vital to set a clear expectation at the start around being attentive. This can be a difficult skill for this age group. It is also difficult to assume a role other than dictator but it is important to model RCP".

- "The only room for improvement would be to have more shared resources so there was a higher degree of interdependency. For example the number of colours or paintbrushes could be limited so there was a high level of consideration".

Workshop 2: Developing RCP agreements on respect, consideration and participation

Aim

To develop the concepts of respect, consideration and participation in relation to responsible citizenship at school.

Activity

Role plays.

Materials

Assorted props for role plays.

Agenda

1. *Circle time – Someone you respect and why* (5 minutes)

    The session is started with an exercise to ground the students in a personal understanding of respect. Students sit in a circle and each person is given the opportunity to tell the others about someone they respect and why. A facilitator can go first and set the tone by providing a brief and succinct account.

2. *Respect, consideration and participation feedback* (5 minutes)

    In this session, one person is chosen from each pot as an example of respect, consideration and participation. The idea is that in subsequent workshops each student within the group will be chosen once from the pot. For example, one of the facilitators announces that "Sandra" was nominated as someone who showed respect. What did "Sandra" do to show respect? The same process is continued for consideration and participation. The idea here is to have a meaningful discussion about the core concepts of RCP. Without focusing on a particular event, general discussion was found to be less productive (even boring) for the students. This process allows the students to act as role models for each other.

3. *RCP Role Plays* (45 minutes)

    The aim of the role plays is to develop the students' understanding of the agreements made in relation to respect, consideration and participation. These role plays also help to develop important skills that the students will need for the production of the video. Tell the students that the role plays are important preparation for the videos.

    The group is broken into three smaller groups. Each agreement becomes the focus of one group:

    -   *Respect*: This group is asked to think of a role play which develops the character of a person who showed respect. The role play should illustrate an example of how that person shows respect.

    -   *Consideration*: This group is asked to role play a time when someone showed consideration. The role play should emphasise how it felt to show consideration and be considered.

    -   *Participation*: This group is asked to role play a time when someone was given an opportunity to participate in an activity, and to share how that felt.

    Once each group presents their role play, the groups can be given a new agreement to work on. If the groups are quick, each group can have a chance to work with each of the three agreements. We didn't spend much time talking about (or debriefing) each skit. We let them speak for themselves.

4. *Nuggets, bows and seeds: Respect, consideration and participation nominations*

   Again, each student has a chance to nominate three people: one person who showed respect, one person who showed consideration, and one person who encouraged participation.

5. *RCP wrap-up* (5 mins)

Facilitators' comments

- "The repetition of the aims so soon after the first session helped to reinforce the concepts of the program to the students. I perceived that they were more relaxed with us and the idea of being in the program in this session. Therefore the sense of belonging, of being together, being a group was developed".

- "The appropriateness came from having the students start to take ownership of the process and feel like they were doing more than being told – they had a degree of freedom".

- "The use of the symbols, colour and resources meant that the group could feel comfortable in creating their own unique space. The facilitators provided the framework and the group completed the detail".

Workshop 3: Responsibility in our school community

Aim

To further develop the concepts of respect, consideration and participation in relation to enabling responsible citizenship at school.

Activity

Poster-making.

Materials

Three painting stations (each with a variety of colours of paint; paint brushes; pencils; water; other materials for creating fun and imaginative posters); roll of paper.

Agenda

1. *Respect, consideration and participation feedback* (5 minutes)

    As with Workshop 2, in this session one person is chosen from each of the three pots. The facilitator announces that "Tom's" name was put in the pot during the last session, what did Tom do that showed respect. This is again repeated for consideration and participation.

2. *Exploring RCP* (5 minutes)

    Explore the idea of RCP with the students based on their experiences in the program so far. Include the following points in your discussion. Ask the students which is the most difficult agreement. The students generally come up with consideration, but explore others as well. Consideration often comes up because we often feel we are being considerate of another person's needs and feelings but we get it wrong. Sometimes we just don't know. Ask the students: How would someone really know when they are being considerate? They will usually come up with "talking about it" or "asking the person". Through asking how someone feels about something or telling others how we feel about something we can be more considerate of others. So, who's responsible in making sure everybody's needs and feelings are considered in a respectful way? Everybody! Everyone must work together, listen and talk to each other, to be considerate.

3. *Exploring responsibility* (5 minutes)

    Explore responsibility with the students and include the following points in your discussion. Who's responsible for the kind of person you are and how you live your life? Each of us is! Sometimes people think that "being in charge" or "being the boss" is what responsibility means but that's not the true meaning of responsibility. What does responsibility really mean? Help the students generate a list that could include these points:

    *   Tell the truth – don't exaggerate or make things up.

    *   People can count on you.

    *   Don't hurt other people – verbally or physically.

    *   Do your school work and jobs to the best of your ability.

    *   Let people know your needs and feelings.

    *   Be part of the solution to problems.

    *   Being responsible makes good things happen at home and at school.

4. *What would a school that encouraged everyone to be responsible look like?* (40 minutes)

    The group brainstorms their ideal school community. Prompt questions could be: What would a classroom that allows everyone's interests to be developed look like? Where would people work/play/eat? How many different rooms would the school have? What would it look like? It would have to: *respect* different people with different talents; *consider* their needs/feeling; and encourage everyone to *participate*.

    Divide the students into three groups (different groups than before) and get each group to paint a picture of a responsible school. Each group should be given the opportunity to present their school to the others. It is important to let the students know that their posters will be displayed and they will have to explain how they've incorporated RCP into their school.

5. *Nuggets, bows and seeds nominations* (5 minutes)

6. *RCP wrap-up* (5 minutes)

Facilitators' comments

- "The major step here was handing over creative licence to the group and putting the program into a real life context. The creative licence came from giving the group a blank sheet and paint. The previous session had involved more directed learning. This subtle step was significant in empowering the group to take on the responsibility of work".

- "The posters were about making the whole process real and tangible. There was a clear end goal or vision that the group (through the subgroups) were creating or at least aspiring to. The language and aims of RCP were part of the thinking that the students put into the posters".

- "There were good signs of participation within the subgroups as they shared ideas for the posters".

Workshop 4: Examining our feelings – Oops! and Ouch!

Aim

The aim of this workshop is for the students to share their feelings about experiences of times when they have hurt someone else's feeling (an oops!) and times when their feelings have been hurt (an ouch!). Then to examine how respect, consideration and participation work to make things right.

Activity

Role play.

Materials

A variety of props for role plays.

Agenda

1. *Respect, consideration and participation feedback* (5 minutes)

2. *Introduction to oops! and ouch!* (5 minutes)

   Explain that respect, consideration and participation are important to practise at all times. Ask the students when RCP is most difficult to practise? They are often most difficult to practise when things go wrong and someone gets hurt. One good approach to making things right, when things go wrong, involves respect, consideration and participation. For example, the questions could be asked: Who do we need to respect or consider when an oops! happens? Who needs to be involved so that everyone feels better?

   For everyone to feel better, it is important to:

   - Respect everyone involved.

   - Consider what happened.

   - Consider how everyone was affected (their feelings).

   - Participate together to find a solution.

3. *Thinking about an oops! and an ouch!* (15 minutes)

   We broke into three small groups to explore these issues with one facilitator for each group. In small groups, the facilitator describes and gives an example of an oops! (when I hurt someone) and an ouch! (when I got hurt). Each of the students then tell a story about an oops!, and then an ouch!. As a prompt, the facilitator asks:

   - What happened?

   - How did you feel? How did you REACT? The facilitator makes notes on butcher paper of feelings and reactions for both Oops! and Ouch! For example, think of a time when you experienced an ouch!, a time that someone hurt your feelings. What did the ouch! feel like? What feelings did you have? What did you need to feel better? The feelings typically include: sad, angry, ashamed, embarrassed, scared, hurt lonely, dumb, afraid, left out, rejected.

To feel better the students typically tell us that they need to feel forgiven and accepted.

- Think of a time when you experienced an oops!, a time that you hurt someone's feelings. What did the oops! feel like? What feelings did you have? What did you need to feel better? Again, the feelings typically include bad, ashamed, guilty, embarrassed, scared, sorry, horrible, left out, lonely. To feel better the students again needed to feel forgiven and accepted.

4. *Oops! and ouch! role plays* (30 minutes)

   While still in the three discussion groups, each group was asked to role play an incident when there was an oops! and ouch!. They were then encouraged to think of ways to put RCP to work to make things better. Each group presented their skit to the other students.

5. *Nuggets, bows and leaves nominations* (5 minutes)

6. *RCP wrap-up* (5 minutes)

Facilitators' comments

- "The activity was hugely appropriate as it was about creating a story for presentation to the whole group. We provided the basis and they had to make the show – a perfect scaled down model of what was to come with the video".

- "I think that we were making progress because of the repetition of the messages. However we had created a 'space' where the rules and expectations were different to the classroom".

- "Again the sequence was very good as the students had more structure to work on with the role plays compared to the posters. The level of complexity of their tasks was increasing towards the level required for the video".

Workshop 5: REACT keys – What to do about Oops! and Ouch!

Aim

To introduce the REACT keys as a way of responding when an oops! and an ouch! have occurred, always remembering RCP. These keys are based on five principles of restorative justice.

Activity

Poster-making.

Materials

Three painting stations (each with a variety of colours of paint; paint brushes; pencils; water; and different textual materials); colourful cardboard paper for making the keys.

Agenda

1. *Respect, consideration and participation feedback* (5 minutes)

2. *Introduce REACT keys* (10 minutes)

   This exercise introduces the REACT Keys. The keys build on the RCP agreements of being a responsible citizen at school. Many of these points would have come up in the previous workshop. Point this out to the students when explaining the REACT keys. This tells them that, to a large extent, they know what to do, you are just confirming that they are doing the right thing. The REACT keys are helpful when harm occurs in the school and at home.

   • Repair the harm done (Principle 5 – Restitution)

   • Expect the best from others (Principle 2 – Separate the person from the behaviour)

   • Acknowledge the harm done (Principle 4 – Acknowledge emotional, social and physical harm)

   • Care for others (Principle 1 – Building communities of care)

   • Take responsibility for behaviour (Principle 3 – Personal resolution to move forward).

   Ask the students: ways to repair the harm done; why it is important to expect the best from others; why it is important to acknowledge feelings, care for others, and take responsibility for behaviour? What would happen if an oops! and ouch! occurred and these things didn't happen.

3. *Make a set of REACT keys* (30 minutes)

   Two sets of colourful keys are made, one for each of the videos that will be produced. The keys should be made out of cardboard and be large and vivid. They will be used in the videos.

4. *Presentation of REACT keys* (5 minutes)

    Each group will be given an opportunity to show their keys to the other group.

5. *Nuggets, bows and seeds nominations* (5 minutes)

6. *RCP wrap-up* (5 minutes)

Facilitators' comments

- "This session was another creative exercise for the group to make more meaningful symbols to increase their sense of belonging. Since there were two groups with numerous keys, each person could get involved in the production".

- "This was another step towards the group understanding the methods of conflict resolution in the context of the program. The keys form one of the fundamental bases of the program and their introduction in a creative manner allows them to be integrated in a positive manner".

Workshop 6: VIDEO – Oops!, Ouch! and REACT in action

Aim

To show students an example of a video in which an oops! and an ouch! occurs and how the harm was repaired.

Activity

Video viewing.

Materials

Video and video player.

Agenda

1. *Respect, consideration and participation feedback* (5 minutes)

    Note: This is the last time the RCP feedback was used. By this time each student should have been drawn from a pot to illustrate an example of RCP. To continue with the feedback, it was felt, would become tedious for them. Also, the logistics of the program in subsequent weeks would make it cumbersome to continue, as the two video groups will now work quite independently. The focus will be on the production of their videos.

2. *VIDEO: oops!, ouch! and REACT KEYS in action* (20 minutes)

    The students watch a video about an oops! and an ouch! that happened in a school. Many different videos are available. Choose one that tells a relevant story for your school.

3. *Video discussion* (15 minutes)

    This exercise takes place after the video is watched. Participants sit in a circle with the five keys scattered in the middle of the circle on the floor. The facilitator asks what the oops! and the ouch! was in the video, who was affected by the action taken and what REACT keys they saw in action, how the keys helped make the situation better, and, through using the keys, what was achieved. Also ask the students what would have happened if the keys were not used.

4. *Preparation for video production* (10 minutes)

    Groups of six to seven members work best for the production of the video. Split the group into two smaller groups if necessary. The groups should be equally diverse. It is useful to divide the students at the end of this session, as they need time to settle into their new groups otherwise it will take up valuable time in the next session. Introduce the students to storyboards (laying out their story scene by scene on large blocks of paper) and get them to start thinking about the theme of their video.

Facilitators' comments

*   "The video was a useful tool for contextualising the ideas and aims in a school setting. Since the video can look very professional through the use of computer software it makes for a very impactful story for the students to learn from".

*   "The video gave some clear messages for the group to review. It served as a story to be safely analysed by the group, rather than unsafe talking about an actual group conflict. They were able to identify, for example, the Oops and Ouches, to be able to see them in a proper context".

Workshops 7, 8 and 9: Planning, rehearsing and producing an RCP video

Aim

To plan, rehearse and produce an RCP video. In theory, one session each should be used for: (a) planning; (b) rehearsing; and (c) producing. In practise, it is a bit of each along the way, albeit more planning in the beginning and more producing in the end.

Activity

Video planning, rehearsing and producing.

Materials

Story boards, props, video cameras, video tapes.

Agenda

These workshops are less formatted as the students must now take responsibility for their learning within the program. Participants are encouraged to use storyboards to develop the plot. There is only one guiding principle: the production must be about what they learnt in the program. In other words, the production must be based on the RCP agreements and be about an oops! and an ouch! and incorporate the REACT keys into the story. All students must have a role to play in the production.

Facilitators' comments

Planning an RCP *video*

- "The splitting of the group into smaller sub-groups changed the dynamic. There was naturally an element of competition that developed between the two. This did lead to some instances of disrespect towards the other team. On the positive side the fact that there were less members meant that people had to start pulling their weight and participating more".

- "From a facilitator's perspective it was important to be able to hand over the sense of responsibility for the task that they were taking on. Therefore a 'planning a video' poster gave a clear image of their task".

- "There was a clear need here to find a line between fun and work as well as handing over responsibility and not overwhelming the group. The group needed to be enthusiastic and yet focused".

- "There was a fair amount of tension in the initial stages of decision making about the story line, content and who was going to do what".

- "The students certainly did have a sense of the video aims at this point. They were able to create storylines that fitted in with the RCP aims. There were plenty of bogus stories put forward that were more about showing off than making a story with a message".

Rehearsing an RCP Video

- "The sense of belonging was high at this stage. The subgroups had a task that they were excited about completing. They were enjoying the position of responsibility and level of creative freedom that they had".

- "Each person was certainly caught up in the excitement and made a contribution as best they could. Naturally it was hard for the quieter ones to participate as readily as the more vocal or more popular group members".

- "I saw my role as providing a framework and letting the group work within that. This was perhaps a high-risk strategy as there were clear deadlines to be met and often little appreciation of the time pressures. I did not want to reduce their sense of responsibility or achievement by stepping in to help or enforce rules. The exception was if the group was trying to include inappropriate material in the video such as violence or bad language".

- "At this stage it was proving useful to have flexible end times to the sessions. The primary reason for this was that the group would take some time to get into the story after the previous session and the creative process was not working according to the deadlines".

Making an RCP video

- "The way I had facilitated the previous session meant that the group knew that today was the only chance they had to finish the production. Therefore they had a real desire to participate in the process. They wanted to make it happen and be successful".

- "Everyone certainly did participate, however there were plenty of disagreements about how to proceed, which I needed to manage".

- "Mostly the group were considerate and respectful, though the pressure for results did mean that there were some minor confrontations".

Before the final workshop the facilitators edited the videos. The students can also participate in this task, when time and resources permit.

Workshop 10: RCP wrap-up

Aim

The aim of this workshop is to bring the learning together and conclude the process such that each participant is acknowledged for their achievements and that they have had an opportunity to reflect upon and decide what has been useful for them. It is important to recognise the students' achievements and celebrate their achievements with them.

Activity

Videos, presentations and celebration.

Materials

Videos, video player, certificates, RCP badges, and party food.

Pre-workshop

Send invitations home for the parents to come and watch the videos and participate in the wrap-up of the program. The students also wrote a short note for the school's newsletter:

Responsible Citizenship in 5S

All students in 5S have been able to participate in the Responsible Citizenship Program. RCP is funded by the Criminology Research Council and students attend 10 workshops over five weeks. RCP also stands for Respect, Consideration and Participation. That is their motto because that is what their program helps to build. It is run by Jack, Ali and Dr Brenda Morrison of the ANU Research School of Social Sciences. The compact resolution word is REACT which stands for:

Repair the harm done

Expect the best from others

Acknowledge feelings of everybody

Care for others

Take responsibility.

Next week all parents of 5S are invited to our final session and video presentation.

Agenda

The videos are shown and each group has an opportunity to talk about their video with the audience. Make the audience as broad as possible, in particular invite the students' parents along. Other classes could also be included. A large group session follows where each participant decides what they have learnt from RCP. Presentations are made to each participant in the program. Each student was called forward and presented with a personalised RCP certificate, which they could hang on their wall or put in their portfolio. The students were also given a badge, which played on the RCP theme yet again. Just before the presentations began, we asked the students what RCP meant and they gave us the standard response, the Responsible Citizenship Program. Then we told them that what RCP really meant: that each and every one of the students was a *Really Cool Person.*

An informal evaluation of the workshop also takes place where participants can share their favourite and least favourite activities. In the final closing each participant has the opportunity to say what they have learnt from RCP.

Upon completion of the program, the class teacher finds time for the students to write about their own reflections on the program and what they have learnt. One activity that is productive is for each student to write a Citizenship Charter. The students could also do this as homework, with their parents, especially after the parents have watched the video.

Facilitators' comments

- "This was a major celebration and a bringing together of the first and second groups, so there was a high level of belonging across all the groups. At last the groups could share in their unique experiences and compare/contrast their thoughts and feelings".

- "There was a great sense of achievement that came with having reached the conclusion of the program which meant the students were feeling positive about themselves and others".

- "A celebration of this nature was integral to the completion of such a project. I cannot think of a way to improve upon it. The symbols, the video, the awards and sense of occasion all contributed to a grand finale".

References

Aber, JL, Brown, JL & Henrich, CC (1999) *Teaching Conflict Resolution: An Effective School-Based Approach to Violence Prevention*, New York: National Center for Children in Poverty.

Abramson, L & Moore, D (2002) "The Psychology of Community Conferencing" in J Perry, (ed), *Restorative Justice: Repairing Communities through Restorative Justice*, Alexandria, VA: American Correctional Association, 123-140.

Advancement Project (2005) "Education on Lockdown: The schoolhouse to jailhouse track", <www.advancementproject.org/reports> accessed 1 September 2005.

Ahmed, E & Braithwaite, V (2004) "Bullying and Victimization: Cause for Concern for both Families and Schools", *Social Psychology of Education*, 7(1), 35-54.

Ahmed, E, Harris, N, Braithwaite, J & Braithwaite, V (2001) *Shame Management through Reintegration*, Melbourne: Cambridge University Press.

Alberto, PA & Troutman, AC (1999) *Applied behavior analysis for teachers*, 5th edn, Upper Saddle River, NJ: Merrill/Prentice Hall.

Amstutz, LS & Mullet, JH (2005) *The Little Book of Restorative Discipline for Schools*, Intercourse, PA: Good Books.

Anderson, C (2004) "Double Jeopardy: The Modern Dilemma for Juvenile Justice", *University of Pennsylvania Law Review*, 152(3), 1181-1219.

Anderson, E (1999) *Code of the Street: Decency, Violence and the Moral Life of the Inner City*, New York: Norton.

Annan, K (2000) "Foreword" in C Bellamy, *The state of the world's children*, New York: UNICEF.

Aronson, E (2000) *Nobody left to hate: Teaching compassion after Columbine*, New York: WH Freeman.

Australian Drug Foundation (1999) ADF Position on the Role of Zero Tolerance in Australian Drug Strategy <www.adf.org.au/article.asp?ContentID=zero_tolerance> accessed 1 September 2005.

Ayres, I & Braithwaite, J (1992) *Responsive Regulation: Transcending the Deregulation Debate*, New York: Oxford University Press.

Ayers, W, Dohrn, B & Ayers, R (2001) *Zero Tolerance: Resisting the Drive for Punishment in Our Schools*, New York: New Press.

Azrin, NH & Holz, WC (1966), "Punishment" in WK Honig (ed), *Operant behavior:*

Areas of research and application, New York: Appleton-Century-Crofts.

Bacon, Francis (nd) in *The Harvard Classics Vol III, Part 1, Francis Bacon – Essays, Civil and Moral*, New York: PF Collier & Son, <www.bartleby.com/3/1/> accessed 2 July 2006.

Bailey, K (2006) "Legal knowledge related to school violence and safety", in SR Jimerson & MJ Furlong (eds), *The handbook of school violence and school safety: From research to practice*, Mahwah, NJ: Lawrence Erlbaum Associates.

Bagshaw, D (1994) "Peer Mediation Strategies in Schools" in Oxenberry, K, Rigby, K,

& Slee, PT (eds), *Children's Peer Relation: Conference Proceedings*, Adelaide: Institute of Social Research, University of South Australia.

Barton, CB (2003) *Restorative Justice: The Empowerment Model*. Sydney: Hawkins Press.

Baumeister, RF & Leary, MR (1995) "The need to belong: Desire for interpersonal attachments as a fundamental human motivation", *Psychological Bulletin*, 117, 497-529.

Baumeister, RF, Twenge, JM & Nuss, C (2002) "Effects of social exclusion on cognitive processes: Anticipated aloneness reduces intelligent thought", *Journal of Personality and Social Psychology*, 83, 817-827.

Bazemore, G & Umbreit, M (1994) *Balanced and restorative justice: Program summary*. Balanced and restorative justice project. Washington, DC: US Department of Justice, Office of Juvenile Justice and Delinquency Prevention.

Bellah, RN, Madsen, R, Sullivan, WM, Swidler, A & Tipton, SM (1992) *The Good Society*, New York: Vintage Books.

Bennett, WJ (1999) *The index of leading cultural indicators: American society at the end of the 20th century*, Colorado Springs, CO: Waterbrook Press.

Bentley, KM & Li, A (1995) "Bully and victim problems in elementary schools and students' beliefs about aggression", *Canadian journal of School Psychology*, 11, 153-165.

Berdondini, L & Smith, PK (1996) Cohesion and power in the families of children involved in bully/victim problems at school: An Italian replication" *Journal of Family Therapy*, 18, 99-102.

Besag, VE (1989) *Bullies and victims in schools. A guide to understanding and management*, England: Open University Press.

Blamey, R & Braithwaite, V (1997) "The validity of the security-harmony social values model in the general population", *Australian Journal of Psychology*, 49, 71-77.

REFERENCES

Blaya, C (2002) "Social climate and violence in French and English secondary education systems" in E Debarbieux and C Blaya (eds), *Violence in Schools and Public Policies*, Oxford: Elsevier Science.

Blood, P (1998) "Good Beginnings: Lewisham Primary School Connect Project", unpublished manuscript held by Circle Speak, Sydney.

Blood, P (2000) "Responding to harmful behaviour in schools: When they get it wrong, do we get it right?", unpublished manuscript held by Circle Speak, Sydney.

Blood, P (2004) "A whole school model of restorative practices: An integrated approach", unpublished manuscript held by Circle Speak, Sydney.

Blood, P & Thorsborne, M (2005) "The Challenge of Culture Change: Embedding Restorative Practices in Schools", Paper presented at the Sixth International Conference on Conferencing, Circles and other Restorative Practices: *Building a Global Alliance for Restorative Practices and Family Empowerment*, Sydney, 3-5 March 2005.

Blum, RW & Libbey, HP (2004) "School connectedness: Strengthening health and education outcomes for teenagers", *Journal of School Health*, 74(7), 231–234.

Bond, L, Carlin, J, Thomas, L, Rubin, K & Patton, G (2001) "Does bullying cause emotional problems? A prospective study of young teenagers", *British Medical Journal*, 323(7311), 480–484.

Boulton, MJ & Smith, PK (1994) "Bully/victim problems among middle school children: stability, self-perceived competence, and peer acceptance", *British Journal of Developmental Psychology*, 12, 315-329.

Bowers, L, Smith, PK & Binney, V (1992) "Cohesion and power in the families of children involved in bully/victim problems at school", *Journal of Family Therapy*, 14, 371-387.

Bowers, L, Smith, PK Binney, V (1994) "Perceived family relationships of bullies, victims and bully/victims in middle childhood", *Journal of Social and Personal Relationships*, 11, 215-232.

Braithwaite, V, Ahmed, E, Morrison, B & Reinhart, M (2003) "Researching prospects for restorative justice practice in schools: The Life at School Survey 1996-1999" in L Walgrave (ed), *Repositioning Restorative Justice*, Devon, UK: Willan Publishing.

Braithwaite, J (1989) *Crime, shame and reintegration*, Cambridge: Cambridge University Press.

Braithwaite, JB (1999) "Restorative Justice: Assessing optimistic and pessimistic accounts" in M Tonry (ed), *Crime and Justice: A Review of Research*, (25), Chicago: University of Chicago Press.

Braithwaite, JB (2001) "Youth Development Circles", *Oxford Review of Education*, 27, 239-252.

Braithwaite, JB (2002) *Restorative Justice and Responsive Regulation*, Oxford: University Press.

Braithwaite, JB (2002a) *Restorative Justice and Responsive Regulation*. Oxford: Oxford University Press.

Braithwaite, JB (2002b) *Democracy, community and problem solving*, <http://restorativepractices.org/library/vt/vt_brai.html> accessed 1 September 2005.

Braithwaite, J (2004) "Emancipation and hope", *The Annals of the American Academy of Political and Social Science*, 592(1), 79-98.

Braithwaite, J & Mugford, S (1994) "Conditions of successful reintegration ceremonies: Dealing with Juvenile Offenders", *The British Journal of Criminology*, 34, 139-171.

Braithwaite, V (1994) "Beyond Rokeach's Equality-Freedom Model: Two-dimensional Values in a One-dimensional World", *Journal of Social Issues*, 50, 67-94.

Braithwaite, V (2000) "Values and restorative justice in schools" in H Strang & J Braithwaite (eds), *Restorative Justice: Philosophy to Practice*. Aldershot, UK: Ashgate.

Braithwaite, VA & Blamey, R (1998) "Consensus, stability and meaning in abstract values", *Australian Journal of Political Science*, 33, 363-380.

Braithwaite, V, Braithwaite, JB, Gibson, D & Makkai, T (1994) "Regulatory styles, motivational postures and nursing home compliance", *Law and Policy*, 15, 327-54.

Braithwaite, VA & Law, HG (1985) "Structure of human values: Testing the adequacy of the Rokeach Value Survey", *Journal of Personality and Social Psychology*, 49, 250-263.

Breheney, C, Mackrill, V, Grady, N (1996) *Making Peace at Mayfield*, Melbourne: Eleanor Curtain Publishing.

Brewer, DD, Hawkins, JD, Catalano, RF & Neckerman, HJ (1995) "Preventing serious, violent, and chronic juvenile offending: A review of evaluations of selected strategies in childhood, adolescence, and the community" in *Sourcebook on Serious, Violent, and Chronic Juvenile Offenders*, edited by JC Howell, B Krisberg, JD Hawkins, and JJ Wilson. Thousand Oaks, CA: Sage Publications.

Brooks, K, Schiraldi, V, Ziedenberg, J (2000) *Schoolhouse Hype: Two Years Later*, Washington, DC: Justice Policy Institute and Children's Law Center.

Burks, VS, Dodge, KA & Price, JM (1995) "Models of internalizing outcomes of early rejection", *Development and Psychopathology*, 7, 683-695.

REFERENCES

Calhoun, C, Light, D & Keller, S (1989) *Sociology*, 5th edn, New York: Alfred A. Knopf.

Calhoun, A (2000) *Calgary Community Conferencing School Component 1999-2000: A Year in Review*, <www.calgarycommunityconferencing. com/rand_e/september_report.html> accessed 4 June 2004.

Callahan, D (2004) *The Cheating Culture: Why More Americans Are Doing Wrong to Get Ahead*, Orlando: Harcourt.

Cameron, L & Thorsborne, M (2001) "Restorative Justice and School Discipline: Mutually Exclusive?", in H Strang and J Braithwaite (eds), *Restorative Justice and Civil Society*, Cambridge: Cambridge University Press.

Canter, L & Canter, M (1992) *Assertive discipline: Positive behavior management for today's classroom*, California: Canter & Associates, Inc.

CBC (Canadian Broadcasting Corp) (2002) "BC girl convicted in school bullying tragedy", CBC News, 26 March, <www.cbc.ca/story/ news/national/2002/03/25/wesley020325.html> accessed 4 April 2002.

CBC (Canadian Broadcasting Corp) (2005) "Landmark win for bullying victim", CBC News, 25 October, <www.cbc.ca/canada/british-columbia/story/2005/10/25/bc_jubran-bully20051025.html> accessed 1 September 2006.

Charach, A, Pepler, D & Zeigler, S, (1995) "Bullying at School: A Canadian perspective", *Education Canada*, 35, 12-18.

Christie, N (1977) "Conflicts as Property", *British Journal of Criminology*, 17, 1-26.

Civil Rights Project (2000) "Opportunities Suspended: The Devastating Consequences of Zero Tolerance and School Discipline", <www. civilrightsproject.harvard.edu> accessed 6 July 2006.

Clarke, AM, Montgomery, RB, Viney LL (1971) "The psychology of punishment and its social implications", *Australian Psychologist*, 6, 4-18.

Claassen, R (2002) *An Introduction to "Discipline that Restores"*, Centre for Peacemaking and Conflict Studies, Fresno Pacific University, <http://disciplinethatrestores.org/IntroDTR.pdf> accessed 4 June 2004.

Claassen, R (1993) "Discipline that Restores", *Conciliation Quarterly Newsletter*, 12, 2.

Clough, P (2001) "Schoolyard Survival 101: It's all about the group", *The Province*, <www.theprovince.com/bullying/01_02.html> accessed 24 January 2001.

Cohen, R (2003) "Students Helping Students", in T Jones and R Compton (eds), *Kids Working it Out*, San Francisco, CA: Jossey-Bass.

Collett, J (1999) "Perceptions of suspended secondary students towards their school disciplinary absences", *Australian Journal of Guidance and Counselling"*, 9(2), 39-54.

Cornell, DG, Sheras, PL, Kaplan, S, McConville, D, Douglass, J, Elkon, A, et al (2004) "Guidelines for student threat assessment: Field-test findings", *School Psychology Review*, 33, 527-546.

Cornell, C (1999) "When kids kill other kids: The root of the problem", *The Script*, XXIX(5), July <http://www.transactioneleanalyse.nl/LinkClick.aspx?fileticket=hEBdEEB0uQU%3D&tabid=981&mid=1966> accessed 1 September 2006.

Costenbader, V & Markson, S (1994) "School suspension: A survey of current policies and practices", *NASSP Bulletin*, (October) 103-107.

Cox, T (1995) "Stress coping and physical health" in A Broome & S Llewelyn (eds), *Health Psychology: Process and Application*. London: Singular Publication Group.

Craig, W (1998) "The relationship among aggression types, depression, and anxiety in bullies, victims, and bully/victims", *Personality and Individual Differences*, 24, 123-130.

Craig, W & Pepler, D (1997) "Observations of Bullying and Victimization in the School Yard", *Canadian Journal of School Psychology*, 13(2), 41-60.

Cunningham, CE (1997) *The effects of primary division, student-mediated conflict resolution programs on playground aggression*, Department of Psychology, Chedoke-McMaster Hospitals, Hamilton, Ontario.

De Leo, D & Evans, R (2004) *International Suicide Rates & Prevention Strategies*, Cambridge MA: Hogrefe & Huber.

Debarbieux, E (2003) "School violence and globalisation", *Journal of Educational Administration*, 41(6), 582-602.

Dewey, J (1900) *The School and Society*, Chicago: University of Chicago Press.

Dewey, J (1916) *Democracy and Education*, New York: Free Press.

Dickens, C (1837) *Oliver Twist*, London: Chapman & Hall.

Dickens, C (1838) *Nicholas Nickleby*, London: Chapman & Hall.

Doyle, W (1986) Classroom organization and management in Merlin C Wittrock (ed), *Handbook of Research on Teaching*, 4th edn, New York: MacMillan Publishing.

Duke, DL (1989) "School organization, leadership, and student behavior" in OC Moles (ed), *Strategies to reduce student misbehavior*, Washington, DC: Office of Educational Research and Improvement, US Department of Education.

Durkheim, E [1897] (1952) *Suicide*, New York: Free Press.

REFERENCES

Durkheim, E [1893] (1997) *The Division of Labor in Society*, New York: Free Press.

Education Queensland (1996) "Community Accountability Conferencing: Trial Report", unpublished manuscript held by Education Queensland.

Education Queensland (1998) "Community Accountability Conferencing: 1997 Pilot Report", unpublished manuscript held by Education Queensland.

Egan, SK & Perry, DG (1998) "Does low self-regard invite victimisation?", *Developmental* Psychology, 34, 199-309.

Einfeld, M (1998) "Schools as a Microcosm of Society", Paper presented at Australian Council of State School Organizations, 8 May, Canberra.

Elias, N (1987, original 1983) *Involvement and detachment: Contributions to the sociology of knowledge*, [translation], Oxford: Blackwell.

Elias, M, Hunter, L & Kress, J (2001) "Emotional Intelligence in Education", in J Ciarrochi, J Forgas, J Mayer (eds), *Emotional Intelligence in Everyday Life: A Scientific Inquiry*, Philadelphia, PA: Psychology Press.

Elias, MJ, Zins, JE, Graczyk, PA & Weissberg, RP (2003) "Implementation, sustainability, and scaling up of social-emotional and academic innovations in public schools", *School Psychology Review*, 32, 303-319.

Elster, J (1999) *Alchemies of the mind: Rationality and the emotions*, Cambridge: Cambridge University Press.

Emler, N & Reicher, S (1995) *Adolescence and Delinquency: The Collective Management of Reputation*, Oxford: Blackwell.

Espelage, DL, Bosworth, K & Simon, TS (2001) "Short-term stability and change of bullying in middle school students: An examination of demographic, psychosocial, and environmental correlates", *Violence and Victims*, 16(4), 411-426.

Evertson, CM & ET Emmer (1982) "Effective Management at the Beginning of the School Year in Junior High Classes", *Journal of Educational Psychology*, 74(4), 485-498.

Evertson, CM & Weinstein, CS (2006) *Handbook of Classroom Management: Research, Practice, and Contemporary Issues*, NJ: Lawrence Erlbaum Associates.

Farrington, DP (1993) "Understanding and preventing bullying" in M Tonry (ed), *Crime and Justice 17*, Chicago: University of Chicago Press.

Feather, NT (1975) *Values in education and society*, New York: Free Press.

Feshbach, S (1971) "The dynamics of morality of violence and aggression", *American Psychologist*, 26, 281-292.

Fine, M & Smith, K (2001) "Zero Tolerance: Reflections on a Failed Policy that Won't Die" in W Ayers, B Dohrn and R Ayers (eds), *Zero Tolerance: Resisting the drive for punishment in our schools*, New York: The New Press.

Fine, ES, Lacey, A & Baer, J (1995) *Children as Peacemakers*, Portsmouth, New Hampshire: Heinemann.

Finkelhor, D, Ormrod, R, Turner, H, Hamby, S (2005) "The Victimization of Children and Youth: A Comprehensive, National Survey", *Child Maltreatment*, 10, 5-25.

Finnegan, RA, Hodges, EVE & Perry, DG (1998) "Victimization by peers: Associations with children's reports of mother-child interaction", *Journal of Personality and Social Psychology*, 75, 1076-1086.

Fisher, R & Shapiro, D (2005) *Beyond Reason: Using Emotions as you Negotiate*, New York: Penguin Books.

Foucault, M (1981) "Questions of Method: An interview with Michel Foucault" *Ideology and Consciousness*, 8, 3-14.

Fowles, J (1998) *Wormholes: Essays and Occasional Writings*, New York: Henry Holt.

Fowler, WJ (1995) "School Size and Student Outcomes', *Advances in Educational Productivity*, 5, 3-26.

Fraser Region Community Justice Initiatives (2004) "Community Justice Initiatives and the Langley School District #35", *Conversation Peace: Creating a Culture of Peace in Schools*. Langley, British Columbia: Community Justice Initiatives and the Langley School District #35.

Fromm, E (1949) *Man for himself: An enquiry into the psychology of ethics*, London: Routledge & Kegan Paul.

Fuentes, A (2003) "Discipline and Punish" *The Nation*, 15 December, pp 17–20.

Fuller, R (2004) *Somebodies and Nobodies: Overcoming the Abuse of Rank*, Gabriola Island, British Columbia: New Society Publishers.

Furlong, M J & Sharkey, J (2006) "A review of methods to assess student self-report of weapons on school campuses" in SR Jimerson & MJ Furlong (eds), *The handbook of school violence and school safety: From research to practice*, Mahwah, NJ: Lawrence Erlbaum Associates.

Gager, PJ & Elias, MJ (1997) "Implementing prevention programs in high-risk environments: Application of the resiliency paradigm", *American Journal of Orthopsychiatry*, 67(3), 363-373.

Gagnon, JC & Leone, PE (2002) "Alternative strategies for school violence prevention" in RJ Skiba & GG Noam (eds), *Zero tolerance: Can suspensions and expulsion keep schools safe? New Directions for Youth Development No 92*, San Francisco: Jossey-Bass.

REFERENCES

Gastic, B (2006) "At what price? Safe school policies and their unintentional consequences for at-risk students", Paper presented at the Annual Meeting of the American Educational Research Association, San Francisco, April.

Gerler, ER (2004) *Handbook of School Violence*, New York: Hawthorn Press.

Galloway, DM & Roland, E (2004) "Is the direct approach to bullying always best?" in PK Smith, D Pepler & K Rigby (eds), *Bullying in Schools: How Successful can Interventions be?* Cambridge: Cambridge University Press.

Garbarino, J & DeLara, E (2002) *And Words Can Hurt Forever: How to Protect Adolescents from Bullying, Harassment, and Emotional Violence*, New York: Free Press.

Garbarino, J & Bedard, C (2001) *Parents Under Siege: Why You Are the Solution, Not the Problem, in Your Child's Life*, New York: Free Press.

Garfalo, J, Siegel, L & Laub, M (1987) "School-related victimization among adolescents: An analysis of National Crime Survey narratives" *Journal of Quantitative Criminology*, 3, 321-337.

Gentry, DB & Benenson, WA (1993) "School-to-Home Transfer of Conflict Management Skills among School-age Children", *Families in Society: The Journal of Contemporary Human Services*, 4(2), 67-73.

Gershoff, ET (2002) Parental corporal punishment and associated child behaviors and experiences: A meta-analytic and theoretical review. *Psychological Bulletin*, 128(4), 539-579.

Gibbs, N & Roche, T (1999) "The Columbine Tapes" *Time*, 154(25), 40-51.

Giddens, A (1990) *The Consequences of Modernity*, Cambridge: Polity Press.

Gilbert, P (1998) "What is shame?" in P Gilbert & B Andrews (eds), *Shame: Interpersonal Behaviour, Psychopathology and Culture*, New York: Oxford University Press.

Gilbert, P (2000) "Sensitivity to social put-down: It's relationship to perceptions of social rank, shame, social anxiety, depression, anger and self-other blame", *Personality and Individual Differences*, 29, 757-774.

Gilbert, P (2003) "Evolution, social roles, and the differences in shame and guilt", *Social Research*, (Special Issue: Shame), 70(4).

Gilbert, P (2005) *Compassion: Conceptualisations, Research and Use in Psychotherapy*, London: Routledge.

Gilliam, WS (2005) *Prekindergarteners Left Behind: Expulsion Rates in States' Prekindergarten Systems*. New Haven, CT: Yale University Child Study Center.

Gilligan, J (1996) *Violence: Our Deadly Epidemic and Its Causes*, New York: Grosset/Putnam Books.

Gilligan, J (2001) *Preventing violence*, London: Thames & Hudson.

Glaser, D (1969) *The Effectiveness of a Prison and Parole System*, Indianapolis, Indiana: Bobbs-Merrill.

Goleman, DP (1995) *Emotional Intelligence: Why It Can Matter More Than IQ for Character, Health and Lifelong Achievement*, Bantam Books, New York.

Goleman, DP (2003) *Destructive Emotions: How can We Overcome Them?: A Scientific Collaboration With the Dalai Lama*, New York: Bantam Books.

Gossen, D (1992) *Restitution: Restructuring School Discipline*, Chapel Hill: New View Publications.

Gottfredson, DC & Gottfredson, GD (1985) "Youth Employment, Crime, and Schooling: A Longitudinal Study of a National Sample" *Developmental Psychology* 21, 419–32.

Gottfredson, D (1997) "School-based crime prevention" in LW Sherman et al (eds), *Preventing crime: What works, what doesn't, what's promising: A report to the United States Congress*, Washington, DC: US Department of Justice, Office of Justice Programs.

Gottfredson, DC, Gottfredson, GD & Hybl, LG (1993) "Managing adolescent behavior: A multiyear, multischool study", *American Educational Research Journal*, 30(1), 179-215.

Greenberg, MT, Weissberg, RP, Utne O'Brien, M, Zins, JE, Fredericks, L, Resnik, H et al (2003) "Enhancing school-based prevention and youth development through coordinated social, emotional, and academic-learning", *American Psychologist*, 58, 466-474.

Hargreaves, A & Fullan, M (1998) *What's worth fighting for out there?* Toronto: Ontario Public School Teachers' Federation.

Harmon, M (1995) *Responsibility as Paradox: A Critique of Rational Discourse on Government*, Thousand Oaks, CA: Sage Publications.

Harris, JR (1999) *The Nurture Assumption*, New York: Touchstone Books.

Harris, N (2001) "Shaming and shame: Regulating Drink-Driving" in E Ahmed, N Harris, J Braithwaite & V Braithwaite (2001) *Shame Management through Reintegration*, Melbourne: Cambridge University Press.

Harris, N (2006) "Reintegrative shaming, shame and criminal justice", *Journal of Social Issues*, 62(2), 327-346.

Harris, N, Braithwaite, J & Walgrave, L (2004), "Emotional Dynamics in Restorative Conferences", *Theoretical Criminology*, 8(2): 191-210.

Harter, S, Low, SM, Whitesell, NR (2003) "What have we learned from Columbine: the impact of the Self-System on suicidal and violent ideation among adolescents", *Journal of School Violence*, 2(3), 3-26.

REFERENCES

Hatch, T (2000) "What does it take to break the mold?", *Teachers College Record*, 102(3), 561-89.

Hayden, C (1996) "Primary exclusion: Evidence for action", *Educational Research*, 38, 213-225.

Hayden, C (1997) "Exclusion from Primary School: children in need and children with special educational need", *Emotional and Behavioural Difficulties*, 2(3), 36-44.

Hayden, C (2003) "Responding to Exclusion from School" *Journal of Educational Administration*, 41(6), 626-639.

Hayden, C & Blaya, C (2005) "", *Policy Studies*, 26(1), 67-83.

Hayden, C & Ward, D (1996) "Faces behind the Figures: interviews with children excluded from primary school", *Children and Society*, 10(4), 199-209.

Heaviside, S, Rowand, C, Williams, C & Farris, E (1998) *Violence and discipline problems in US Public Schools: 1996-97 (NCES 98-030)*, Washington, DC: U.S. Department of Education, National Center for Education Statistics.

Higson, R (2005) "School of hard knocks", *The Weekend Australian Magazine*, 29-30 January, pp 12-16.

Hinkle, WG & Henry, S (2000) *School Violence*, Thousand Oaks, CA: Sage Publications.

Hobbes, T, [1651] (1991) reproduced in Tuck, R (ed), *Leviathan* Cambridge, UK: Cambridge University Press.

Hoffman, J (2001) "Much ado about zero: can hard-line policies stop school violence, or do they ignore the real problem?" *Today's Parent*, (April), 76-80.

Hogan, R (1973) "Moral conduct and moral character: A psychological perspective", *Psychological Bulletin*, 79, 218-232.

Hopkins, B (2004) *Just Schools: A Whole School Approach to Restorative Justice*, London and New York: Jessica Kingsley Publishers.

Hudson, C & Pring, R (2000) "Banbury Police Schools Project: Report of the Evaluation" unpublished manuscript, held by the Thames Valley Police.

Huesmann, LR, Eron, LD, Lefkowitz, MM & Walder, LO (1984) "Stability of aggression over time and generations", *Developmental Psychology*, 20, 1120-1134.

Hughes, T (1857) *Tom Brown's School Days*, London: Macmillan.

Hutchinson, FP (1996) *Educating beyond violent futures<* USA & Canada: Routledge.

Ierley, Alice and Claassen-Wilson, David (2003) *Making Things Right: Restorative Justice for School Communities* in TS Jones and R Compton (eds), *Kids Working It Out: Stories and Strategies for Making Peace in Our Schools*, San Francisco: Jossey-Bass.

Ierley, A & Ivker, C (2002) "'Restoring School Communities', Restorative Justice in Schools Program: Spring 2002 Report Card", unpublished manuscript, held by the School Mediation Center, Boulder, Colarado.

Ireland, JL & Archer, J (2004) "The association between measures of aggression and bullying among juvenile and young offenders" *Aggressive Behavior*, 30, 29-42

James, W (1890) *The principles of psychology*, New York: Henry Holt & Co.

Jessor, R & Jessor, SL, (1977) *Problem Behaviour and Psychosocial Development: A Longitudinal Study of Youth*, New York: Academic Press.

Jimerson, SR & Furlong, MJ (2006) *Handbook of School Violence and School Safety: From Research to Practice.* NJ: Lawrence Erlbaum Associates.

Johnstone, G (2002) *Restorative Justice: Ideas, Values, Debates*, Devon: Willan Publishing.

Johnstone, G & VanNess, D (2002) *Handbook of Restorative Justice*, Devon: Willan Publishing.

Johnson, DW & Johnson, RT (1995) *Reducing School Violence through Conflict Resolution*, Alexandria, Virginia: Association for Supervision and Curriculum Development.

Johnson, DW & Johnson, RT (1995) "Why violence prevention programs don't work – and what does?" *Educational Leadership*, 52(5), 63-68.

Johnson, DW, Johnson, R, Cotton, B, Harris, D & Louison, S (1995) "Using conflict managers to mediate conflicts in an inner-city elementary school", *Mediation Quarterly*, 12(4), 379-390.

Johnson, DW, Johnson, R & Dudley, B (1992) "Effects of peer mediation training on elementary school students", *Mediation Quarterly*, 10(1), 89-99.

Jones, T & Compton, R (eds), (2003) *Kids Working it Out: Stories and Strategies for Making Peace in Our Schools*, San Francisco, CA: Jossey-Bass.

Juvonen, J, Nishina, A & Graham, S (2000) "Peer Harassment, Psychological Adjustment and Schooling Functioning in Early Adolescence" *Journal of Educational Psychology*, 92(2), 349-359.

Kant, I [1803] (1900) *Kant On Education (Ueber Paedagogik)*, (trans Annette Churton, introduction by CA Foley Rhys Davids), Boston: DC Heath and Co, <http://olldownload.libertyfund.org/EBooks/Kant_0235.pdf>, Ch 5.

REFERENCES

Kaplan, J & Carter, J (1995) *Beyond behavior modification: A cognitive-behavioral approach to behavior management in the school,* Austin, TX: Pro-Ed.

Katz, J (1999) *How Emotions Work,* Chicago: University of Chicago Press.

Kaufman, G (1992) *Shame: The Power of Caring.* Rochester, Vermont: Schenkman Books Inc.

Kaufman, G (1996) *The psychology of shame: theory and treatment of shame-based syndromes,* New York: Springer.

Kauffman, G & Raphael, L (1991) *Dynamics of Power: Fighting Shame and Building Self-Esteem,* 2nd edn, Rochester, Vermont: Schenkman Books Inc.

Kaufman, G, Raphael, L & Espeland, P (1999) *Stick up for yourself: Every kid's guide to personal power and positive self-esteem,* Minnesota: Free Spirit Publishing.

Kaukiainen, A, Bjprlqvist, K, Lagerspetz, K, Osterman, K, Salmivalli, C, Rothberg, S & Ahibom, A (1999) "The relationships between social intelligence, empathy, and three types of aggression", *Aggressive Behavior,* 25, 81-89.

Kelling, GL & CM Coles (1996) *Fixing Broken Windows: Restoring Order And Reducing Crime In Our Communities,* New York: The Free Press.

King, Martin Luther Jr [1968] (1998) "Remaining Awake Through a Great Revolution" in C Carson & P Hollaran (eds), *A Knock at Midnight: Inspiration from the Great Sermons of Reverend Martin Luther King, Jr,* New York: IPM/Warner Books.

Kingery, PM (2000) *Zero tolerance and school safety: A critical analysis,* Washington, DC: Hamilton Fish Institute, The George Washington University.

Kochenderfer-Ladd, B & Wardrop, JL (2001) "Chronicity and instability of children's peer victimization experiences as predictors of loneliness and social satisfaction trajectories", *Child Development,* 72, 134-151.

Koh, ACE (1998) "The Delinquent Peer Group: Social Identity and Self-Categorization Perspectives", unpublished PhD dissertation, Australian National University.

Kohn, A (1996) *Beyond Discipline: From Compliance to Community,* Alexandria VA: Association for Supervision and Curriculum Development.

Kumpulainen, K & Rasanen, E (2000) "Children involved in bullying at elementary school age: their psychiatric symptoms and deviance in adolescence. An epidemiological sample", *Child Abuse Neglect,* 2, 1567-77.

Kunc, M (1992) "The Need to Belong: Rediscovering Maslow's Hierarchy of Needs" in RA Villa, JS Thousand, W Stainback & S Stainback (eds), *Restructuring for Caring and Effective Education: An Administrative Guide to Creating Heterogeneous Schools* Baltimore: Paul H Brookes.

Kupersmidt, JB, Coie, JD & Dodge, KA (1990) "Predicting disorder from peer social problems" in SR Asher & JD Coie (eds), *Peer rejection in childhood,* Cambridge: Cambridge University Press.

Lambert, L (2003) *Leadership capacity for lasting school improvement,* Alexandria, VA: ASCD.

Lantieri, L & Patti, J (1996) Waging peace in our schools. Boston: Beacon Press.

Larson, J (1994) "Violence Prevention in the Schools: A Review of Selected Programs and Procedures", *School Psychology Review,* 23(2), 151-164.

Le Grand, J & Bartlett, W (1993) *Quasi-Markets and Social Policy,* Basingstoke: Macmillan.

Leary, M. R, Kowalski, R. M, Smith, L & Phillips, S (2003) Teasing, rejection, and violence: Case studies of the school shootings. *Aggressive Behavior, 29,* 202-214.

Lewis, H (1971) *Shame and guilt in neurosis,* New York: International University Press.

Lewis, HB (1987) *The role of shame in symptom formation.* Hillsdale, NJ: Lawrence Erlbaum Associates.

Lewis, HB (1995) "Shame, repression, field dependence and psychopathology" in JL Singer (ed), *Repression and Dissociation: Implications for Personality Theory, Psychopathology and Health,* Chicago, IL: University of Chicago Press.

Lingard, B, Mills, M, Hayes, D (2000), "Teachers, school reform and social justice: challenging research and practice", *The Australian Educational Researcher,* 27(3), 93-109.

Lipsey, M (1991) "The effect of treatment of juvenile delinquents: Results from meta-analysis" in F Losel, D Bender & T Bliesener (eds), *Psychology and Law,* New York: Walker De Gruyter, 131-143.

Louis, KS, Kruse, S & Marks, H (1996) "Schoolwide professional community" in Fred Newmann and Associates (ed), *Authentic Achievement: Restructuring Schools for Intellectual Quality,* San Francisco: Jossey-Bass.

Lowenstein, L (1978) "Who is the bully?", *Bulletin of the British Psychological Society,* 31, 147-149.

Louv, R (2005) *Last Child in the Woods: Savings Our Children from Nature-Deficit Disorder,* Chapel Hill, NC: Algonquin Books.

REFERENCES

MacHale, D (2002) *Wisdom,* London: Prion Books.

Manning, M, Heron, J & Marshall, T (1978) "Styles of hostility and social interactions at nursery, at school, and at home: An extended study of children" in LA Hersov, M Berger & D Shaffer (eds), *Aggression and Antisocial Behavior in Childhood and Adolescence*, Oxford: Pergamon.

Marsh, P (2004) "Supporting Pupils, Schools and Families: An Evaluation of the Hampshire Family Group Conferences in Education Project", unpublished manuscript held by the University of Sheffield.

Marshall, T (1997) "Seeking the Whole Justice" in S Hayma (ed), *Repairing the Damage: Restorative Justice in Action,* London: ISTD.

Martens, W (2005) "A Multicomponential Model of Shame', *Journal for the Theory of Social Behavior,* 35(4), 399-411.

Maxwell, G and Morris, A (1994) "The New Zealand Model of Family Group Conferences" in C Alder and J Wundersitz (eds), *Family Conferencing and Juvenile Justice: The Way Forward or Misplaced Optimism?* Canberra: Australian Institute of Criminology.

Morris, A and Maxwell, G (2003) "Restorative justice for adult offenders: the New Zealand Experience" in L Walgrave (ed), *Repositioning Restorative Justice,* Devon: Willan Publishing.

Maxwell, G and Morris, A (2006) "Youth Justice in New Zealand: Restorative Justice in Practice?" *Journal of Social Issues,* 62(2), 239- 258.

Maxwell, JP (1989) "Mediation in the Schools: Self-regulation, Self-esteem, and Self-discipline", *Mediation Quarterly,* 7(2),149-155.

May, MA & Doob, LW (1937) "Competition and Cooperation", *Social Science Research Council Bulletin,* New York.

Mayer, GR & Sulzer-Azaroff, B (1990) "Interventions for vandalism" in G Stoner, MK Shinn & HM Walker (eds), *Interventions for Achievement and Behavior Problems*, Washington, DC: National Association of School Psychologists Monograph.

Mayer, JD, Caruso, DR & Salovey, P (1999) "Emotional intelligence meets traditional standards for an intelligence", *Intelligence,* 27, 267-298.

McCold, P (1997) "Restorative Justice – Variations on a Theme" in L Walgrave (ed), *Restorative Justice For Juveniles: Potentialities, Risks, and Problems,* Leuven: Leuven University Press.

McCold, P (2005) "Evaluation of a Restorative Milieu: Replication and Extension for 2001-2003 Discharges", Paper presented at the annual meeting of the American Society of Criminology, Nashville, Tennessee, 16–19 November 2004, *Restorative Practices e-Forum,* 25 January, <www.realjustice.org/library.ern2.html> accessed 7 March 2005.

McDonald, J & Moore, D (2001) "Community conferencing as a special case of conflict transformation" in H Strang & J Braithwaite (eds), *Restorative Justice and Civil Society*, Cambridge: Cambridge University Press.

McGarrell, EF & Hipple, NK (2005) "Indianapolis Family Group Conferencing with Youthful Offenders: The Effect of Group Assignment on Re-Offending", Paper presented at *Empirical Findings and Theory Developments in Restorative Justice: Where Are We Now?* 23-25 February, University House, Australian National University.

McGeer, V (2004) "The art of good hope", *The Annals of the American Academy of Political and Social Science*, 592(1), 100-127.

McKenzie, A (1999) "An Evaluation of School Community Forums in New South Wales Schools", Paper presented at the *Restorative Justice and Civil Society Conference*, February, Australian National University, Canberra.

McNeely, CA, Nonnemaker, JM & Blum, RW (2002) "Promoting School Connectedness: Evidence for the National Longitudinal Study of Adolescent Health", *Journal of School Health*, 72(4), 138-146.

Mellor, A (1990) *Spotlight 23: Bullying in Scottish Secondary Schools*, Edinburgh: Scottish Council on Research in Education.

Middleton, G (2000) "School suspends girls named in suicide note", *The Province*, 17 November, p A3.

Miller, S (1994) "Kids Learn about Justice by Mediating the disputes of Other Kids", in J Wolowiec (ed), *Everybody Wins: Mediation in the Schools*, Chicago, IL: American Bar Association.

Minnesota Department of Children, Family and Learning (2002) "In-school behavior intervention grants", *A three-year evaluation of alternative approaches to suspensions and expulsions*, Report to the Minnesota Legislature.

Mirsky, L (2003) "SanerSaferSchools: Transforming School Culture with Restorative Practices", *Restorative Practices E-Forum*, 20 May <http://fp.enter.net/restorativepractices/ssspilots.pdf> accessed 2 July 2004.

Moilanen, R (2004) "Just say no again: The old failure of new and improved anti-drug education", *Reason*, vol 16 <www.reason.com/news/show/29003.html accessed 1 September 2005>.

Moloney, J (1998) *Buzzard breath and brains*, St Lucia, Qld: University of Qld Press.

Moore, DB & O'Connell, TA (1994) "Family Conferencing in Wagga Wagga: A Communitarian Model of Justice" in C Alder and J Wundersitz (eds), *Family Conferencing and Juvenile Justice: The Way Forward or Misplaced Optimism?*, Canberra: Australian Institute of Criminology.

Moore, MH, Petrie, CV, Braga, AA & McLaughlin, BL (2002) *Deadly Lessons: Understanding Lethal School Violence*, Washington, DC: National Research Council.

Morrison, BE (2001) "Developing the schools capacity in the regulation of civil society" in H Strang and J Braithwaite (eds), *Restorative Justice and Civil Society*, Cambridge: Cambridge University Press.

Morrison, BE (2002) "Bullying and victimisation in schools: A restorative justice approach" *Trends and Issues in Crime and Criminal Justice*, 219, (February), Canberra: Australian Institute of Criminology.

Morrison, BE (2003) "Regulating Safe School Communities: Being Responsive and Restorative", *Journal of Educational Administration*, 41(6), 689–704.

Morrison, BE (2005) Restorative Justice in Schools in E Elliott and RM Gordon (eds), *New Directions in Restorative Justice: Issues, Practice, Evaluation*, Devon: Willan Publishing.

Morrison, BE (2006a) "School Bullying and Restorative Justice: Toward a Theoretical Understanding of the Role of Respect, Pride, and Shame", *Journal of Social Issues*, 62(2), 371-392.

Morrison, BE (2006b) "Schools and Restorative Justice" in G Johnstone and D Van Ness (eds), *Restorative Justice Handbook*, Devon: Willan Publishing.

Morrison, BE, Blood, P & Thorsborne, M (2005) "Practicing Restorative Justice in School Communities: Addressing the Challenge of Culture Change" in G Bazemore & S O'Brien (eds), *Public Organization Review: A Global Journal*, 5(4), 335-357.

Morrison, BE & Martinez, M (2001) "Restorative justice through social and emotional skills training: An evaluation of primary school students", unpublished manuscript held at the Australian National University, Canberra.

Morrison, BE & Samycia, V (2001) *Contextualizing the barriers to the use of restorative practices in schools: Perspectives from within the school system*, <www. http://www.sfu.ca/cfrj/database/scholar/210_02_05.htm>.

Mulvey, E & Cauffman, E (2001) "The inherent limits of predicting school violence", *American Psychologist*, 56, 797-802.

Munro G & Midford, R (2001) "'Zero tolerance' and drug education in Australian schools", *Drug and Alcohol Review*, 20(1), 105-109.

Murphy, HA, Hutchinson, JM & Bailey, JS (1983) "Behavioral school psychology goes outdoors: The effect of organized games on playground aggression", *Journal of Applied Behavioral Analyses*, 16, 29-35.

Mynard, H, Joseph, S, Alexander, J (2000) "Peer-victimization and post-traumatic stress in adolescents", *Personality and Individual Differences*, 29, 815-821.

Nansel, TR, Overpeck, M, Pilla, R.S, Ruan, WJ, Simons-Morton, B & Scheidt, P (2001) "Bullying behaviors among US youth: prevalence and association with psychosocial adjustment", *Journal of the American Medical Association*, 285, 2094-100.

Nathanson, D (1987) *The many faces of shame,* New York: Guildford Press.

Nathanson, D (1992) *Shame and pride: Affect, sex and the birth of the self,* New York: WW Norton.

Nathanson, DL (1997) "Affect theory and the compass of shame" in MR Lansky (ed), *The widening scope of shame,* Hillsdale, NJ: The Analytic Press.

National Research Council (2003) *Deadly Lessons: Understanding Lethal School Violence.* National Academies Press, <http://www.nap.edu/> accessed 1 September 2005.

Neary, A & Joseph, S (1994) "Peer victimization and its relationship to self-concept and depression among schoolgirl", *Personality and Individual Differences*, 16, 183-186.

Newman, KS (2004) *Rampage: The Social Roots of School Shootings,* New York: Basic Books.

New Zealand Herald (2006) "Justice Centre for AUT", 15 September, <www.nzherald.co.nz/section/1/story.cfm?c_id=1&objectid=10401403> accessed 17 September 2006.

Nicholl, C (1998) *Community policing, community justice, and restorative justice: exploring the links for the delivery of a balanced approach to public safety,* Washington, DC: US Department of Justice.

O'Callaghan, E (2005) "The MacKillop Model of Restorative Practice", Paper presented at *Building a Global Alliance for Restorative Practices and Family Empowerment, Part 3, IIRP Sixth International Conference on Conferencing, Circles and other Restorative Practices*, 3-5 March Penrith, NSW, <www.safersanerschools.org/library/au05_ocallaghan.html> accessed 1 September 2005.

O'Connell, P, Pepler, DJ & Craig, W (1999) "Peer involvement in Bullying: insights and challenges for intervention", *Journal of Adolescence*, 22, 86-97.

O'Connell, P, Sedighdeilami, F, Pepler, DJ, Craig, W, Connolly, J, Atlas, R, Smith, C, and Charach, A (1997) "Prevalence of bullying and victimization among Canadian elementary and middle school children" unpublished manuscript, held by Ontario Mental Health Foundation.

O'Connell, T (1995) "Community Accountability Conferences: An Effective School-based Strategy for Violence and Drug Matters", unpublished discussion paper.

O'Connell, T, Wachtel. B & Wachtel, T (1999) *Conferencing Handbook.* Pipersville, PA: The Piper's Press.

O'Leary, J (2000) "School bullying 'could cost millions'", *The Times,* 4 January, p 10.

O'Moore, AM (1986) "Bullying in Britain and Ireland: An overview" in E Roland & E Munthe (eds), *Bullying: An International Perspective,* London: Fulton.

O'Moore, AM & Hillery, B (1991) "What do teachers need to know?" in M Elliott (ed), *Bullying: A practical guide to coping in schools,* Harlow, UK: David Fulton.

O'Toole, ME (2000) *The School Shooter: A Threat Assessment,* Quantico, VA: Federal Bureau of Investigation.

Olweus, D (1978) *Aggression in the schools: Bullies and whipping boys,* Washington, DC: Hemisphere.

Olweus, D (1980) "Familial and temperamental determinants of aggressive behavior in adolescent boys: A causal analysis" *Developmental Psychology,* 16, 644-660.

Olweus, D (1984) "Aggressors and their victims: Bullying at school" in N Frude & H Gault (eds), *Disruptive behavior in. schools,* New York: Wiley.

Olweus, D (1987) "School-yard bullying-Grounds for intervention", *School Safety,* 6, 4-11.

Olweus, D, (1991) "Bully/victim problems among school children: Some basic facts and effects of a school-based intervention program" in D Pepler and K Rubin (eds), *The development and treatment of childhood aggression,* Hillsdale, NJ: Lawrence Erlbaum Associates

Olweus, D (1993) *Bullying at School: What We Know and What we Can Do,* Oxford, Blackwell.

Parke, RD & Walters, RH (1967) "Some Factors Influencing the Efficacy of Punishment Training for Inducing Response Inhibition", *Monographs of the Society for Research in Child Development,* 32(1), 1-45.

Parker, JG & Asher, SR (1987) "Peer relations and later personal adjustment: Are low-accepted children at risk?" *Psychological Bulletin,* 102(3), 357-389.

Parsons, C (1999) *Education, exclusion and citizenship,* London: Routledge.

Patterson, GR (1986) "The contribution of siblings to training for fighting: A microsocial analysis" in D Olweus, J Block and M Radke-Yarrow (eds), *Development of antisocial and prosocial behavior: Research, Theories, and Issues,* New York: Academic Press.

Patusky, C & Botwinik, L (2006), "The Philadelphia SchoolStat Model; A Data-Driven Management System for Public School Districts", Fels Institute of Government, University of Pennsylvania <www.fels.upenn.edu/News%20Pages/SchoolStatWhitePaperAug2006.pdf> accessed 1 September 2006.

Peachey, DE (1989) "The Kitchener Experiment" in M Wright & B Galaway (eds), *Mediation and Criminal Justice: Victims, Offenders and Community,* London, Ontario: Sage Publications.

Pepler, DJ & Craig, WM (1997) "Bullying: Research and Intervention", *Youth Update,* 15(1), 4-6. Institute for the Study of Antisocial Youth, Oakville, Ontario.

Petrosino, A, Turpin-Petrosino, C & Buehler, J (2003) "Scared Straight and Other Juvenile Awareness Programs for Preventing Juvenile Delinquency: A Systematic Review of the Randomized Experimental Evidence", *The Annals of the American Academy of Political and Social Science,* 589(1), 41-62.

Pfeffer, CR (1990) "Clinical perspectives on treatment of suicidal behavior among children and adolescents" *Psychiatric Annals,* 20,143–150.

Pikas, A (1989) The common concern method for the treatment of mobbing in E Roland and E Munthe (eds), *Bullying: An international perspective.* London: Fulton.

Porter, L (2000) *Behaviour in Schools: Theory and Practice for Teachers.* London: Open University Press.

Porter, L (2002) *Educating young children with special needs,* Sydney: Allen & Unwin.

Porter, L (2001) *Children are people too: A parent's guide to young children's behavior.* Adelaide: Small Poppies Press.

Pranis, K (2001) *Building Justice on a Foundation of Democracy, Caring and Mutual Responsibility* <www.doc.state.mn.us/rj/pdf/rjbuildingjustice.pdf> accessed 1 September 2005.

Pranis, K (2005) *The Little Book of Circle Processes,* Intercourse, PA: Good Books.

Pranis, K. Stuart, B & Wedge, M (2003) *Peacemaking Circles: From Crime to Community,* St Paul, MN: Living Justice Press.

Prothrow-Stith, D, (1993) *Deadly Consequences: How Violence is Destroying our Teenage Population,* New York: Harper Perennial.

Putnam, RD (1995) "Bowling Alone: America's declining social capital", *Journal of Democracy,* 6, 65-78.

Putnam, R.D (2000), *Bowling Alone: The Collapse and Revival of American Community,* New York: Simon & Schuster.

Putnam, RD with Feldstein, L & Cohen, D (2003), *Better Together: Restoring the American Community,* New York: Simon & Schuster, New York.

Randall, PE (1996) *A Community Approach to Bullying,* Stoke on Trent: Trentham Books.

Reddy, M, Borum, R, Vossekuil, B, Fein, R, Berglund, J & Modzeleski, W (2001) "Evaluating risk for targeted violence in schools: Comparing risk assessment, threat assessment, and other approaches", *Psychology in the Schools,* 38(2), 157-172.

Retzinger, SM (1991) "Shame, anger and conflict: Case study of emotional violence", *Journal of Family Violence,* 6(1), 37-59.

Retzinger, SM & Scheff, TJ (1996) "Strategy for community conferences: Emotions and social bonds" in B Galaway & J Hudson (eds), *Restorative Justice: International Perspectives,* New York: Criminal Justice Press.

Rican, P, Klicperova, M, Kozeny, J & Koucka, T (1993) "Families of bullies and their victims: A children's view", *Studia Psychologica,* 35, 261-266.

Riestenberg, N (2000) "Aides, administrators and all the teachers you can get: A restorative training guide for schools", unpublished manuscript, held by the Minnesota Department of Children, Family and Learning.

Riestenberg, N (2003) "Restorative schools grants final report (January 2002-June 2003): A summary of the grantees' evaluation", unpublished manuscript, held by the Minnesota Department of Children, Family and Learning.

Riestenberg, Nancy (2005) "PEASE Academy: The Restorative Recovery School", *Restorative Practices e-Forum,* 19 July <www.safersanerschools.org/library/peaseacademy.html> accessed 5 August 2005.

Riestenberg, N (2005) "Classroom meeting and re-entry meetings: Circle visible and invisible", unpublished manuscript, held by the Minnesota Department of Children, Family and Learning.

Rigby, K and Cox, IK (1996) "The contributions of bullying and low self-esteem to acts of delinquency among Australian teenagers" *Personality and Individual Differences,* 21(4), 609-612.

Rigby, K, Cox, I. K & Black, G (1997) "Cooperativeness and bully/victim problems among Australian schoolchildren", *Journal of Social Psychology,* 137(3), 357-368.

Rigby, K & Slee, PT (1993) "Dimensions of interpersonal relating among Australian school children and their implications for psychological well-being", *Journal of Social Psychology*, 133(1), 33-42.

Rigby, K & Slee, PT (1999) "Suicidal ideation among adolescent school children, involvement in bully/victim problems and perceived low social support", *Suicide and Life-threatening Behavior*, 29, 119-130.

Rigby, K (1993) "School children's perceptions of their families and parents as a function of peer relations", *Journal of Genetic Psychology*, 154, 501–513.

Rigby, K (1994) "Psychological Functioning in Families of Australian adolescent schoolchildren involved in bully-victim problems", *Journal of Family Therapy*, 16(2), 173-187.

Rigby, K (1996) *Bullying in schools and what to do about it*, Melbourne: The Australian Council for Educational Research Ltd.

Rigby, K (1997) "What Children Tell Us About Bullying In Schools", *Children Australia*, 22(2), 28-34.

Rigby, K (1998) "Suicidal ideation and bullying among Australian secondary school children', *Australian Educational and Developmental Psychologist*, 15(1), 45-61.

Rigby, K (1999) "Peer victimisation at school and the health of secondary students', *British Journal of Educational Psychology*, 22(2), 28-34.

Rigby, K (2002) *New Perspectives on Bullying*, London and Philadelphia: Jessica Kingsley Publishers.

Ribgy, K (2003) "Consequences of bullying in school" *Canadian Journal of Psychiatry*, 48(9), 583-590.

Rigby, K (2004) "Addressing bullying in schools: Theoretical perspectives and their implications", *School Psychology International*, 25(3), 287-300.

Ritchie, J & O'Connell (2001) "Restorative Justice and the Need for Restorative Environments in Bureaucracies and Corporations", in H Strang and J Braithwaite (eds), *Restorative Justice and Civil Society*, Cambridge: Cambridge University Press.

Roberts, WB & Morotti, AA (2000) "The bully as victim: Understanding bully behaviors to increase the effectiveness of interventions in the bully-victim dyad", *Professional School Counseling*, 4(2), 148-155.

Roberts, JV & Stalans, L ((1997) *Public Opinion, Crime and Criminal Justice*, Boulder, CO: Westview Press.

Rokeach, M (1973) *The nature of human values*, New York: Free Press.

Roland, E & Idsoe, T (2001) "Aggression and Bullying", *Aggressive Behaviour*, 27, 446-462.

Roland, E (2002) "Bullying, depressive symptoms and suicidal thoughts", *Educational Research*, 44, 55-67.

Roosevelt, E, (1953) The Eleanor Roosevelt Papers Project, <www. gwu.edu/~erpapers/abouteleanor/er-quotes/> accessed 14 June 2006.

Ross, DM (1996) *Childhood Bullying and Teasing: What School Personnel, Other Professionals, and parents Can Do*, Alexandria, VA: American Counseling Association.

Royer, E (1995) "Behaviour disorders, exclusion and social skills: punishment is not education", *Therapeutic Care and Education*, 4(3), 32-6.

Russell, T D (2003) "Between town and gown: The rise and fall of restorative justice on Boulder's University Hill", *Utah Law Review*, 1, 91-136.

Salmivalli, C (1999) "Participant role approach to school bullying: Implications for interventions", *Journal of Adolescence*, 22, 453-459.

Salmivalli, C, Lagerspetz, K, Bjorkqvist, K, Osterman, K & Kaukiainen, A (1996) "Bullying as a group process: Participant roles and their relations to social status within the group" *Aggressive Behavior*, 22, 1-15.

Salmivalli, C, Huttunen, A & Lagerspetz, KMJ (1997) "Peer Networks and Bullying in Schools", *Scandinavian Journal of Psychology*, 38, 305–312.

Scheff, TJ (1990) *Microsociology: Discourse, Emotion and Social Structure*, Chicago: University of Chicago Press.

Scheff, TJ (1994) *Bloody Revenge: Emotions, Nationalism and War*, Boulder, CO: Westview Press.

Scheff, T & Retzinger, S (1991) *Emotions and Violence*, Lexington, MA: Lexington Books.

Scheff, T (2000) "Shame and the Social Bond: A Sociological Theory", *Sociological Theory*, 18, 84-99.

Schorr, LB (1997) *Common purpose: Strengthening families and neighborhoods to rebuild America*, New York: Anchor Books.

Schumacher, E (1977) *A guide for the perplexed*, London: Jonathon Cape.

Scott, WA (1965) *Values and organizations: A study of fraternities and sororities*, Chicago: Rand McNally.

Shannon, M & McCall, D (2001) "Zero Tolerance Policies in Context: A Preliminary Investigation to Identify Actions to Improve School Discipline and School Safety", prepared for the Canadian Association of Principals, <www.safehealthyschools.org/whatsnew/capzerotolerance. htm> accessed 1 May 2005.

Sharpe, S (2003) *Beyond the Comfort Zone: A Guide to the Practice of Community Conferencing*, Calgary, AB: Calgary Community Conferencing.

Shaw, G & Wierenga, A (2002) "Restorative Practices: Community Conferencing Pilot" unpublished manuscript, held at the Faculty of Education, University of Melbourne.

Sherman, L (2003) "Reason for emotion: Reinventing justice with theories, innovations, and research – The American Society of Criminology 2002 Presidential Address", *Criminology*, 41(1), 1-37.

Sherman, LW and Strang, H (2004) "Verdicts or Inventions? Interpreting Results From Randomized Controlled Experiments in Criminology", *American Behavioral Scientist*, 47(5) (January), 575-607.

Sherman, LW, Barnes, G, Strang, H, Woods, D, Inkpen, N, Newbury-Birch, D, Bennett, S & Angel, C (2004) "Restorative Justice: What we know and how we know it Working Paper #1", Jerry Lee Program on Randomized Controlled Trials In Restorative Justice, University of Pennsylvania, Lee Center of Criminology; and Australian National University, Centre for Restorative Justice, <www/sas.upenn.edu/jerrylee/rjWorking Papers1.pdf> accessed 30 November 2004.

Sherman, LW, Barnes, G, Strang, H, Woods, D, Inkpen, N, Bennett, S & Angel, C (2005) "Effects of face-to-face restorative justice on victims of crime in four randomized, controlled trials", *Journal of Experimental Criminology*, 1, 367–395.

Shields, A & Cicchetti, D (2001) "Parental maltreatment and emotion dysregulation as risk factors for bullying and victimization in middle childhood", *Journal of Clinical Child Psychology*, 30, 349-363.

Skiba, RJ & Noam, GG (eds), (2001) *Zero Tolerance: Can Suspension and Expulsion Keep Schools Safe? New Directions for Youth Development: Theory Practice Research No 92*, San Francisco, CA: Jossey-Bass.

Skiba, RJ & Knesting, K (2001) "Zero Tolerance, zero evidence: An analysis of school disciplinary practice", *Zero Tolerance: Can Suspension and Expulsion Keep Schools Safe? New Directions for Youth Development: Theory, Practice, and Research No 92*, San Francisco, CA: Jossey-Bass.

Skiba, R & Peterson, R (1999) "The dark side of zero tolerance", *Phi Delta Kappan*, 80, 372-378.

Skiba, RJ & Rauch, MK (2006) "Zero tolerance, suspension, and expulsion: Questions of equity and effectiveness" in CM Evertson & CS Weinstein (eds), *Handbook of classroom management: Research, practice, and contemporary issues*, Mahwah, NJ: Lawrence Erlbaum Associates.

Slee, P (1995) "Peer victimization and its relationship to depression among Australian primary school students", *Personality and Individual Differences*, 18, 57-62.

Slee, P (1998) "Bullying Amongst Australian Primary Students – Some Barriers To Help-Seeking And Links With Sociometric Status" in P Slee & K Rigby (eds), *Children's Peer Relations*, London: Routledge Publications.

REFERENCES

Slee, PT & Ford, DC (1999) "Bullying is a serious issue – it is a crime!", *Australia & New Zealand Journal of Law & Education*, 4(1), 23-39.

Smith, JD, Schneider, BH, Smith, PK & Ananiadou, K (2004) "The effectiveness of Whole-School Antibullying Programs: A Synthesis of Evaluation Research", *School Psychology Review*, 33, 548-561.

Smith, MB (1963) "Personal values in the study of lives" in RW White (ed), *The study of lives*, New York: Atherton Press.

Smith, PK & Shu, S (2000) "What good schools can do about bullying: findings from a survey in English schools after a decade of research and action', *Childhood*, 7, 193-212.

Smith, PK, Morita, Y, Junger-Tas, Y, Olweus, D, Catalano , R & Slee, P (eds), (1999) *The Nature of School Bullying: A CrossNational Perspective*, London and New York: Routledge.

Smith, P.K, Pepler, D.K & Rigby, K (eds), (2004) *Bullying in schools: How successful can interventions be?* Cambridge: Cambridge University Press.

Smith, PK & Sharp, S (1994) *School Bullying: Insights and Perspectives*, New York: Routledge.

Sorokin, P (1962) *Social and cultural dynamics*, vol 1, New York: Bedminster Press.

Soutter, A & McKenzie, M (1998) "The Evaluation of the dispute resolution project in Australian Secondary Schools", *School Psychology International*, 19(4), 307-316.

Soutter, A & McKenzie, M (2000) "The use and effects of anti-bullying and anti-harassment policies in Australian schools", *School Psychology International*, 21(1), 96-104.

Strang, H (1999) "Crimes Against Schools: The Potential for a Restorative Justice Approach", *International Forum On Initiatives For Safe Schools: School Violence Prevention And Juvenile Protection – What Works?*, Seoul, Korea, June.

Strang, H & Braithwaite, J (2001) *Restorative justice and civil society*, Cambridge, UK: Cambridge University Press.

Strang, H (2002) *Repair or Revenge: Victims and Restorative Justice*, Oxford, Oxford University Press.

Strang, H & Braithwaite, J (2001) *Restorative Justice and Civil Society*, Cambridge University Press.

Strang, H & Sherman, LW (2003) "Repairing the harm: Victims and restorative justice", *Utah Law Review*, 1, 15-42.

Strang, H, Sherman, LW, Angel, CM, Woods, DJ, Bennett, S, Newbury-Birch, D & Inkpen, N (2006) "Victim Evaluations of Face-to-Face Restorative Justice Conferences: A Quasi-Experimental Analysis", *Journal of Social Issues*, 62(2), 281-306.

Staples, S (2000) "Violence: Rage against a broken world" in WG Hinkle & S Henry (eds), *School Violence*, Thousand Oaks, CA: Sage Publications.

Strassberg, Z, Dodge, FA, Pettit, GS & Bates, JE (1994) "Spanking in the home and children's subsequent aggression toward kindergarten peers", *Development and Psychopathology*, 6, 445-462.

Straus, MA, Gelles, RJ & Steinmetz, SK (1981) *Behind closed doors: Violence in the American family*, Garden City, New York: Anchor Books.

Stephenson, P & Smith, D (1989) "Bullying in two English comprehensive schools" in E Roland and E Munthe (eds), *Bullying: An International Perspective*, London: Fulton.

Stirling, M (1993) "How many children are being excluded?", *British Journal of Special Education*, 19(4), 128-130.

Stone, D, Patton, B, Heen, S (2002) *Difficult Conversations: How to Discuss What Matters Most*, New York: Viking/Penguin.

Sugai, G & Homer, RH (1999) "Discipline and behavioral support: Preferred processes and. practices", *Effective School Practices*, 17,10-22.

Sutton, J, Smith, PK & Swettenham, J (1999a) "Bullying and theory of mind: A critique of the 'social skills deficit' view of anti-social behaviour", *Social Development*, 8, 117-127.

Sutton, J, Smith P.K & Swettenham, J (1999b) "Social cognition and bullying: Social inadequacy or skilled manipulation?" *British Journal of Developmental Psychology*, 17, 435-450.

Tajfel, H, Turner, JC (1979) "An integrative theory of intergroup conflict" in S Worchel and WG Austin (eds), *The social psychology of intergroup relations*, Monterey: Brooks/Cole.

Tangney, JP (2003) "Self-relevant emotions" in MR Leary & JP Tangney (eds), *Handbook of self and identity*, New York: Guilford Press.

Tangney, JP, Boone, AL & Dearing, R (2005) "Forgiving the self: Conceptual issues and empirical findings" in EL Worthington, Jr (ed), *Handbook of forgiveness*, New York: Brunner-Routledge.

Tangney, JP & Dearing, R (2003) *Shame and guilt*, New York: Guilford.

Tebo, MG (2000) "Zero Tolerance, Zero Sense", *American Bar Association Journal*, (May) <www.ABAnet.org> accessed 1 May 2001.

The Guardian (1996) "Clive Soley: Education at comprehensive rife with bullying had helped him cope with life", 10 November, p 5.

REFERENCES

Thorsborne, M & Vinegrad, D (2002) *Restorative Practices in Schools: Rethinking Behaviour Management,* unpublished manuscript, held by Margaret Thorsborne and Associates, Buderim, Queensland.

Thorsborne, M & Vinegrad, D (2004) *Restorative Practices in Classrooms: Rethinking Behaviour Management,* unpublished manuscript, held by Margaret Thorsborne and Associates, Buderim, Queensland.

Tolan, PH & Guerra, NG (1994) *What works in reducing adolescent violence: An empirical review of the field,* Boulder: University of Colorado. Center for the Study and Prevention of Violence.

Tompkins, SS (1962) *Affect, imagery, consciousness: Vol I. The positive affects,* New York: Springer.

Tomkins SS (1963) *Affect, imagery, consciousness: Vol II.* New York: Springer.

Tompkin, SS (1987) "Shame" in DL Nathanson (ed), *The many faces of shame,* New York: Guildford Press.

Tomovic, VA (1979) *Definitions in Sociology: Convergence, Conflict and Alternative Vocabularies,* Diliton Publications, Inc: St Catherines, Ontario.

Trevaskis, DK (1994) *Mediation in Schools,* ERIC Digest ED 378108, University of South Maine.

Troy, M & Sroufe, LA (1987) "Victimization among preschoolers: role of attachment relationship history", *Journal of American Academy of Child and Adolescent Psychiatry,* 26, 166-172.

Turner, JC (1996) "Henri Tajfel: An introduction" in WP Robinson (ed), *Social groups and identities: Developing the legacy of Henri Tajfel,* Oxford: Butterworth Heinemann.

Turner, JC, Hogg, MA, Oakes, PJ, Reicher, SD & Wetherell, MS (1987) *Rediscovering the social group: A self-categorization theory.* New York: Basil Blackwell, Inc.

Tutu, D (1999) *No Future Without Forgiveness.* London: Rider.

Twenge, JM, Baumeister, RF, Tice, DM & Stucke, TS (2001) "If you can't join then, beat them: Effects of social exclusion on aggressive behavior", *Journal of Personality and Social Psychology,* 81, 1058-1069.

Twenge, JM, Catanese, KR & Baumeister, RF (2003) "Social exclusion and the deconstructed state: Time perception, meaninglessness, lethargy, lack of emotion, and self-awareness", *Journal of Personality and Social Psychology,* 85, 409-423.

Twenge, JM, Baumeister, RF, DeWall, CN, Ciarocco, NJ & Bartels, JM (2006) "Social exclusion decreases prosocial behavior", manuscript submitted for publication.

Tyler, TR & Blader, S (2000) *Cooperation in groups: Procedural justice, social identity, and behavioral engagement,* Philadelphia: Psychology Press.

Tyler, T (2006) "Restorative Justice and Procedural Justice: Dealing with Rule Breaking", *Journal of Social Issues,* 62(2), 307-326.

Udry, JR (2003) "National Longitudinal Study of Adolescent Health (Add Health)", Waves I & II, 1994-1996; Wave III 2001-2002, Chapel Hill, NC: Carolina Population Center, University of North Carolina at Chapel Hill.

Umbreit, MS (1998) "Restorative Justice Through Victim-Offender Mediation: A Multi-Site Assessment", *Western Criminology Review* 1(1) <http://wcr.sonoma.edu/v1n1/umbreit.html> accessed 1 May 2005.

Van Ness, D (1986) *Crime and its victims: What we can do,* Downers Grove, IL: Intervarsity Press.

Van Stokkom, B (2002) "Moral emotions in restorative justice conferences: Managing shame, designing empathy", *Theoretical Criminology,* 6(3), 339-360.

Varnham, S (2005) "Citizenship in schools: the gap between theory and practice", *Education and the Law,* 17(1-2), 53-64.

Varnham, S (2005) "Seeing things differently: restorative justice and school discipline", *Education and the Law,* 17(3), 87-104.

Vossekuil, B, Reddy, M, Fein, R, Borum, R & Modzeleski, W (2000) *USSS Safe School Initiative: An Interim Report on the Prevention of Targeted Violence in Schools,* Washington, DC: US Secret Service, National Threat Assessment Center.

Vulliamy, G & Webb, R (2001) "The social construction of school exclusion rates: implications for evaluation methodology", *Educational Studies,* 27, 357-70.

Wachtel, T & McCold, P (2001) "Restorative justice in everyday life: Beyond the formal ritual" in H Strang and J Braithwaite (eds), *Restorative Justice and Civil Society,* Cambridge: Cambridge University Press.

Walker, HM, Colvin, G & Ramsey, E (1995) *Anti-Social Behaviour at School: Strategy and Best Practices,* Pacific Grove, CA: Brooks Cole Publishing Co.

Wallace, N (2004) "Crossbow attacker jailed", *Sydney Morning Herald,* 5 June, p 4.

Webber, JA (2003) *Failure to Hold: The Politics of Youth Violence,* Lanham, MD: Rowman and Littlefield.

Weber, M (1946) "Politics as a vocation" in HH Gerth & CW Mills (eds), *From Max Weber: Essays in Sociology,* New York: Oxford University Press.

REFERENCES

Weissberg, RP (2004) "Statement to the Subcommittee on Substance Abuse and Mental Health Services", United States Senate Committee on Health, Education, Labor, and Pensions, hearing on *Providing Substance Abuse Prevention and Treatment Services to Adolescents*, 15 June, Washington DC.

Wetzstein, C (1999) "Index of 'Cultural Indicators' Sees Trends Decidedly Mixed", *Washington Times*, 12 October, p A10.

Weitekamp, E (1999) "The History of Restorative Justice" in G Bazemore & L Walgrave (eds), *Restorative Juvenile Justice: Repairing the Harm of Youth Crime*, Monsey: Criminal Justice Press.

Welsh, WN (2000) "Effects of school climate on school disorder" in WG Hinkle & S Henry (eds), *School Violence*, Thousand Oaks, CA: Sage Publications.

Whitman J (2003) *Harsh Justice: Criminal Punishment and the Widening Divide Between America and Europe*, New York: Oxford University Press.

Whitney, I & Smith, PK (1993) "A survey of the nature and extent of bullying in junior/middle and secondary schools", *Educational Research*, 35, 3-25.

Wilcox, T, Brigham, F & Nicolai, B (1998) "Increasing Self-Discipline with the ABC Event Frame", *Bulletin of the National Association of Secondary School Principals*, 82, 16-24.

Wilkins, R (1993) "Training children and adolescents in the skills of interpersonal conflict resolution: A developmental theory and training strategy" in D Evans, M Myhill and J Izard (eds), *Student Behaviour Problems: Positive Initiatives and New Frontiers, Selected papers from the 1993 National Conference on Student Behaviour Problems*, Melbourne: ACER.

Williams, K, Chambers, M, Logan, S & Robinson, D (1996) "Association of common health symptoms with bullying in primary school children", *British Medical Journal*, 313, 17-19.

Williams, KD, Forgas, JP & von Hippel, W (eds), (2005) *The social outcast: Ostracism, social exclusion, rejection, and bullying*, New York: The Psychology Press.

Wilson, SJ, Lipsey, MW & Derzon, JH (2003) "The effects of school-based intervention programs on aggressive and disruptive behavior: A meta-analysis", *Journal of Consulting and Clinical Psychology*, 71(1), 136-149.

Woehrle, LM (2000) *Summary Evaluation Report: A study of the Impact of the Help Increase the Peace Project in the Chambersburg Area School District*, Baltimore, MD: American Friends Service Committee.

Wolfgang, ME, Figlio, RM & Sellin, T (1972) *Delinquency in a Birth Cohort*, Chicago, IL: University of Chicago Press.

Wright, Martin (1996) *Justice for Victims and Offenders*, Philadelphia, PA: Open University Press.

Wu, S, Pink, W, Crain, R & Moles, O (1982) "Student Suspension: A Critical Reappraisal", *The Urban Review*, (14)4, 245-304.

Youth Justice Board for England and Wales (2004) *National Evaluation of the Restorative Justice in Schools Programme*, <www.youth-justice-board.gov.uk> accessed 1 May 2005.

Zehr, H (1990) *Changing Lenses: A new focus for criminal justice*, Scottsdale, PA: Herald Press.

Zehr, H (2000) "Journey to Belonging", Paper delivered at *Just Peace? Peace making and peacebuilding for the New Millenium*, international conference, Massey University, Albany, NZ, 24-28 April.

Zehr, H (2002) "Journey to Belonging" in EGM Weitekamp & HJ Kerner (eds), *Restorative Justice: Theoretical Foundations*, Devon, UK: Willan Publishing.

Zehr, H (2002) *The Little Book of Restorative Justice*, Intercourse, PA: Good Books.

Zehr, H (2006) "Restorative Justice: Promise and Challenge", 2006 International Peace Award Keynote Address, <www.cofchrist.org/peacecolloquy/2006/pc06peacekeynote.asp?pr=yes> accessed 1 November 2006

Zins, J, Weissberg, RW, Wang, MC & Walberg, H (eds), (2004) *Building school success on social emotional learning: What does the research say?*, New York: Teachers College Press.

Index

Islam

Its law and society

Jamila Hussain

Recent events have brought Islam and Muslims to the centre of the West's attention, leading many to ask what it means to be Muslim, keen to know what is fact and what is misconception.

Jamila Hussain explains the basic principles of the religion of Islam and its law, the Shariah, and how the Shariah is lived in the context of many different cultures throughout the World. The discussion includes: A brief survey of Islamic history and civilisation; The development of Islamic law and how it is applied in modern conditions; A Western Muslim community such as in Australia; The position of women in Islam and the growth of Islamic feminism; Family law and inheritance; Modern reproductive technology; Criminal law and evidence; Banking and commercial law; Islamic laws of war and peace and the conduct of Muslims in times of war.

Now in its second edition, this book is ideal for those who wish to acquire an introductory knowledge of Islamic culture and law in general and within Australian society in particular.

2003 · ISBN 978 1 86287 499 2 · pb · 260 pp · $39.95

The Labour Market ate My Babies

Barbara Pocock

In this book, young Australians from all over the country, city and the bush, rich and poor, talk about the good and bad of parental work - the trade off between money and time, consumer riches versus time for each other.

Barbara Pocock, acclaimed author of *The Work/Life Collision*, argues that the modern labour market is having a huge impact on today's youth and eating into our capacity to care. Children have become a 'market'. Caring for kids and selling to kids is big business, as stressed, time-poor parents struggle to care for their children and salve their guilt with presents and pocket money.

How will this future generation of workers weigh up the labour market and organise their lives? *The Labour Market Ate My Babies* argues that a sustainable future requires new policy approaches to work that incorporate the perspectives of children.

> It's good to get money coming in and probably it's good to work as hard as you can when you're younger so when you're older you can retire with some money. But there should probably be a limit to how much before your relationships with other people start to strain because you are never there (Adam, 16)

2006 · ISBN 978 1 86287 604 0 · pb · 254 pages · $44.95

Achieving Social Justice
Indigenous Rights and Australia's Future
Larissa Behrendt

Writing with great power and clarity, Behrendt proposes practical short-term reforms, as well as longer term aspirational initiatives leading to institutional change that will facilitate greater rights protection and the exercise of self-determination including a preamble to the Constitution * a treaty * the national self-image * economic redistribution * alternative institutional forms * regional framework agreements * a more energised politics * Constitutional protection.

> *A magnificent synthesis of Indigenous history and insights ... based in profound scholarship yet highly readable and accessible, it deserves the widest possible readership* Dr William Jonas AM

> *[A} remarkably lucid and readable book* Professor Ann Curthoys

> *A clear and unambiguous statement of what is wrong with the status quo from an Aboriginal perspective* Fred Chaney AO

> *the clearest articulation we have of what Indigenous Australians want and need – and how it might be achieved* QUT Law Journal

2003 • ISBN 978 1 86287 450 3 • pb • 208pp • $29.95

Environment and Sustainability Policy
Creation, Implementation, Evaluation
Stephen Dovers

Dovers argues that better public policy is the key to creating a more sustainable environment and shows what this might involve. This is an intensely practical book, intellectually original and rigorous, and written in a concise and accessible style.

> *... a seminal contribution to the literature on learning for sustainability, a truly comprehensive analysis of the issues and policy implications.*
> Paul J Perkins, Chair, National Environmental and Education Council, Australia

> *Dovers masterfully explains how researchers, land managers, and environmental professionals ... can work more effectively together to achieve environmental sustainability. This book is essential reading for anyone involved in Natural Resource Management.*
> Professor David Bowman, Charles Darwin University

2005 • ISBN 978 1 86287 540 1 • pb • 208 pages • $49.95